MODERNISM AND THE FRANKFURT SCHOOL

Edinburgh Critical Studies in Modernist Culture
Series Editors: Tim Armstrong and Rebecca Beasley

Available:

Forthcoming:

MODERNISM AND THE FRANKFURT SCHOOL

Tyrus Miller

EDINBURGH
University Press

© Tyrus Miller, 2014, 2020

Edinburgh University Press Ltd
The Tun – Holyrood Road
12 (2f) Jackson's Entry
Edinburgh EH8 8PJ
www.euppublishing.com

First published in hardback by Edinburgh University Press 2014

Typeset in Sabon and Gill Sans by
Servis Filmsetting Ltd, Stockport, Cheshire
and printed and bound in Great Britain by
CPI Group (UK) Ltd, Croydon CR0 4YY

A CIP record for this book is available from the British Library

ISBN 978 0 7486 4018 8 (hardback)
ISBN 978 1 4744 7321 7 (paperback)
ISBN 978 0 7486 9471 6 (webready PDF)

The right of Tyrus Miller to be identified as Author of this work has been
asserted in accordance with the Copyright, Designs and Patents Act 1988,
and the Copyright and Related Rights Regulations 2003 (SI No. 2498).

CONTENTS

SERIES EDITORS' PREFACE

This series of monographs on selected topics in modernism is designed to reflect and extend the range of new work in modernist studies. The studies in the series aim for a breadth of scope and for an expanded sense of the canon of modernism, rather than focusing on individual authors. Literary texts will be considered in terms of contexts including recent cultural histories (modernism and magic; sonic modernity; media studies) and topics of theoretical interest (the everyday; postmodernism; the Frankfurt School); but the series will also re-consider more familiar routes into modernism (modernism and gender; sexuality; politics). The works published will be attentive to the various cultural, intellectual and historical contexts of British, American and European modernisms, and to inter-disciplinary possibilities within modernism, including performance and the visual and plastic arts.

LIST OF ABBREVIATIONS

AC
Herbert Marcuse, "On the Affirmative Character of Culture," in *Art and Liberation*, Collected Papers, Volume 4, ed. Douglas Kellner (New York: Routledge, 2007)

AP
Walter Benjamin, *The Arcades Project*, trans. Howard Eiland and Kevin McLaughlin (Cambridge, MA: The Belknap Press of Harvard University Press, 1999)

DBS
Alexander Kluge, *The Devil's Blind Spot*, trans. Martin Chalmers and Michael Hulse (New York: New Directions, 2004)

EC
Herbert Marcuse, *Eros and Civilization: A Philosophical Inquiry into Freud* (Boston: Beacon Press, 1955, 1966)

ISW
Theodor W. Adorno, *In Search of Wagner*, trans. Rodney Livingstone (London: New Left Books, 1981)

MM
Theodor W. Adorno, *Minima Moralia: Reflections From Damaged Life*, trans. E.F.N. Jephcott (London: New Left Books, 1974)

ODM
Herbert Marcuse, *One-Dimensional Man: Studies in the Ideology of Advanced Industrial Society* (Boston: Beacon Press, 1964)

PoM
Albrecht Wellmer, *The Persistence of Modernity: Essays on Aesthetics, Ethics, and Postmodernism*, trans. David Midgley (Cambridge, MA: The MIT Press, 1991)

QUF
Theodor W. Adorno, *Quasi Una Fantasia: Essays on Modern Music*, trans. Rodney Livingstone (London: Verso, 1992)

SF
Theodor W. Adorno, *Sound Figures*, trans. Rodney Livingstone (Stanford: Stanford University Press, 1999)

SM
Herbert Marcuse, *Soviet Marxism: A Critical Analysis* (New York: Columbia University Press, 1958)

SW I
Walter Benjamin, *Selected Writings,* Volume I: 1913–1926, ed. Marcus Bullock and Michael W. Jennings (Cambridge, MA: The Belknap Press of Harvard University Press, 1996)

SW II
Walter Benjamin, *Selected Writings,* Volume II: 1927–34, ed. Michael W. Jennings, Howard Eiland, and Gary Smith (Cambridge, MA: The Belknap Press of Harvard University Press, 1999)

SW III
Walter Benjamin, *Selected Writings*, Volume III: 1935–38, ed. Howard Eiland and Michael W. Jennings (Cambridge, MA: The Belknap Press of Harvard University Press, 2002)

SW IV
Walter Benjamin, *Selected Writings*, Volume IV: 1938–1940, ed. Howard Eiland and Michael W. Jennings (Cambridge, MA: The Belknap Press of Harvard University Press, 2003)

TAG
Peter Bürger, *Theory of the Avant-Garde* (Minneapolis: University of Minnesota Press, 1984)

VMS
Albrecht Wellmer, *Versuch über Musik und Sprache* [Essays on Music and Language] (Munich: Carl Hanser Verlag, 2009)

MODERNISM AND THE FRANKFURT SCHOOL

The several different incarnations of the *Institut für Sozialforschung* (Institute for Social Research) that existed in various locations in Europe and the United States from the 1920s to the 1970s, as well as its broader intellectual legacy and afterlife in the work of a wide range of thinkers, have come to be known collectively as "the Frankfurt School." It is a vague and in many respects imprecise designation, since it suggests more cohesion and homogeneity than can readily be ascribed to the successive phases of the Institute's existence, its defining thinkers affiliated in different periods, and its thematic emphases in research and publication. Further contributing to the term's imprecision is the broad impact the work of the Institute had on a range of disciplines and individuals, both in academic and in activist circles. The Frankfurt School represented one of the most influential tendencies in social, political, and cultural thought of the twentieth century, and it is notoriously difficult to circumscribe its boundaries and reach. Few, for example, would consider the late Edward Said a "Frankfurt School" thinker; yet his last book masterfully applied and extended Theodor Adorno's notion of "late style," originally developed in connection with Beethoven's late piano concertos and his *Missa Solemnis*,[1] to a number of literary and musical examples.[2] I will deal with such definitional complications largely by brushing them aside, in order not to get distracted from my primary concerns. Other studies have dealt with the complex formation, internal divisions, and canonization of "the Frankfurt School," and that is not my task here. From the outset, I will simply register the limits of the designation's conceptual and historiographic precision, and go on to employ it pragmatically to focus in on the main concerns of this study: the theory of modernism and the avant-garde articulated by three key thinkers who are typically considered defining figures in the founding "Frankfurt School": Walter Benjamin, Theodor Adorno, and Herbert Marcuse.

I may be pitied, however, if my attempt to jump out of the definitional frying pan with regard to the Frankfurt School has landed me in the still-hotter flames around the definitional and periodizing issues associated with modernism and the avant-garde. Here I will offer a similarly pragmatic working definition and, as with the Frankfurt School, beg off addressing the knotty questions of exact conceptual and period boundaries for the terms I will use to designate a wide range of artistic examples. Once again, these complications are peripheral to my concerns here, though – as I hope is demonstrated in my earlier books *Late Modernism* and *Singular Examples*, which deal with interwar modernism and post-World War II neo-avant-gardes – not without importance in the broader spectrum of modernist studies.[3] I will rely here on a more casuistic approach, taking up examples that derive primarily from direct references in the work of the Frankfurt School or closely related examples. Moreover, because throughout the book I move freely between examples from the various arts, as appropriate to the Frankfurt School's multimedial and intermedial aesthetics, I must leave the definitional and periodizing framework rather loose and flexible.

By *modernism* I designate a diverse set of formally, thematically, and stylistically innovative artistic and literary works, primarily from the twentieth century. When I use the term *avant-garde*, I understand a particular inflection of modernism that emphasized the struggle of new artistic tendencies for legitimacy in ways that drew inspiration from modern forms of political organization and activities, such as mass demonstrations, propagandistic publicity, and party structures. (In my last chapter, I also discuss the work of Peter Bürger, who asserts a more rigorous distinction between modernism and the avant-garde.) Modernist and avant-garde artists, I argue, responded to a new experiential background of highly intensified social and technical modernity by questioning the historical conventions of the arts and, reciprocally, by seeking experimentally to invent new, aesthetically binding principles exemplified in singular works. Their freshly invented formal and stylistic idioms not only communicated narrative, poetic, visual, musical, cinematic, or dramatic artistic contents; they also asserted implicit supplementary claims about the nature of art, the validity of unfamiliar artistic idioms, and the protocols by which these should be interpreted and experienced. Whereas consensually accepted artistic conventions – usually confined to particular media – had once governed the communicative contract between artist, artwork, and audience, in the changed context of artistic modernism and the avant-garde, this communicative relation had to be staked on an artist's gambit that his or her invention was indeed artistically valid, even if the grounds for that validity were opaque, questionable, and contentious. In this circumstance, it is the artwork itself that reflexively posits and "argues for" the standards by which it itself is to be judged a valid work of art. The audience may grasp and accept these standards and hence immediately value the work as innovative art, or – as was more often the case – it may greet the work with incomprehension, indifference, or sheer hooting rage. Small circles of individuals, such as fellow artists and intellectuals, often served as the early advocates of new criteria of the arts, polemicizing for new standards and carrying out the work of pedagogy and propaganda for those works that were to be measured by them. Some modernist and avant-garde works were eventually institutionalized in museums, literary canons, academic curricula, and concert hall programs, thus gaining widespread legitimacy with a broader public. Others fell out of sight even for the art world elite, and where they have not been completely lost to posterity, they have become objects of mainly archival, academic, or antiquarian interest. In a few cases, as with the recovery and reinterpretation of Soviet avant-garde art by American and European artists of the 1960s, a once-forgotten strain of modernism could serve as inspiration for a new wave of modernist innovation, translated across gaps of chronology and historical context.

I will be focusing on the specific ways in which key Frankfurt School thinkers – and a few of their intellectual heirs – dealt with the issue of artistic modernism and interpreted key examples from the modernist and avant-garde arts, from literature and music to photography and architecture. By extension, too, I suggest how their treatment of artistic modernism might inform present-day modernist studies, even beyond their specific range of themes, problems, and examples. I make no pretense to writing an intellectual history of the Frankfurt School; nor can I discuss the broad range of theoretical ideas encompassed by even a few key thinkers of the Frankfurt School, much less of the Frankfurt School as a whole, which, with its multifaceted, interdisciplinary approach, aimed to encompass the complex totality of modern society in a unitary, collaborative, critical program. This qualification of my aims also implies that some thinkers crucial to the Frankfurt School will receive little or no consideration here, because of their limited direct contribution to the analysis of modernism, however much they may have contributed to the full Frankfurt School analysis of social and political *modernity*. These figures would include, for example, the *Institut*'s main director, Max Horkheimer, who appears here solely in my introduction to the Frankfurt School project and not in an independent chapter; other key Frankfurt School thinkers receiving little or no discussion are the economist Friedrich Pollock, the legal scholars Otto Kirchheimer and Franz Neumann, the literary sociologist Leo Löwenthal, and – a more problematic omission – the prolific social theorist and philosopher

Jürgen Habermas, who warrants another book unto himself. Readers will need to avail themselves of other studies in the steadily growing body of scholarship on the Frankfurt School to learn more about their role.

This book, instead, concentrates on the role, historically and in the present, of the Frankfurt School in the analysis of artistic and literary modernism. The Frankfurt School's general theoretical orientation and the individual thinkers connected with it have already exercised an enormous influence across a broad spectrum of contemporary cultural scholarship. The works of, for example, Walter Benjamin and Theodor Adorno regularly feature in undergraduate and graduate courses in theory; various essays from Benjamin, Adorno, Marcuse, and others in the Frankfurt School are obligatory critical reading alongside primary texts of literature, film, visual art, music, architecture and urbanism, political theory, and history, across a truly global range of periods and cultural contexts. The field of modernist studies, which has undergone a sort of renaissance and upsurge in the last two decades, has been no exception in this regard. In particular, social, political, and other contextual approaches to the innovative literature and arts of the twentieth century have vastly expanded the range of research questions, materials, and critical methodologies included in the general field of modernist studies. More and more scholarship – in resonance with the interdisciplinary and interartistic emphases of the Frankfurt School – moves adeptly between histories and examples from the various arts, breaking down the silos between literary studies, art history, visual studies, film studies, musicology, and studies of architecture and urbanism. Similarly, modernist studies draw upon the intellectual histories and theoretical resources of psychoanalysis and social psychology, sociology, anthropology, philosophy, cultural studies, feminist and gender studies, science and technology studies, media and communications studies, and many more disciplines, thus constituting current modernist studies as an open-ended, evolving interdisciplinary field of inquiry. The more that modernist studies in recent years have taken shape as a distinct field of inquiry, the more intensely have contemporary scholars looked to the Frankfurt School legacy of interdisciplinary social and cultural research to explain key problems that arise in their research and teaching.

This interest in the Frankfurt School is, of course, just part of a voracious, eclectic search for new ideas and new problems that has enlivened humanistic fields in the wake of the turn to theory; this is true for modernist studies as well. Yet for the study of modernism, I would argue, motivation exists for a particularly intense engagement with Frankfurt School critical theory. For the Frankfurt School thinkers gave close, multifaceted attention in their work to the nature of advanced modernity and its social, political, and aesthetic implications. In their attempts to grasp the secrets of modernity, the principals of the Frankfurt School were often drawn to artistic modernism as an especially fruitful, concentrated focus of inquiry. Literary figures from

Charles Baudelaire to André Breton, playwrights from Henrik Ibsen to Samuel Beckett, musicians from Gustav Mahler to John Cage, painters such as Paul Klee and Pablo Picasso, architects including Adolf Loos and Le Corbusier, and many more figures from other related arts constitute key reference points in the texts of the major Frankfurt School theorists. Walter Benjamin not only penned critical essays and theoretical works, but also as a writer practiced a modernist-influenced form of what now might be called "creative non-fiction": memoirs, dream protocols, aphorism collections, and other hybrid literary forms. He also developed a unique montage-like way of handling historical writing, especially utilizing numerous quotations from diverse sources, framed by a topical apparatus. Theodor Adorno had even more direct relations to modernist artistic practice. He trained in the 1920s in Vienna as a composer under Alban Berg, leaving behind a small corpus of atonal works and the torso of a *Singspiel*, *The Treasure of Indian Joe* (1932), based on Mark Twain and influenced by Kurt Weill's celebrated *Three-Penny Opera* and *The Rise and Fall of the City of Mahagonny*. He brought this inside knowledge of modernist composition to bear not only on his fine-grained, sensitive analyses of music, but also on his philosophical, critical, and literary analysis in subsequent years. Although Herbert Marcuse's writing was more formally conventional than that of Benjamin or Adorno, he was formally educated as a literary scholar and throughout his life maintained a lively dialogue with both historical and contemporary arts and literature, as scholars such as Charles Reitz and Douglas Kellner have documented.[4]

Though the broader Frankfurt School intellectual program was shaped by a number of historical and theoretical elements – from the rise of fascism to the critique of positivism to the increasing administrative integration of post-World War II society during the Cold War – a very broad, multi-medial, trans-European scope of artistic works and aesthetic programs informed the thinking of their core researchers. Some of their individual theoretical hypotheses about particular social phenomena, such as their analyses of the psychology of prejudice (e.g. *The Authoritarian Personality*, 1950), may legitimately have come to seemed dated because of the fading of the Freudian theoretical paradigm and the overwhelming inflection of their work by the German catastrophe of Nazism, the Holocaust, and the fascist-period intellectual emigration. By contrast, Frankfurt School aesthetics, across the span of many diverse writings over many decades, have remained far more enduring in their applicability and re-interpretability. Frankfurt School aesthetics always engaged with issues of modernity that went well beyond the specific topical context of Germany or the particular experiences of exile, the war, or Cold War reconstruction. Through their aesthetics, the Frankfurt School sought not only to explain problems of their present context, but also to understand the social preconditions and implications of the broad efflorescence of the arts throughout the late nineteenth and early twentieth century, grasping its transformative meaning for social behavior, individual experience, conceptual thought, and the characteristics of contemporary political power.

Arguably, then, there is a special "elective affinity" between the culture of artistic modernism, which responded to and artistically reshaped lived experiences of modernity through innovative aesthetic form, and Frankfurt School critical theory, which likewise takes modern experience and its various cultural expressions as a primary object of critical reflection. Just as modernist artists responded to new modern experiences by reconceiving the style, form, mode of reception, and criteria of judgment for works of art, so too the key figures of the Frankfurt School developed daringly innovative, interdisciplinary critical approaches to the emerging phenomena of modern life. Moreover, in many cases they attended to the compositional forms and stylistic idioms of cultural theory and analysis as integral dimensions of a renovated critical thought. Montage, constellation, aphorism, portrait, essay, construction, and composition were key terms in the epistemic and methodological vocabulary of the Frankfurt School thinkers: experimental means by which they sought to capture modern experience in its subtle distinctiveness, its complexity, and its latent qualities, as well as its explicit social, ideological, and aesthetic features. Not accidentally, many of these stylistic and formal modes were part of the technical repertory developed by modern writers and artists. The modern arts, thus, served the Frankfurt School thinkers not only as a privileged matter for critical reflection, but also as a source of critical heuristics, conceptual models, and compositional frameworks for a theoretical activity appropriate to the multifaceted character of its object: modernity itself, ultimately, in all its multifaceted challenge. Coming out of and responding to the same matrix of problems in modern experience, modernist artists and Frankfurt School theorists exhibit parallel, complementary styles of thought in their respective figural and theoretical idioms. Considered together, modernism and critical theory may thus also illuminate one another productively, bringing into view their mutual potentials and limits as means by which twentieth-century intellectuals have addressed urgent questions of cultural life.

PHASES IN THE FRANKFURT SCHOOL'S DEVELOPMENT

The first *Institut für Sozialforschung* was founded in Frankfurt in 1924 through the support of the wealthy merchant Felix Weil and under the direction of the labor historian Carl Grünberg, with an orthodox Marxist political orientation. This first phase, prior to Max Horkheimer's assuming of the directorship in 1930, following Grünberg's suffering of a stroke, is incidental to our concerns, since the Institute had little engagement with issues of arts and aesthetics at the time. The first Institute included a number of important left-wing intellectuals centered in the social sciences, including the economists Henryk Grossmann and Friedrich Pollock, the latter of whom would continue to play an important role as a theorist of state capitalism, planning, and automation in later phases of the Frankfurt School, as well as Karl August Wittfogel, a Communist Party member and China expert, who after World War II would become a notable Cold War anti-communist.

It was only after Horkheimer assumed the directorship that the Frankfurt School program of "Critical Theory" and the various motifs that contributed to the loose but distinctive intellectual-history outlines of a "Frankfurt School" of thought began to take shape.[5] As Rolf Wiggershaus notes in his comprehensive account, *The Frankfurt School: Its History, Theories, and Political Significance*,[6] there were five features that together allow us to ascribe the status of a "school" to the otherwise disparate and chronologically variable output of its affiliated thinkers. Moreover, as he notes, only in the early period of Horkheimer's directorship can we discern a strong, consistent presence of all five. These include:

1. An institutional framework: the *Institut für Sozialforschung*.
2. A charismatic leader armed with a theoretical vision and managerial skills: Max Horkheimer.
3. A manifesto: Horkheimer's 1931 inaugural lecture, "The Present State of Social Philosophy and the Tasks Facing an Institute of Social Research."
4. A new paradigm: "Critical Theory," as a new model of self-reflexive, interdisciplinary social science with explicit emancipatory goals.
5. A journal and other publication ventures: the *Zeitschrift für Sozialforschung* (*Journal for Social Research*) and the books associated with the *Institut*.[7]

A fuller discussion of these five elements would take us too far afield. However, because I have already employed the term "Critical Theory" in connection with the Frankfurt School, I will briefly discuss Horkheimer's influential programmatic essay "Traditional and Critical Theory,"[8] which as Wiggershaus rightly notes, set out a broad paradigm for the activity of the Institute.

Horkheimer's essay, which appeared in 1937, seeks to distinguish a functional difference between theory as conventionally understood in the sciences and "critical theory," as should be pursued by the Institute. Traditional theory, he argues, seeks to establish a limited set of abstract, interlinked principles to represent a phenomenon. These principles can then be experimentally compared to the facts discovered about the phenomenon and either be verified or be subjected to revision, to better accommodate facts that cannot be accounted for under the existing theory. Traditional theory thus always stands in a hypothetical relation to facts, which help to confirm or disconfirm the hypotheses the theory generates. Traditional theory, Horkheimer argues, has played an important role in the scientific, technological, and industrial development of bourgeois society. As the means by which new facts are incorporated into conceptual frameworks and rationalized, it is key to maintaining an effective pragmatic relationship to the evolving modern world. Nevertheless, from a social perspective, traditional theory also has a defining limitation: it takes the existing division of labor for granted and embeds theoretical activity within it as a specialized form of intellectual labor rather than reflecting on whether the division of labor is optimal or should be changed. In effect, it operates "rationally" only within the unquestioned framework of production and knowledge established by the operations of capitalism, rather than asking how the capitalist division of labor itself might be changed to make it more rational and just – and how theory might have to operate differently to help bring this about.

Critical theory, in contrast, engages directly with the historical alterability of knowledge, which changes along with the evolving roles, orientations, and positions of those who are producers of knowledge within the social division of labor. Knowledge does not just grow and change over time, as new facts are discovered, old concepts are improved, and new conceptual frameworks emerge. It also changes its function and fundamental character, as society evolves. Alterations in society and changes in the function and nature of knowledge have a systematic relationship to one another, which it is the task of critical theory to reflect on and make the object of intentional planning and practice. Horkheimer writes:

> The continuous change of social relationships, due immediately to economic developments and finding its most direct expression in the formation of the ruling class, does not affect only some areas of the culture. It also affects the way in which the culture depends on the economy and, thus, the key ideas in the whole conception. This influence of social development on the structure of the theory is part of the theory's doctrinal content . . . Since the theory is a unified whole which has its proper means only in relation to the contemporary situation, the theory as a whole is caught up in an evolution.[9]

Horkheimer's formulation about the social evolution of theories found echoes in the work of other Frankfurt School colleagues in connection to the social role of art as well. Benjamin, for example, diagnosed a broad "refunctioning" of art associated with the spread of the technical reproducibility of images and the growth of mass politics, in which art was taking on new socially critical, political, and pedagogical roles. Horkheimer and Adorno diagnosed an analogous, if negative refunctioning of art within the "culture industry," which had drawn art into a commodified, industrially produced and disseminated economy of cultural goods, thus neutralizing any critical effects it might once have had. So too Adorno and Marcuse ascribed critical functions to art's sheer resistance to being reduced to facts and information, when, in the social background, more and more previously autonomous domains of thought were being subordinated to "one-dimensional" administrative and economic mechanisms. In the view of critical theory, all intellectual activities, whether theoretical or artistic work, evolve historically and change their social function in observable relation to social changes. In this sense, thus, Horkheimer's program for a critical theory also broadly informed the key premises of the Frankfurt School's aesthetics and theory of modernism.

Another crucial difference, definitive for Horkheimer of critical theory, is that theory should not simply accept the given division of labor and get on with its hypothetical work of fitting facts into the existing framework. Instead, theory should reflect on the given social framework and motivate its restructuring for the better. Critical theory does not merely represent a large-scale hypothesis about "what is" today, about the existing constellation of facts, but rather offers a hypothesis about "what could be" in the future: what, realistically, could be changed in the interest of greater human freedom and rationality and what social forces specifically might bring about that change. In this respect, critical theory was to favor a work of "constructive thinking" over "empirical verification";[10] it sets itself in a certain counterfactual tension with the state of things in its presently existing form. Horkheimer even suggests that critical theory is a kind of stubborn "obstinacy" in the face of present facts, a rigorous exercise of imagination that creates an image of an emancipated future, highlighting those elements of the present that cannot yet allow this future to come to fruition or that even pose active obstacles to its realization.[11] He writes:

> One thing which this way of thinking has in common with fantasy is that an image of the future which springs indeed from a deep understanding of the present determines men's [sic] thoughts and actions even in periods in which the course of events seems to be leading far away from such a future and seems to justify every reaction except belief in fulfillment. It is not the arbitrariness and supposed independence of fantasy that is the common bond here, but its obstinacy. Within the most advanced group it is the theoretician who must have this obstinacy.[12]

As the Frankfurt School found less and less in the existing social world to nourish this obstinacy in the face of an unpromising present, modernist art – as a willfully persistent practice of questioning the given world and imagining artistic alternatives to it – took on an ever-greater importance in its intellectual orbit.

Returning to Wiggershaus's five elements as anchoring points for an enduring if – throughout most of its historical existence – primarily virtual "School," we can go on to identify six major phases of the Frankfurt School's development following Horkheimer's assumption of the directorship. Helmut Dubiel, in *Theory and Politics: Studies in the Development of Critical Theory*,[13] differentiates three initial phases of the Horkheimer-led *Institut für Sozialforschung*, and I follow his analysis here:

1. Materialism, 1930–37, in which the Institute's activities retained a relatively strong connection to Marxism, including in its desire to contribute theoretical perspectives to the workers' movement and to see its own emancipatory hopes realized in fascism's defeat and the advance of socialism.
2. Critical Theory, 1937–40, in which the Institute continued its theoretical work of the early 1930s, but viewed the relation between its own critical theory and any definite agent of social change as ever more tenuous and troubled.
3. The Critique of Instrumental Reason, 1940–45, in which the emphasis of the Institute's investigation shifted from the critique of the capitalist social context in which theory was produced and applied to the underlying anthropological interests that science, social and political structures, cultural products, and psychological dispositions expressed.

Supplementing this initial typology with the longer trajectory of the Frankfurt School after the end of World War II – and here, drawing upon Wiggershaus's study – I would identify three further phases of its evolution:

4. Return to Germany and Restoration, 1945–55, in which the work of the Institute was reestablished in the new context of post-World War II reconstruction, the Cold War and the division of Europe into rival East and West blocs, and the post-Auschwitz horizon for art, philosophy, and ethics.
5. Critical Theory and Democratic Culture, 1955–69, in which Frankfurt School theory gained increasing public resonance and influence, including among younger radical thinkers, artists, and activists who would eventually challenge the authority of the first-generation Frankfurt School.
6. The Communicative Turn, 1969 on, in which, following the death of Adorno and under the leading influence of Jürgen Habermas, the aporias and shortcomings of first-generation Frankfurt School thought would be confronted with a new paradigm of Critical Theory rooted in language, communication, and the progressive democratization of society.

These latter three phases, like Dubiel's earlier three, are only approximately dated; but they do suggest certain key historical thresholds and thematic emphases that are useful in understanding when and in what context artistic modernism became an important topic for the Frankfurt School. For example, in the fifth period in the above typology Adorno's intellectual influence soared to its peak. Questions of artistic modernism were accordingly invested with both aesthetic and political urgency. In contrast, following the communicative turn, aesthetics – and hence of the problems of modernism – were relatively demoted in the Frankfurt School theoretical program. True, Peter Bürger's important *Theory of the Avant-Garde* and Alexander Kluge and Oskar Negt's *Public Sphere and Experience*, two key contributions to modernist theory from a Frankfurt School-oriented perspective, date from the 1970s. Yet neither could be said to have exerted decisive impact on the broad intellectual program of Habermas and his followers. For the most part, Habermas and the major Habermasians have focused their attention elsewhere than on art and aesthetics, whether classical or modernist: Habermas has written on a vast range of problems in philosophy, theory of science, social theory, law, religion, and contemporary politics. Axel Honneth and Hans Joas have made important contributions to action theory, problems of social recognition, and the historical study of philosophical anthropology and pragmatism. Even Albrecht Wellmer, who, as I discuss in my final chapter, writes cogently on modernist aesthetics and on contemporary music from a post-Habermasian perspective, has devoted much of his published work to the philosophy of language, discourse ethics, and political theory, with little immediate reference to art and aesthetics.

One key consideration with regards to the significance of artistic modernism in the various periods of the Frankfurt School's existence was the seminal role of Walter Benjamin. In many respects, Benjamin developed his concerns with artistic modernism *in advance of* and with significant *independence from* his somewhat limited formal contacts with the *Institut für Sozialforschung*. Through his focus on artistic and aesthetic questions, Benjamin is best thought of as an influential source of new themes for the emerging Frankfurt School theory of modernity, rather than as an applier of an already-formed Frankfurt School theory to artistic questions or as the fortunate beneficiary of its intellectual community and support. Despite this caveat, however, his work was to some extent shaped by his affiliation with the *Institut für Sozialforschung* throughout the 1930s, which helped financially support his "Arcades Project" research on nineteenth-century Paris, the "primal history of modernity" that he left uncompleted at his death by suicide in 1940. Benjamin's connection with the Frankfurt School can only be understood, ultimately, as a richly mediated one, above all through the editorial labor and powerful interpretation it received from Theodor Adorno. Adorno took crucial inspiration from Benjamin, and in turn, shepherded Benjamin's legacy in ways that would prove controversial for the 1960s German left. In part through Benjamin's direct connection with the Institute, but in even greater part through Adorno's tending of his work posthumously, Benjamin contributed to the composite intellectual physiognomy of the Frankfurt School.

Independently, of course, Adorno must take equal billing with Benjamin in any account of the Frankfurt School's relation to artistic modernism. Adorno, along with Benjamin, was closest to the actual practice of artistic modernism through his engagement with atonal musical composition as a student of Alban Berg in Vienna and his direct acquaintance with key modern musicians including Arnold Schönberg, Ernst Krenek, Hanns Eisler, Kurt Weill, and Virgil Thomson, as well as with the young "New Music" composers associated with Darmstadt's post-war summer course and festival. Through Adorno's rising star as Horkheimer's close collaborator and his direct shaping role in the *Institut* from the mid-1940s on, modernist art and aesthetics rose to particular importance in the post-war Frankfurt School. In studies and essay collections such as *The Philosophy of the New Music*, *In Search of Wagner*, *Prisms*, *Dissonances*, *Quasi una Fantasia*, and *Notes to Literature*, as well as his *Aesthetic Theory*, Adorno made a monumental contribution to modern musicology and to the aesthetics of modern art and literature, offering a direct connection between artistic modernism and the comprehensive social and philosophical concerns he articulated in works such as *Dialectic of Enlightenment* and *Negative Dialectics*.

Finally, the general cultural context of the 1960s lent new vigor to controversies around modernist art and aesthetics, both because the period saw a thoroughgoing recovery and reinterpretation of radical avant-garde culture of the 1910s–1930s in a rapidly politicizing context, and because counter-cultural tendencies had charged both art and the aesthetics of daily life (clothes, hair, rock music, drug use, etc.) with a new political significance. Benjamin's work took on new relevance in this context, seeming to offer a revolutionary path out of an official modernism that had become ever more administrated, institutionalized, and attenuated by Cold War constraints and concerns. Adorno, who staked the very possibility of resisting the onslaught of the culture industry and the liquidation of subjectivity on a fragile critical modernism, was challenged to articulate his anti-systematic aesthetics in quasi-systematic form, in the *Aesthetic Theory* he left unfinished at his death in 1969. And Herbert Marcuse, for whom aesthetics had been, at most, a background concern in his critical philosophy and theory of society, increasingly articulated his vision of a liberated society in ways that blended Friedrich Schiller's romantic ideals of aesthetic education and the aesthetic state with post-scarcity utopian ideals of a "new sensibility" based on freedom, solidarity, and sensuous fulfillment in daily life. Although works of art were in Marcuse's view at most indices of the capacities of human beings to imagine the world differently, and neither direct manifestations of emancipated life (e.g. "Living Theater") or figural models to be actualized in practice, the important role he ascribed to aesthetic experience nevertheless lent innovative art an increasingly central place in his writings. Moreover, Marcuse's theories exercised an influence on and helped provide theoretical legitimacy for a range of counter-cultural and liberationist artistic practices that he himself, with his relatively cautious artistic tastes, did not directly endorse.

TOPICS AND CONTEXTS OF FRANKFURT SCHOOL THOUGHT: REIFICATION, TECHNOLOGY, UTOPIA

In this section, I will seek to contextualize the work of the three main figures treated in this book – Walter Benjamin, Theodor Adorno, and Herbert Marcuse – within a topical context that extends beyond them and, indeed, even beyond the Frankfurt School more broadly. In a brief montage rather than a detailed exposition, I will consider three key topics that circulate within their work and that tie them (and their Frankfurt School colleagues) to a larger ambit of thought about the capitalist modernity to which they relate their theory of modernism. Moreover, this topical approach allows me to focus, in passing, on three exemplary thinkers who are not strictly speaking part of the "Frankfurt School," but who nevertheless stand close to their concerns and who each had biographical, intellectual, and political ties with *Institut* members. The topics I will discuss include: *reification*, which will be considered in relation to the Marxist philosopher Georg Lukács and his influential 1923 book *History and Class Consciousness*; *technology*, which I will consider though a brief discussion of Siegfried Kracauer's essays "Photography" and "The Mass Ornament"; and *utopia / non-synchronicity*, which will be discussed through a short exposition of the thinking of Ernst Bloch.

Reification (Georg Lukács)

In his 1923 book *History and Class Consciousness*,[14] the Hungarian Marxist Georg Lukács, in exile following the collapse of the Hungarian Commune in 1919, advanced a theoretical concept that would become central to the cultural analyses of the Frankfurt School: reification (*Verdinglichung*), or the becoming thing-like of social dynamics and processes. Although its subsequent theoretical productiveness may owe more to its suggestive richness than to its conceptual rigor,[15] there is no question that this concept, more than any other, was pivotal for the Frankfurt School's analysis of culture and its aesthetics. Horkheimer made reference to it in his overall framing of "critical theory," and Benjamin, Adorno, and Marcuse each offered original interpretations and applications of Lukács's reification concept. (In a short article from 1929, notably, Benjamin would name *History and Class Consciousness* as one of the four greatest books of German scholarly literature of the recent past.[16] The others were Alois Riegl's *Late Roman Art Industry* from 1901, Adolf Meyer's

Building in Iron from 1907, and Franz Rosenzweig's *Star of Redemption* from 1921.)

With his concept of reification, Lukács sought to give a comprehensive explanation of how knowledge and action are systematically constrained under capitalist modernity. Through a synthesis of theoretical motifs from Karl Marx, Georg Simmel, and his former teacher Max Weber, Lukács believed he could account for several apparently distinct, but actually inter-related processes in modern society: the intensive spread of capitalist social relations to all reaches of society, including to "intellectual" or "spiritual" domains; the growing administrative control of social institutions through bureaucracy; the increasing specialization of the sciences and the intellectual disciplines; and the increasing atomization, distance, and coldness of social relations between modern individuals. The theoretical linchpin that held these processes together for Lukács was Marx's notion of commodity fetishism, by which Marx characterized the apparent magic that the commodity performs in a capitalist economy. Any commodity – whether a bolt of fabric, an auto-mobile tire, a can of soup, or any other of the myriad objects produced for sale and profit – can turn the organized collaborative work of living men and women within a division of labor into a seemingly independent thing that can circulate in new contexts, carry the mark of its value, and be consumed as an object of use – all without any evident reference to those human laborers who produced it. For Lukács, the commodity's transformation of living relations into things was paradigmatic of a whole process of mystification involving reified social relations. Through the processes of reification, the dense struc-tures of social interactions in modern society and the social relations within which knowledge is produced and applied become hidden behind a heap of pseudo-autonomous things, which possess the density and opacity of a new human-produced "second nature."

These second-nature "things" that have become separate from their pro-ducers and which conceal the social interaction that produced them include, however, not just tangible material things, but also intellectual objects: con-cepts, facts, theories, scientific paradigms and methods. The production of knowledge is also, Lukács underscores, a socially mediated process, with complex social interactions in the formation, dissemination, and application of the products of mental labor. But the social conditions of thought tend, like material commodities, to disappear behind the intellectual goods themselves. Producers of knowledge, mental laborers, cultural workers like artists and writers under capitalism are subject to processes of reification just as surely as are industrial and farm workers. Lukács uses this perspective to criticize the contemporary thought-world of his time, which was rife with spurious conceptual objects (e.g. "lived experience," "Weltanschauung") and vacuous positivistic facts with ever an more narrow social reference. Idealism and positivism – predominant tendencies in the social sciences and philosophy of his time – derived for Lukács from a common incapacity to penetrate the thick veil of reified social relations. Idealism's hypostatized concepts and positivism's atomized facts function ideologically: producing systematically distorted knowledge that hides the structural basis of modern capitalist society, the antagonistic class relations of production.

Notably, in his later work Lukács would apply his analysis of reification to literary study. In proto-modernist tendencies such as naturalism and aestheticism, as well as in modernist and avant-garde writing proper, he identified a complementary relation between stylistic tendencies that otherwise seemed to be polar opposites.[17] On the one hand, some modernist and proto-modernist writing seemed to him to be mired in an abstract subjectivism, reveling in the sensations, psychological states, and feelings of the inner world, while losing the solidity and social nature of the world outside the self. Typical in this regard for Lukács was the work of Kafka, where the world has become confusing, anxiety-filled, and unpredictable, insofar as it follows an inner dream-like logic rather than a realistic social logic of action in context, as, for Lukács, the great realist novels of Balzac and Tolstoy did. One might also point, as a complementary example, to Oscar Wilde's *Portrait of Dorian Gray*, which embeds in its overall moral allegory an exhaustive, but ultimately superfluous catalogue of Dorian's self-refinement of the senses, as he runs through the sensations attached to jewels, spices, fabrics, and the other stimulants he throws at his sensuous palate. On the other hand, Lukács argues, reification leads to literary manifestations of an atomized positivism, which cleaves to surface details of social life, registering disconnected and meaning-deprived facts, while failing to penetrate to the underlying relations, dynamics, and structural principles. He found these effects of reification to be exemplified in the naturalist novels of Emile Zola and Upton Sinclair, as well as in the modernist montage-novels of James Joyce, John Dos Passos, and Alfred Döblin. This diagnosis of reification would also underpin Lukács's opposition to the "reportage" and "factographic" tendencies within socialist writing, represented most importantly by Bertolt Brecht and Sergei Tretiakov.[18]

The Frankfurt School modernists would, in significant respects, concur with Lukács's connection of reification and modernism, but not with his prescriptive rejection of modernism on that basis. Benjamin, Adorno, and Marcuse saw artistic modernism not, as did Lukács, as a blind reflection of an ever-more reified world, but rather as a sensitive registration of and response to reification's penetration of the whole fabric of modern experience. The modernist arts could not help but reflect this overwhelming and all-embracing social force; yet for the Frankfurt School, they did not merely express a helpless capitulation to reification. They could also help to critically diagnose the forms of reification and offer singular, sometimes unprecedented tactics for resisting it, making space and moving within a seemingly closed, reified world.

Technology (Siegfried Kracauer)

A key topic of concern for the Frankfurt School thinkers, as for a wide range of twentieth-century philosophers and social theorists, was the nature and impact of technology, which was affecting every part of modern culture, experience, and everyday life. In some cases, as with some of the more pessimistic work of Adorno and Horkheimer about the domination of "instrumental reason" in modern society, fear of technology could be a discernable note in Frankfurt School writing. Typically, however, their analysis of technology was more dialectically ambivalent or even, as in Benjamin's case and in some of Marcuse's work, tilted towards a utopian view of technology's potentials. Benjamin, for example, famously saw in the technology of image reproduction a potential to charge art with a new emancipatory function: the analysis of modern urban life and the political "training" of the masses to meet the emerging challenges of the day. Analogously, Marcuse envisioned a liberatory technology that would free human beings for a more sensuously and existentially fulfilled life free from scarcity. No longer an instrument of exploitation and alienation under capitalism, technology could be made to serve goals of human happiness and the harmonious exchange of society with nature. Even the strongly ambivalent Adorno took in his musical writings a dialectical view of compositional "*Technik*" – meaning primarily not the visible instruments or machinery to produce modern music, but rather the conceptual and procedural rationality that modern musicians from Schönberg to post-war serialist composers employed to construct their musical artworks. Adorno strongly affirmed the imperative to adhere to the highest standard of technical rationality in art, and correlatively, he vehemently denounced any recourse to regression, the archaic, or the "barbaric" – as he detected, for example, in early works of Igor Stravinsky like *The Rite of Spring* and *Petrushka*.

An important immediate precursor of the Frankfurt School's analysis of technology can be found in the essays of Siegfried Kracauer from the late 1920s and early '30s. Kracauer was associated with Walter Benjamin, Ernst Bloch, and other left-wing literary intellectuals around the newspaper *Frankfurter Zeitung*, for which he wrote as a salaried journalist between 1921 and 1933, regularly publishing feuilleton essays, articles, and reviews. He also had a close personal relation to the young Theodor Adorno, who as a teenager adopted Kracauer as an older intellectual mentor and Saturday teacher of Kant. In key texts such as "Photography" and "The Mass Ornament,"[19] both originally published as *Frankfurter Zeitung* essays in 1927, Kracauer introduced a dialectical conception of how, in the present day, technology and culture were interacting in the formation of images. In one respect, the image of the object-world that is produced by technology, like the modernist artwork, is artificial, arbitrary, and alienated from the organic forms and connections to be found in nature. Technology, at first glance, appears to be placing human beings at a greater and greater distance from natural objects and spaces. On closer examination, as Kracauer reveals, the relation of technology and nature is more entangled and complex.

In his "Photography" essay, for instance, Kracauer ponders the difference between an image we hold in memory and a photographic image. The memory-image is an affectively shaped, organic selection of features, in which the elements of the image are emphasized according to their meaningfulness. By contrast, a photograph captures exact visual details, which may be of uncertain meaning or which may not have even been consciously perceived prior to the photography's isolation and highlighting of them. Thus, for instance, we notice a slight asymmetry of the facial features of a person, or a crease in their clothes, or an out-of-place object in the background. As photographic images of the world become more and more prominent – and Kracauer was writing in the period in which photojournalism and cinema had surged into everyday life – they supplant the organic, meaning-based selection that human perception and memory perform in forging images of the world. The visible world appears to be not a necessary, organic totality, but rather a contingent montage of an open-ended set of individual snapshots. Kracauer suggests, however, that it is only with this technologically disclosed contingency that a modern scientific conception of nature, neutral and lawful but devoid of reference to human values and meaning, first fully emerges. At the same time, however, this nature is in no way "natural," in the sense of merely given, independent of human intervention. Nature's emergence as a distinct category in modern thought, Kracauer implies, is thoroughly mediated by technology, which is a product of human society. Technology divests nature of the residues of mythic meaning that human beings project into it, and lets nature simply "be." But even as nature is manifested in this way, the same process leads us to question how necessary and "given" any of nature's forms are for us.

If – as photographically mediated experience suggests to us – nature's configurations are contingent and devoid of intrinsic meaning, and if these constellations can be reconfigured and reconstructed at will through the agency of technology, then human beings can "construct" nature rationally to serve our goals and intentions. We can, by perceiving technology's emancipatory potential, remake nature in a way that conceives it neither, as in the mythical world, as a source of mysterious fate doled out by gods and spirits, nor, as in the age of enlightenment and modern science, as a neutral resource to be dominated and exploited. Rather, through a liberated technology, nature can be configured to conform to human needs and to support collective happiness, which requires consideration of substantive shared human values rather than the abstract quantitative metrics of science and economics. Kracauer describes this dialectical process – pushing the technological denaturing of nature to the point where a second, consciously constructed nature becomes possible – as the "go-for-broke game of the historical process." He concludes:

> The images of the stock of nature disintegrated into its elements are offered up to consciousness to deal with as it pleases. Their original order is lost; they no longer cling to the spatial context that linked them with an original out of which the memory image was selected. But if the remnants of nature are not oriented toward the memory image, then the order they assume through the image is necessarily provisional. It is therefore incumbent on consciousness to establish the *provisional status* of all given configurations, and perhaps even to awaken an inkling of the right order of the inventory of nature.[20]

It is a quick step from this argument to the artistic arguments of Sergei Eisenstein and Bertolt Brecht for the conscious use of montage in constructing modernist works of cinema and theater, and to Walter Benjamin's broad championing of montage practice in the arts and historical writing. They saw in the experimental montage of images the means to analyze the given state of affairs, to reveal its contingency, and to project ways in which it could be changed in the interest of human liberation.

Kracauer would take up an analogous argument in his essay "The Mass Ornament," which discussed the popular culture phenomenon of the revue group The Tiller Girls, who performed line dances of the sort rendered even more spectacular in the films of Busby Berkeley in the late 1920s and early '30s. Although their founding as a dance troupe dated back to the 1890s and they had their start in Manchester rather than in New York or Hollywood, Kracauer implies that they are recent "products of American distraction factories" (and in fact, by the 1920s, there was a Tiller dance school on Broadway supplying Tiller girls to revue acts like the Ziegfeld Follies).[21] These "girl clusters," as Kracauer characterized them, utilized human bodies not as individual, organic wholes, but rather as abstract visual tokens to be assembled into larger *mass* images, in some cases machine-like, in other instances natural and organic, such as waves or flowers opening and closing. In both cases, however, their function is, in Kracauer's view, ornamental. They present an abstract visual "argument," rather than expressing some meaning hidden beneath the explicit surface of the performance:

> The star-formations . . . have no meaning beyond themselves, and the masses above whom they rise are not a moral unit like a company of soldiers. One cannot even describe the figures as the decorative frills of gymnastic discipline. Rather, the girl-units drill in order to produce an

immense number of parallel lines, the goal being to train the broadest mass of people in order to create a pattern of undreamed of dimensions. The end result is ornament, whose closure is brought about by emptying all the substantial constructs of their contents.[22]

Suggestively, Kracauer associates these ornamental, embodied patterns-in-motion with the industrial labor process under capitalism. Capitalism labor, he argues, is an "end in itself"; rather than being produced for some purpose organic to the produced object, it brings forth the product as commodity, thus creating it first and foremost as a unit of value exchangeable with other value-carrying objects of very different uses and material qualities. It is brought forth, in its very material existence, as a "real abstraction," as Karl Marx termed it in *Capital*. Although Kracauer does not remark it explicitly, the real abstractions of the capitalist work-process and these popular culture "mass ornaments" that offered transfigured reflections of industrial machine-labor also had corollaries in the art of modernism and the avant-garde: for example, the fusion of architectural elements or furniture and vegetative and female nude ornamental motifs in Secession / Art Nouveau design; or the imitation of machinery in Futurist art, such as the print shop suggested by the performers of Giacomo Balla's 1914 theater piece *Printing Press* or the "photodynamic," cinematic, and theatrical productions of Anton Gulio Bragaglia, who received an affirmative notice by Benjamin in 1928 in *Die literarische Welt*.[23] These too share with the mass ornament a process of abstraction, fusing bodies, organic or mechanical motifs, and pure visual or sonorous elements into an autonomous, ornamental whole. Their semantic interdeterminacy, their suspended meaning or even nonsensical character, allows them to emphasize their sign- or token-like quality as bearers of social value and power. In one of their manifestos, the Dadaists famously asked "What is Dada?" and facetiously answered "A Fire Insurance"; similarly, they jokingly admonished their audience to "Invest your money in Dada! Dada is the only savings bank that pays interest in the hereafter!" Though done with a mocking laugh, their metaphorical reference of Dada to money was hardly accidental. The Dadaists pointed to the tenuous status of all values, monetary, moral, and aesthetic, in the society of their day. They emphatically underscored that their works were nothing but the abstract bearer of socially guaranteed (or socially refused) value, something "underwritten" against risk, like a piece of fire insurance or an investment, not an object of evident utility or intrinsic significance, guaranteed by tradition, unquestionable authority, or the organic qualities of the thing itself.

Kracauer's judgment on this ornamental abstraction is dialectical. On the one hand, he considers the mass ornament an exemplary cultural manifestation of a technically advanced capitalist society. The dynamics of capitalism tend towards the dissolution of organic forms of association typical of traditional societies in favor of ever more abstract, atomized, and anonymous social bonds, above all the cash-nexus of capitalist economic relations. Insofar as human beings can be abstracted from their qualities as individuals and treated as tokens in an apparatus of machine-mediated production and consumption, they become a "mass." The "mass ornament" makes an artwork out of this atomized human material of an industrially organized society, offering it back to a mass audience as its own aesthetically transfigured image. Yet, on the other hand, Kracauer does not lament this process of abstraction in favor of the organic ties of traditional community. Rather, he argues, what the Tiller Girls reveal is that the process has not gone far enough to break through into a full-scale emancipation of technology's human potential. The ornament is abstract, and hence represents a certain degree of rationalization of the organic human community. It is an image of certain positive facets of the industrial work-process, exhibiting the planning, order, and coordination that are necessary to have a hundred workers cooperate to produce an automobile or a hundred dancing girls forming a picture of a rolling wave or a flower rotating in time to music. At the same time, this planning, order, and coordination remains purely visual and aesthetic; it does not touch on the more substantive aspects of the girls' lives, thoughts, and experience. Kracauer takes the mass ornament, accordingly, as an ambivalent sign: it represents a utopian image of a more rationally ordered collective life, yet insofar as it remains abstract and ornamental, it also diverts and betrays this potential. As Benjamin would later argue explicitly in his celebrated essay "The Work of Art in the Age of Its Technical Reproducibility," only when the mass artwork goes beyond an aesthetic function to engage with the social and political actualities of contemporary life can it serve the goal of human emancipation. The more art defensively entrenches itself in the aesthetic, remaining in the alienated abstraction of the ornament, Kracauer and Benjamin suggest, the more it relinquishes its emancipatory potential. Benjamin would go so far as to argue that this dialectical ambivalence of the mass ornament defined the dividing line between a reactionary cultural politics aligned with fascism and a revolutionary politics of art that could lend aid to human liberation.

Utopia / Non-Synchronicity (Ernst Bloch)

Shortly after World War I, the philosopher Ernst Bloch, a friend of Lukács and part of the *Frankfurter Zeitung* circle of intellectuals, published his book *Spirit of Utopia*.[24] In it, and in subsequent works such as *Heritage of Our Times* (1935),[25] he developed a novel conception of utopia that both influenced and paralleled ideas put forward by the thinkers of the Frankfurt School. Classical utopias, such as Thomas More's *Utopia*, Tommaso Campanella's *City of the Sun*, and Francis Bacon's *New Atlantis*, presupposed a *spatially* located "good place": they were contemporaneous with the present-day world of their authors, but in another place, such as on the island that More's traveler Raphael Hythloday arrives at and returns from to tell his utopian tale. The intellectual historian Reinhart Koselleck identified the late eighteenth century as the threshold of a significant change, the "temporalization of utopia," which shifts the location of utopia from an alternative position in space to that of an alternative *time*, usually the future.[26] Increasingly, the representations of utopian societies become temporal constructions of alternative futures, and, in turn, they invest the fictional works that expound them with an anticipatory function. Bloch would boldly extend this structure of modern utopias to encompass a philosophy of history and religion centered on collective anticipation and hope, a hermeneutics for interpreting works of art and culture as bearers of a future-oriented "utopian function," and even a speculative ontology involving the unfinished nature of the present and the latency of the future in anterior times. Embedded in the very structures of being, Bloch believed, were the foundations of human aspirations and hope for the fulfillment of the future's promise. The manifold products of human thought and labor could thus be interpreted as prefigurative signs pointing towards this future. "Utopia" meant nothing other than the in-dwelling of the future, in unfulfilled traces, in the heritage of the past and the longings of the present, whether these are political, religious, artistic, or individual-existential. Bloch's conception of utopia found important resonances in the work of, especially, Walter Benjamin, who made his own original contribution to the philosophical and political conception of utopia, and put utopian thinkers such as Charles Fourier, Robert Owen, Étienne Cabet, and Tony Garnier at the center of his thinking about urban modernism and modernity.

Bloch explored unconventional ways of thinking and writing, in order to discern and communicate about this hidden utopian reserve in the objects of culture and everyday life. Typical in this regard is his famous discussion of a pitcher, at the beginning of *Spirit of Utopia*, in which, in an expressionistically stylized lyrical prose, he rises to an almost mystical ontological and psychological identification with the pitcher:

> Not every puddle I step in makes me gray; not every railroad track bends me around a corner. But I could probably be formed like the pitcher, see myself as something brown, something peculiarly organic ... and not just mimetically or simply empathetically, but so that I thus become for my part richer, more present, cultivated further toward myself by this artifact that participates in me. That is true of all things that have grown, and here, in drinking pitchers, the people labored to express their pleasure and their deeper sense of contentment, to affix themselves to these implements of their household and the public house.[27]

Objects, in Bloch's view, constitute complex nodes of social experiences. Those that are bound up with experiences of special intensity, love, communion, fidelity, freedom, and enjoyment are especially charged with qualities that define how we would envision a condition of future utopian fulfillment, in which these experiences would be normal and universal rather than exceptional. Therefore, by concentrating intensely on objects charged with such significance, we can assemble the figural and spiritual elements of a fulfilled future and motivate ourselves and others to strive to realize it.[28]

Bloch also suggests that art and literature are intentionally designed to have analogous effects to those produced by objects that, contingent on habitual practice and experience, are associated with utopian wishes. In a sense, artworks are intentionally designed constellations of the unfulfilled future, montages of fragments of utopian "wish-landscapes" that the artist composes into larger wholes and that the viewer, listener, or reader may translate into actuality. Thus, in the same passage dealing with the pitcher, Bloch concludes with an extension of the pitcher into the domain of artistic experience:

> Everything that was ever made in this way, out of love and necessity, leads a life of its own, leads into a strange, new territory, and returns with us formed as we could not be in life, adorned with a certain, however weak sign, the seal of our self. Here, too, one feels oneself looking down a long, sunlit corridor with a door at the far end, as in a work of art. The pitcher is not one, it has nothing of the work of art about it, but a work of art should at least be like this in order really to be one, and that alone would certainly already be a lot.[29]

Bloch's organon for art – its production, its experience, and its interpretation – is thus the object that, in recalling instances of social practice and collective feeling, also projects a utopian future transcending the moment of the artwork's present context.

Bloch's conception of utopian anticipation latent in the past and present holds important implications for cultural interpretation and the writing of history. If the present is not homogeneous, but rather shot through with traces of a still-renewable past and a not-yet realized but latently effective future, then typical notions of "context," which tie the meaning of a historical fact to related historical facts within a common chronological span or period, are undermined by the instability of time itself. In this questioning of received notions of context, Bloch shared an anti-historicist orientation with Walter Benjamin, who in both his work on baroque allegory and in his historiographic notes for the *Arcades Project*, emphasized the potential *divergence* of a cultural or literary artifact from its original context and its ability to generate new historical meanings rather than just reflect those assigned to it by its place in its original historical context. Whether it was an aristocratic house that had fallen into ruin, a king who had gone mad and drawn his kingdom down with him, a sacred or literary work that could no longer be read without a commentary, or the myriad images of obsolete fashion and ephemeral consumer products he had unearthed in his research of nineteenth-century Paris, Benjamin selected objects of study that broke free of their originating context and laid bare its defunct social premises. So too, in an analogous fashion, Bloch favored objects that were *anachronistic*, because they were obsolete and evocative of a bygone age, they were fantastic and eccentric to the present, or they had a strongly anticipatory thrust towards the future. If a material artifact bears within it references that transcend the present either backward into persisting tradition or forward into the latent future, then present context cannot exhaustively determine its meaning. For Bloch, it is important to note, this is not just a matter of an object's taking on a new meaning as it passes from one historical period or context to another. It is rather that, in Bloch's view, the utopian traces in the object play an active role *in the present* to help *produce* new contexts, new situations of possibility, new historical horizons. Just as, psychologically, human beings imagine changed worlds and are motivated to create change by desire and longing, so too for Bloch there is a kind of objective longing intrinsic to culture, a claim the future lays upon the present, an impulse to change that dwells within the present. No cultural object, in Bloch's view, can be adequately interpreted without accounting for this reciprocal, effective implication of the past, present, and future in one another.

In his more mature work, Bloch would develop his earlier conception of utopia into a full-scale theory of non-homogeneous time, or "non-contemporaneity" (*Ungleichzeitigkeit*). In a section of his 1935 book *Heritage of Our Times*, in which Bloch sought to account for the Nazis' use of archaic symbols and appeals to traditions not simply as mystifications but as diversions of genuine popular wishes and longings, he gave theoretical formulation to the problem of non-contemporaneity. Notably, this problem had arisen in the socialist tradition already under the guise of "uneven development," which became acute when the socialist revolution succeeded not in advanced industrial Europe but rather in the industrially backward, largely agrarian expanses of Russia. Socialist thinkers such as Lenin and Trotsky, later Georg Lukács, Antonio Gramsci, Bloch, Raymond Williams and others, confronted the unexpected combination of backward conditions and historical acceleration that the Bolshevik victory represented to an orthodox Marxist sense of history. Bloch developed a dialectic that analyzed the "turbulent Now," not just into two fundamental class elements in contradiction with one another, but rather into a multi-faceted structure of contradiction that grasps a temporally non-homogeneous present: "We had to distinguish between the falsely and the genuinely non-contemporaneous contradiction, the latter and the contemporaneous one, and again in the both the subjective and the objective factor of contradiction."[30] By the false and the genuine non-contemporaneous contradiction, Bloch had in mind the Nazis' appeal to the peasantry and the lower middle-classes through their evocation of community and their protest against the injuries of capitalism upon these social elements, which were distorted and turned to reactionary ends as racial scapegoating and violent nationalism. There are, Bloch underscores, genuine grounds for these "little people" to rebel, as Germany's peasant and village communities, livelihoods, and traditions, already anachronistic under advanced capitalism, have been progressive devalued and destroyed. Moreover, in Bloch's view, such protests are not intrinsically reactionary, as urban liberals and socialists often believed. On the contrary, precisely because they were not acknowledged as legitimate by the left, they could be appropriated by the demagoguery of Hitler, who appeared to lend the sufferings of these plebian elements a voice, a narrative to make them meaningful, and an enemy against which to target their rage. The contemporaneous contradiction, for Bloch, was the present-day struggle of workers against the bourgeoisie, and the forces of socialism against fascism. The two struggles in the contemporaneous and non-contemporaneous dimension were also in contradiction with each other, thus overdetermining the outcomes within each. For example, the contradiction of the contemporaneous and the non-contemporaneous could be, in the situation of interwar Europe, turned to reactionary ends (e.g. using the peasantry against the revolutionary workers) or could be acknowledged and worked through to different results by means of strategic alliances between workers and other popular forces (as Lenin did with his victorious slogan in 1917 of "Land, Bread, Peace," and as the Popular Front sought to achieve in the mid-1930s). Finally, both the contemporaneous and non-contemporaneous had two dimensions, objective and subjective, which could work in contradiction with one another:

> The subjectively non-contemporaneous contradiction is accumulated rage, the objectively non-contemporaneous one the unfinished past; the subjectively contemporaneous one is the free revolutionary action of the proletariat, the objectively contemporaneous one the prevented future contained in the Now, the prevented technological blessing, the prevented new society with which the old one is pregnant in its forces of production.[31]

Thus, for example, the accumulated rage that Bloch identified as the subjective side of the non-contemporaneous contradiction may lead the peasantry and petit bourgeoisie to embrace Nazism; yet for Bloch, that allegiance is precisely what blocks their resolving the unfinished past. The contradiction between objective and subjective, especially in their multi-dimensional dialectical interaction, may lead to a catastrophic outcome, as was the case in the "turbulent Now" of the European 1930s.

In part directly influenced by the thought of Walter Benjamin (to the point that Benjamin unjustly suspected Bloch of plagiarizing his ideas), Bloch embraced a sort of avant-garde montage as his favored mode of writing critical and philosophical texts. These compositional methods borrowed from the modernist and avant-garde arts were intended not just as stylistic ornamentation but as a constructive means to theorize a multi-faceted, temporally non-homogeneous space of culture and politics. In a passage that shows his sympathetic comprehension of Benjamin's use of montage and provisional, experimental thought as a way of grasping the temporal complexity of the present, Bloch writes:

> It is evident in the philosophical cross-drilling of Benjamin . . . that montage takes its material from much improvisation which would have previously been random, from much emphasized interruption which would have previously merely remained unemphasized disturbance; it takes intervening means from despised or suspicious forms and from forms which were formerly second-hand. Also from the ruin-meanings of decaying great works and from the jungle of material that is no longer smoothly arranged . . . Everywhere here there is not much more than programme, fleeting, lonely and often temporary; and yet the attraction of this programme or disjointed participation in its consequences is in most of what the twenties have produced in the way of significant art and perception. Even the pervasion and interchangeability of the parts, which appears in the self-collapse of the bourgeoisie, is superior to the closed unity of its previous "world-picture."[32] (Bloch 1990: 207)

THE FRANKFURT SCHOOL BETWEEN HIGH AND LOW CULTURE

A final context important to address in the introduction is the debate that took place in the 1930s within the Frankfurt School about "high" autonomous art and "low" popular and political-propagandistic art. This debate especially involved Walter Benjamin, from a somewhat marginal position with respect to the *Institut*, and Theodor Adorno, who was beginning to come into his own within it and consolidate his position as an increasingly central partner of Max Horkheimer. (Marcuse's position, which I will defer discussing in detail until later, would vary over the years.) In turn, this debate would prove very influential when the "postmodernism" debates of the 1980s and early '90s strongly focused aesthetic debate on high / low and autonomous / heteronomous distinctions and dialectics in the arts. I will also thus briefly consider here three important Frankfurt School-influenced positions advanced in that latter context, by Andreas Huyssen, Fredric Jameson, and Thomas Crow.

In the mid-1930s, Walter Benjamin and Theodor Adorno were engaged in an intense if sporadic correspondence. Much of it, as one might expect of two exiled German-Jewish intellectuals, centered around the exigencies of staying alive, both intellectually and financially, and their letters teem with reports on mutual friends, suspicions about plots and intrigues, schemes to tap relatives and patrons for funds, and the like. Yet in the midst of this, and not wholly unrelated to these practical matters, was a fundamental debate about the nature, function, and outlook of culture in the present day. Benjamin, to a significant extent, looked favorably on the tendencies which were liquidating the traditional modes of art and its consumption; Adorno defended the critical potential of autonomous works of art, while not unambiguously affirming either, as it were, Mickey Mouse or Goethe. In a much-quoted remark, he rebuffed Benjamin for his undialectical position. Both the cinema and the autonomous artwork, he argued, "bear the stigmata of capitalism, both contain elements of change . . . Both are torn halves of an integral freedom, to which however they do not add up."[33]

In retrospect, it is possible to see that the stakes of the argument were not solely, as has often been claimed, that Benjamin held a collectivist and activistic position that allowed him to favor, over-optimistically, the new mass-reproduced "low" forms of art, while Adorno defensively clung to individual, autonomous, "high" artworks. Insofar as this dichotomized view is accurate at all – and it is only partially so – it appears secondary to a more important distinction. In common but with different emphases, both were seeking to understand the new alignments of cultural products with the life-practice of individuals and groups in society. Within this common project, they advanced divergent hypotheses about the new social structure within which culture would have to be thought. Benjamin saw the decisive feature of the present moment to be the ongoing dissolution of the separated spheres of liberal society, including that which englobed artistic activity within its relative autonomy. The dominant feature of current European society was, in his view, this crisis, and the incipience of a new constellation of power, for better or worse. In this context, the highly mediated place and function of bourgeois art, its role in the formation of the bourgeois self through *Bildung* and private aesthetic experience, could pass over into new functions and help give shape to unprecedented, superindividual agencies in everyday and political life: for example, the proletarian photography groups that formed in continental Europe, Britain, and the United States; the militant theater group, such as Benjamin saw fostered by Bertolt Brecht's didactic dramas, or by the British Worker's Theatre Movement; and the intransigent intellectual society, as represented by Georges Bataille's *Acephale* and *Collège de Sociologie*.[34] Radical intellectuals such as Benjamin hoped to steer this all-encompassing crisis of social experience in an emancipatory direction, rather than allowing its potential to be crushed by fascism, essentially repeating, in still more brutal form, the depressing events of the last major European crisis of 1918–23.

Adorno, in contrast, did not view the crisis itself as the primary structural factor in determining culture's defining features in the present, but rather the new mechanisms of political, economic, and cultural integration that had emerged in the face of it. In particular, and in keeping with his greater remove from the vicissitudes of European politics, Adorno laid great emphasis on the rise of an integrated culture industry, which not only churned out a stereo-typed mass product without spontaneous links to popular groups, but also reprocessed high culture in ways that betrayed the experiential content that it had earlier held for the liberal-democratic bourgeoisie. This is an important and often forgotten point about Adorno's idea of "culture industry." It is explicitly not synonymous with "mass culture," a term Adorno rejected; it rather characterizes a new corporatist administration of *all* culture, whether "high" or "low." Thus if Adorno sought to release the critical potential he perceived in rare, stigmatized instances of autonomous art, as with the works of Samuel Beckett or Arnold Schönberg, it was not because they "preserved a heritage," in the Arnoldian sense of being a solid repository of the best that has been thought and said. Rather, they represented a tenuous margin from which it was possible to make visible the betrayal of the entire spectrum of culture to capitalist administration, from the fragile perspective of works that both resisted the homogenizing demands of the culture market and liquidated, through technical processes that destroyed their aesthetic appearance, their affirmative content as high culture "goods," prestigious commodities in the niche market of the arts.

Subsequent Marxist debates around modernism have reprised these two positions, often taking over as implicit background Benjamin's and Adorno's hypotheses about the nature of the 1930s social transition. For example, both Fredric Jameson and Andreas Huyssen have emphasized Adorno's view of the culture industry's all-encompassing nature, its comprehensive incorpora-tion and redistribution of the entire economy of cultural value, from "high" to "low." In his essay "Adorno in Reverse: From Hollywood to Richard Wagner,"[35] Huyssen takes historical stock of Adorno's assessment of mass culture, sorting out what he considers its core insight from its more limited conjunctural judgments:

> Adorno's bleak description of modern mass culture as dream turned nightmare has perhaps outlived its usefulness and can now take its place as a historically contingent and theoretically powerful reflection on fascism. What has not outlived its usefulness, however, is Adorno's suggestion that mass culture was not imposed on art only from the "outside," but that art was transformed into its opposite thanks precisely to its emancipation from traditional forms of bourgeois art. In the vortex of commodification there was never an outside.[36]

Huyssen suggests that one logical response for contemporary art to this "vortex" would be to attempt to continue the project of modernist resistance, despite the progressive attenuation of its critical substance. Yet he also holds out the possibility of an effective use by artists of both modernism and mass culture, a partial embrace of commodification that stands in productive tension with the artist's ambition and pursuit of the great work. Huyssen suggests that this sort of strategic desublimation of the artwork is necessary to preserve contemporary art against ineffective purism, on the one side, and a definitive yielding of the field to commercialized kitsch, on the other. While Huyssen does not fully spell out in this essay what such a compromise would entail, the amalgamation of modernist and mass cultural elements does inform his idea of pop and other postmodern art movements, which may be in turn both ambivalently affirmative *and* critical in relation to contemporary capitalist society.

In appropriating Adorno, however, Huyssen also reduces the content of his culture industry thesis – which aimed at understanding a radical transformation in the structure of everyday experience – to a circumscribed matter of artistic creation and critical discourses that apportion value among different sorts of cultural production ("mass culture" and "modernism"). Jameson, too, is strongly concerned with the evaluative nature of the terms "mass culture" and "modernism." However, unlike Huyssen, he roots this question of value, as well as questions of narrative form, in the context of changes in everyday life. Thus, in his 1979 essay "Reification and Utopia in Mass Culture," Jameson writes:

> Capitalism systematically dissolves the fabric of all cohesive social groups without exception, including its own ruling class, and thereby problematizes aesthetic production and linguistic invention which have their source in group life. The result . . . is the dialectical fission of older aesthetic expression into two modes, modernism and mass culture, equally dissociated from group praxis.[37]

This shared dissociation, however, takes different shape in the two differentiated modes. In the absence of a more organic relation to group practice, neither modernism nor mass culture can directly express the interests of any social group. These works register and work through social interests and anxieties in displaced, repressed, symptomatic form. Modernist works, however, offer alternative aesthetic heterotopias as "compensatory structures," while mass culture works offer "imaginary resolutions" in narrative and "optical illusions of social harmony."[38] Although Jameson will soon formulate this symptomatic repression of social contradictions in terms of a political unconscious of narrative works in relation to an unrepresentable History, the model offered here might more accurately be described as an aesthetic "psychopathology of everyday life." Both mass culture and modernism represent a sort of ideological slip of the tongue in the ugly face of late capitalist everydayness.

Jameson's discussion of mass culture and modernism, however, suggests only one location in which their invidious division might be reconciled: in the reading and viewing of the Marxist critic. Basically, Jameson goes no further than to argue for suspending evaluative judgments about "high" and "low" and for treating both to symptomatic reading. Huyssen, in contrast, despite his more narrow focus, draws conclusions that point in the direction of a transformed artistic practice. If Huyssen opts for a problematic artistic reconciliation of mass culture and modernism in new artworks, Jameson in this essay basically leaves the split as it is, however much he may critically trace it back to its common source in late capitalism. At the time of their writing, now many years ago, neither Jameson nor Huyssen were particularly sanguine about the possibility of a more thoroughgoing, utopian reconciliation of these divided cultural modes, recollecting and reanimating group life, whose fragmentation had led to the emergence of the split between modernist and mass culture as complementary deformations.

Thomas Crow, in his essay "Modernism and Mass Culture in the Visual Arts,"[39] offers a reading of modernism analogous to that of Huyssen and Jameson, but is both more concrete in his observations about the social content of modernist art and more historically grounded in the empirical development of visual art in France from the late eighteenth century into the twentieth century. Crow notes that such earlier artists as David, Delacroix, and Courbet and the later artists of impressionism and post-impressionism cannot be saliently distinguished in terms of a simple opposition of engaged versus autonomous art, or politically radical versus aesthetically radical orientations. Rather their difference lies with the profound displacement of oppositional impulses that occurred with the reaction which followed the 1848 uprisings and the imposition in 1851 of the Bonapartist dictatorship. Up to 1848, Crow argues, an oppositional art could ally itself with a radical middle class pursuing democratic freedom in the political arena. After the rise of Louis Bonaparte to power, radical middle-class politics was shut down and the aspirations once expressed there were shunted from official public institutions to new spaces of consumption and leisure. In other words, with the destruction of public political culture under the dictatorship, the various regions of everyday life – clothing, leisure, entertainment, habits of consumption – became charged with a new expressive significance, with the task of giving palpable shape to desires for individual autonomy and distinction. Following some observations of Meyer Shapiro, Crow notes that works of modern art have tended to focus in their content precisely on leisure activities such as sports or other collective spectacles; on entertainment scenes of dancers, musicians, and actors; on spaces of personal enjoyment such as cafés and bars; on intimate fields of everyday objects; and finally, on art itself as an activity distinct from work or public life. Modernism, at least as expressed in the visual arts of France at this time, thus follows the general social shift towards consumption and leisure (a conclusion also reached by T.J. Clark in his classic Marxist art history of nineteenth-century French painting, *The Painting of Modern Life*).[40]

This is not, however, Crow's last word on modernism. In a bold move, generalizing beyond his immediate historical case, he compares the oppositional communities of modernist artists, whose revolt against their society gets expressed in terms of artistic questions and an aesthetics of lifestyle, with the contemporary subcultures that have been discussed in the pioneering works of cultural studies. Conceived as a kind of subculture, the modernist avant-garde can be understood to presuppose the disintegration of previous forms of social solidarity, in this case those ties which bound radicalized artists to a radical bourgeois politics pursuing republican democracy against the remnants of the aristocracy and monarchy. With the collapse of this alignment and "the emergence of a persistent avant-garde," Crow writes –

> a small, face-to-face group of artists and supporters became their own oppositional public, one socially grounded within structured leisure. The distinctive point of view and iconographic markers of the subculture came to be drawn from a repertoire of objects, locations and behaviors supplied by other colonists of the same social spaces; avant-garde opposition was and is drawn out of inarticulate and unresolved dissatisfactions which those spaces, though designed to contain them, also put on display.[41]

This equivocation between displaying dissatisfaction and containing it also marks the temporal unfolding of avant-garde revolts, Crow suggests. He explains the clearly apparent cycles of revolt, co-optation, and renewed revolt in terms of the ambiguous nature of a capitalism centered on consumption of goods and culture within leisure-time. While consumerism appeals to an ever-expanding and ever-intensifying realm of sensual experiences available for purchase, Crow notes –

> the emphasis on continual novelty basic to [the culture] industry runs counter to the need of every large enterprise for product standardization and economies of scale. This difficulty is solved by the very defensive and resistant subcultures that come into being as negotiated breathing spaces on the margins of controlled social life. These are the groups most committed to leisure, its pioneers, who for that reason come up with the most surprising, inventive, and effective ways of using it.[42]

In other words, defensive subcultures provide the necessary "avant-garde" negative and renovative energies needed to keep capitalist standardization from petrifying, eventually undermining the economic profit to be gained by the industrialization of consumer and cultural goods. In this light, avant-gardes are not merely contingent, marginal elements in advanced capitalist societies, nor do they pertain only to the specialized, differentiated sphere of "the arts" and its institutions, like the gallery, the literary or artistic journal, or the music festival. Rather, they are intensive microcosms of larger-scale dynamics within capitalism. In their rapid-fire succession of "isms," they mirror the cyclical emergence, stagnation and refreshing of aesthetic styles integral to value in a consumer-centered economy in which the symbolic "design" qualities of a product are often even more important than its material utility.

Crow's analysis, by implication, points up the ambiguity of any "critique of everyday life," of which both modernist avant-gardes and oppositional sub-cultures represent practical instances. Consumerism, like the culture industry, is not an authoritarian command structure, in which tastemakers force-feed consumers the "hottest new thing," despite Adorno's occasional evocations of Pavlovian conditioning and remote-control manipulation through stereotype schemata of experience and the use of psychological testing in advertising. Rather, it is a thoroughly dialectical process: a delicate, dynamically managed balance between, on the one hand, the drive to standardize production and expand distribution by repeating successful models, and on the other hand, the demand for continually renewed novelty, to retain present consumers while reaching ever more new buyers. Clearly, modernism and the avant-gardes created a constantly expanding, open-ended set of novel aesthetic forms and experiences – verbal, visual, sonorous, performative works of art – that were intended as critical alternatives to an everyday life dominated by consumption and inclined to become ever more standardized, stultified, and bureaucratically shackled. Yet insofar as these novel experiences might migrate into fashion, the culture industry, and product design as new "styles" and tokens of "lifestyles," the avant-garde's critical negativity could itself also serve as an important con-tributor to the renewal and expanded reproduction of consumer society. The innovative arts of the twentieth century offered, then, paradoxically, a disrup-tive impetus for consumerism to refresh itself constantly and overcome indus-trialized culture's potentially self-stifling tendencies. Frankfurt School theory, accordingly, had to adapt to this ambiguous dialectical relation of modernism and consumerism, which intensified considerably after World War II. In their aesthetic studies they sought, as I have noted, to draw upon the negative ener-gies of modernism as a critical and utopian resource. Yet the Frankfurt School thinkers also increasingly had to reflect on the "co-optation" of oppositional impulses in society, including those of artistic modernism and the avant-garde. Much of the later Frankfurt School's work, particularly the late Adorno and Marcuse, was taken up with the question of how such negativity gets con-tained and "turned" to serve the long-term interest of the system, how in fact it must be both elicited and set to work by capitalism if the system is to escape its own entropic spiral of diminishing returns.

It is in this spirit, I would argue, that Benjamin and Adorno formulated a certain secret cultural pact between the radical modernist work and the obsolete rubbish of consumer culture. Both the sublimely difficult modernist work and the obsolete popular culture product stand in stubborn anachronistic disalignment with society's rhythms of value and renovation. Each retains a capacity to produce the oppositional experience that Baudelaire called "spleen," a peculiarly modern form of existential dissonance, which these artworks help direct towards society and its processes and which draws the ire of that society in turn. As Adorno concluded in a passage from *Minima Moralia*: "Scarcely less than the hatred for a radical, much too modern composition is that for a film already three months old, to which the latest, though in no way differing from it, is relentlessly preferred" (*MM*, 118; translation modified). The work of the Frankfurt School critic, he implies, is to reconnect the short-circuit between the incommunicable modernist work and the all-too-communicable popular one, to release the sparks of emancipatory energy residing in neither one alone, but realizable in the sudden flash between them.

NOTES

1.. Theodor W. Adorno, "Late Style in Beethoven," in *Essays on Music*, ed. Richard Leppert, trans. Susan H. Gillespie (Berkeley and Los Angeles: University of California Press, 2002), pp. 564–7.
2. Edward Said, *On Late Style: Music and Literature Against the Grain* (New York: Vintage, 2007).
3. Tyrus Miller, *Late Modernism: Politics, Fiction, and the Arts Between the World Wars* (Berkeley and Los Angeles: University of California Press, 1999); and Tyrus Miller, *Singular Examples: Artistic Politics and the Neo-Avant-Garde* (Evanston: Northwestern University Press, 2009). For more on questions of modernism and periodization, see also Tyrus Miller, *Time Images: Alternative Temporalities in Twentieth-Century Theory, History, and Art* (Cambridge: Cambridge Scholars Publishing, 2009).
4. Charles Reitz, *Art, Alienation, and the Humanities: A Critical Engagement with Herbert Marcuse* (Albany: State University of New York Press, 2000); Douglas Kellner, *Herbert Marcuse and the Crisis of Marxism* (Berkeley and Los Angeles: University of California Press, 1985); Kellner, "Marcuse, Art, and Liberation" in Herbert Marcuse, *Art and Liberation*, Collected Papers, Volume 4, ed. Douglas Kellner (New York: Routledge, 2007), pp. 1–70.
5. For Horkheimer's essays from the early years of his directorship, including his inaugural speech, see Max Horkheimer, *Between Philosophy and Social Science: Selected Early Writings*, trans. G. Frederick Hunter, Matthew S. Kramer, and John Torpey (Cambridge, MA: The MIT Press, 1993).
6. Rolf Wiggershaus, *The Frankfurt School: Its History, Theories, and Political Significance*, trans. Michael Robertson (Cambridge, MA: The MIT Press, 1995).
7. Freely adopted from Wiggershaus, *The Frankfurt School*, p. 2.
8. Max Horkheimer, "Traditional and Critical Theory," trans. Matthew J. O'Connell,

in Horkheimer, *Critical Theory: Selected Essays* (New York: Continuum, 1972), pp. 188–243.

9. Horkheimer, "Traditional and Critical Theory," p. 238.
10. Horkheimer, "Traditional and Critical Theory," p. 221.
11. Political theorist Oskar Negt and author-filmmaker Alexander Kluge would return to Horkheimer's motif of "obstinancy" in detail in their monumental *Geschichte und Eigensinn* (History and Obstinancy) (Frankfurt a/M: Zweitausendeins, 1981).
12. Horkheimer, "Traditional and Critical Theory," p. 220.
13. Helmut Dubiel, *Theory and Politics: Studies in the Development of Critical Theory*, trans. Benjamin Gregg (Cambridge, MA: The MIT Press, 1985).
14. Georg Lukács, *History and Class Consciousness*, trans. Rodney Livingstone (Cambridge, MA: The MIT Press, 1971).
15. For a recent treatment of the theme of reification within the Frankfurt School, see Axel Honneth, *Reification: A New Look at an Old Idea* (Oxford: Oxford University Press, 2012).
16. Walter Benjamin, "Bücher, die lebendig geblieben sind," in *Gesammelte Schriften* III, ed. Hella Tiedeman-Bartels (Frankfurt a/M: Suhrkamp Verlag, 1980), pp. 169–71.
17. See, for this argument, Georg Lukács, *The Meaning of Contemporary Realism*, trans. John and Necke Mander (London: Merlin Press, 1963).
18. See "'Tendency' or Partisanship?" and "Reportage or Portrayal," in Georg Lukács, *Essays on Realism*, trans. Rodney Livingstone (Cambridge, MA: The MIT Press, 1983), pp. 33–44 and 44–75.
19. "Photography" and "The Mass Ornament," in Siegfried Kracauer, *The Mass Ornament: Weimer Essays,* ed. and trans. Thomas Y. Levin (Cambridge, MA: Harvard University Press, 1995), pp. 46–63 and 74–86.
20. Kracauer, "Photography," p. 62.
21. My thanks to Tim Armstrong for pointing out the Tiller Girls' Manchester origins and their more complex history than Kracauer's account suggests.
22. Kracauer, "The Mass Ornament," p. 77.
23. Walter Benjamin, "Bragaglia in Berlin," in *Gesammelte Schriften* IV, 1,2, ed. Tillman Rexroth (Frankfurt a/M: Suhrkamp Verlag, 1980), pp. 522–3.
24. Ernst Bloch, *Spirit of Utopia*, trans. Anthony A. Nassar (Stanford: Stanford University Press, 2000).
25. Ernst Bloch, *Heritage of Our Times*, trans. Neville and Stephen Plaice (Berkeley and Los Angeles: University of California Press, 1990).
26. Reinhard Koselleck, "The Temporalization of Utopia," in Koselleck, *The Practice of Conceptual History: Timing History, Spacing Concepts*, trans. Todd Samuel Presner and others (Stanford: Stanford University Press, 2002), pp. 84–99.
27. Bloch, *Spirit of Utopia*, p. 9.
28. In his essay on Bloch's *Spirit of Utopia*, Theodor W. Adorno would explicitly comment on Bloch's philosophical exploration of singular experiences, in "The Handle, the Pot, and Early Experience," in Adorno, *Notes to Literature* II, trans. Shierry Weber Nicholsen (New York: Columbia University Press, 1992), pp. 211–19.
29. Bloch, *Spirit of Utopia*, p. 9.
30. Bloch, *Heritage of Our Times*, p. 113.
31. Bloch, *Heritage of Our Times*, p. 113.
32. Bloch, *Heritage of Our Times*, p. 207.
33. Letter of Theodor W. Adorno to Walter Benjamin, 18 March 1936, in Adorno et al., *Aesthetics and Politics* (London: New Left Books, 1977), p. 123.
34. For the connections between the Bataille circle and the Frankfurt School, see

Tyrus Miller, "Mimesis, Mimicry, and Critical Theory in Exile: Walter Benjamin's Approach to the Collège de Sociologie," in *Exile, Borders, Diasporas*, ed. Elazar Barkan and Marie-Denise Shelton, in the "Cultural Sitings" series (Stanford: Stanford University Press, 1998), pp. 123–33; and Tyrus Miller, "Mimesis of the New Man: The 1930s from Ideology to Anthropolitics," in *Encounters with the 30s* (Madrid: Reina Sofia/La Fabrica: 2012).

35. Andreas Huyssen, "Adorno in Reverse: From Hollywood to Richard Wagner," in *After the Great Divide: Modernism, Mass Culture, Postmodernism* (Bloomington: Indiana University Press, 1986), pp. 16–43.

36. Huyssen, "Adorno in Reverse," p. 42.

37. Fredric Jameson, "Reification and Utopia in Mass Culture," in Jameson, *Signatures of the Visible* (London: Routledge, 1992), p. 23.

38. Jameson, "Reification and Utopia in Mass Culture," pp. 25–6.

39. Thomas Crow, "Modernism and Mass Culture in the Visual Arts," in *Modern Art in the Common Culture* (New Haven, CT: Yale University Press, 1996), pp. 3–38.

40. Timothy J. Clark, *The Painting of Modern Life: Paris in the Age of Manet and His Followers* (Princeton: Princeton University Press, 1984).

41. Crow, "Modernism and Mass Culture in the Visual Arts," pp. 20–1.

42. Crow, "Modernism and Mass Culture in the Visual Arts," p. 34.

2

WALTER BENJAMIN

INTRODUCTION: BENJAMIN AND MODERNISM

Walter Benjamin poses his readers and interpreters with a puzzle. A gifted man of letters, cultural theorist, and historian – and by today, one of the most generative thinkers associated with the early Frankfurt School – Benjamin was nevertheless the author of only a few completed, book-length works typical of the mainstream humanistic intellectuals, academics, or philosophers of his time. His corpus of writings consists preponderantly of book reviews, translations, individual essays, and even more miscellaneous notes and sketches, many left unpublished during his lifetime because of the difficult circumstances of inflation, economic depression, and spreading fascism. Benjamin would also swell and resift fragments of long unfinished research projects for years. Initially for circumstantial reasons, but increasingly by intentional design, Benjamin maintained a many-sided, but irregular output of occasional studies, which offer intriguingly partial glimpses of his concerns rather than explicit, discursively exhaustive expositions.

Benjamin's production has typically been divided into his "early" esoteric-theologically oriented works (circa 1913–23), his "middle" period of work as a left literary intellectual of Weimar Germany (circa 1924–33), and his "late" period of Marxist-influenced writings in exile in Paris and elsewhere (circa 1934–40). The first period includes a few highly significant essays and programmatic texts such as his unpublished exposition of "Two Poems by

Friedrich Hölderlin" (1914–15), his sketch of a theological language-theory called "On Language as Such and on the Language of Man" (1916), and his anarchist-influenced "Critique of Violence" (1921), as well as his dissertation on "The Concept of Criticism in German Romanticism" (1919–20), his introduction to a set of Baudelaire translations, "The Task of the Translator" (1921), and his path-breaking study of "Goethe's *Elective Affinities*" (1919–22). The middle period includes such works as the books *The Origins of German Tragic Drama* (1928) and *One-Way Street* (1928), as well as major essays on "Surrealism" (1929), "The Image of Proust" (1929), "Karl Kraus" (1931), "Doctrine of the Similar" (1933), "On the Mimetic Faculty" (1933), and "Experience and Poverty" (1933). The final period, perhaps the most impressive and influential, includes Benjamin's vast unfinished research for an "archeo-history of the modern," the so-called *Arcades Project* for a materialist history of nineteenth-century Paris, his programmatic essays on the politics of art in "The Author as Producer" (1935) and "The Work of Art in the Age of Its Technical Reproducibility" (1936), further essays on Kafka (1934) and Leskov ("The Storyteller," 1936), and a study of the socialist cultural historian "Edward Fuchs, Collector and Historian" (1937). In addition, in connection with the *Arcades Project* research, Benjamin developed three pieces of a separate book on the great French poet and art critic Charles Baudelaire – "Paris, Capital of the Nineteenth Century" (1935), "The Paris of the Second Empire in Baudelaire" (1938), and "On Some Motifs in Baudelaire" (1939), as well as aphoristic reflections "On the Concept of History" (1940).

The fragmentariness of Benjamin's corpus relates, in ways that I will seek to illuminate further, to a wider context of modernist artistic tendencies such as cubism, expressionism, Dadaism, and surrealism in which fragmentation was a characteristic cultural style of thought. More than just a literary or artistic technique, fragmentation was a cultural infrastructure and mode of thinking shared across competing, otherwise strongly differentiated movements in early twentieth-century arts and writing. Benjamin too participates in this cultural style. In its complex temporality of development, Benjamin's textual corpus implicitly exemplifies his critical concept of modernity. It enfolds reflections on expressionism backwards in historical time into his examination of the German Baroque; it anticipates in earlier texts themes that will fully emerge many years later with different examples and reference points; it cycles back from explicitly Marxist positions of the 1930s to the esoteric-theological motifs of his youth; and it couples the archeo-mythic with the ultra-modern in surprising, counter-intuitive ways. It is also a tissue of anticipations, interruptions, and returns, with few clearly defined beginnings, middles, and ends.

This inner rhythm of his writing, I would suggest, is more than just a contingent product of Benjamin's precarious life and livelihood, though no doubt it is a register of that as well. Benjamin stressed how primordial myth and ultra-newness were intertwined in "modern times"; how modernity manifested complex rhythms of recurrence and continual reinvention; how the apparent continuity of progressive history concealed catastrophic breaks and harbored the potential for messianic leaps; and how connections between historical arti-facts and events could be established by trans-historical montages often span-ning huge gaps in scale and chronological time. One might say that Benjamin, like Ernst Bloch, came increasingly to understand the underlying structure of artistic modernism, such as the principles of montage and multiple regimes of time, as being first situated in the extra-artistic realm of social, histori-cal, and natural life: rooted in the *ontological* character of time itself, which brings material objects and spaces of very different temporal provenance into collision.

Early on, in his more "esoteric," theologically influenced writings, Benjamin boldly represented this ontology as a non-subjective and more-than-human "life" that encompassed history, including both nature and the apparently "artificial" life of texts, institutions, concepts, and technologies. Thus, in his renowned essay "The Task of the Translator," from 1923, he argued that translations were manifestations of the "life" of important texts, and went on to expound:

> The idea of life and afterlife in works of art should be regarded with an entirely unmetaphorical objectivity. Even in times of narrowly preju-diced thought there was an inkling that life was not limited to organic corporeality . . . The concept of life is given its due only if everything has a history of its own, and is not merely the setting for history, is credited with life. In the final analysis, the range of life must be determined by the standpoint of history rather than that of nature, least of all by such tenuous factors as sensation and soul. (*SW* I, 254–5)

So too, in his final writings "On the Concept of History," he viewed natural history and human history not as separate domains, but rather as aspects of ontologically real time grasped at different degrees of concentration or exten-sion, from the explosively charged present outward through the various spans of human time into the all-encompassing life of the cosmos. Time and mate-rial reality, for Benjamin, constantly lent themselves to a work of constructive shaping and reshaping, of figuration and refiguration, whether through the theological labor of a creating God or the analytical labor of the commentator, the collector, the translator, and the montage-artist and historian.

In turn, given that Benjamin saw this work of figural construction as part of the ontological structure of creation itself, the primary task of the revolution-ary modernist historian, like any authentically modernist artist, was to reflect this created reality "mimetically." Yet unlike in classical notions of mimesis, Benjamin's mimesis-concept did not imply a realist, representational mirror, but rather conscious montage-construction, experimentally modeling what is happening "out there" in the world of modern social phenomena, such as urban life in the great metropolises of Europe. By his own understanding, then, the modernistic stylizations of Benjamin's own writings were not just fashionable literary choices or attempts to measure himself, as a writer, against the best literary models of the day (though no doubt, he also wished to do this). Rather, he believed that he, like the modernist writers he admired, must respond urgently to the pressures and emerging tendencies of the day, in which the stakes were literally that of the life and death of millions of people. As the notion of a continuum from the present to cosmic eternity suggests, Benjamin did not understand even his most fragmentary, his most ephemeral and topical observations as disconnected from his long-term historical vision and even theological hopes. Whenever he was documenting the nature of modern times, Benjamin was also channeling modernity through his every experience as an intellectual, as a writer, and as a frail, fallible creature hungry for redemption.

Finally, in his considerations of aesthetic modernism, as with his other objects of study, Benjamin's first and foremost concern was neither the work's "form" nor its "content," but rather the "experience" that it captures, organizes, and renders collectively shareable (or "communicable," *mitteilbar*, to use a key word in Benjamin's early conceptual vocabulary).[1] Whether he was writing about a book, a film, a dramatic performance, or a work of architecture, Benjamin sought to understand how the artistic artifact implied – and often actualized – a space of encounter and activity, at once spiritual and material, of which certain sorts of experience might become the enduring trace. Benjamin understood the social world as full of objects on which experience could be brought to bear and which, in their very particular objecthood, held in tension various possibilities for giving rise to experience. Modernist works of art, because of their intentional design, stressed this latter modeling and generative function, this occasioning of "learning processes" (*Lernprozesse*), as later Frankfurt School thinkers like Jürgen Habermas and Alexander Kluge would put it. Such works served as anticipatory testing-grounds for kinds of experience that the social world as a whole was not yet fully prepared to realize, and in turn they lent concreteness and impulse to the inchoate forces of renewal just beginning to be perceptible in the broader social realm.

MODERNISM AND THE TRANSFORMATION OF EXPERIENCE

In some of his best-known essays, including his texts on Kafka, Proust, Leskov, and Baudelaire, as well as his seminal essay on technology and aesthetics, "The Work of Art in the Age of Its Technical Reproducibility," Benjamin traced a modern disintegration of the communal experience transmitted as tradition and its replacement by a typically contemporary individual, psychological, interior experience. The achievement of the authors that Benjamin made the focus of his attention in these essays lies, in his view, in their having provided a literary record of that massive transition. They register with unrelenting truthfulness the implications of this seismic shift in experience, yet they also, in the details of their narratives, and often in unconscious or paradoxical ways, retain valuable traces of the anterior communal experience that was already in their time on the verge of disappearing into oblivion: for instance, Kafka's reference to a specifically Central European Jewish heritage stretching back to the Middle Ages. The modernity of their stories, novels, parables, and poems lends a disenchanting critical view of much that was repressive and archaic in the older forms of tradition; yet precisely in disenchanting tradition, they also redeem a precious, utopian residue of truth content in danger of being swept away by that same modernity.

Typical in this regard is Benjamin's judgment, in a letter to Gershom Scholem, on Kafka. Kafka's work, he writes, "represents a sickening of tradition" (*SW* III, 326) the tradition from which, for example, the ability to know and transmit proverbial wisdom derives. Yet as uncompromisingly as Kafka acknowledges this sickening of tradition, he also makes an unusual and literarily productive response to it:

> This consistency of truth has been lost. Kafka was by no means the first to be confronted with this realization. Many had come to terms with it in their own way – clinging to truth, or what they believed to be truth, and, heavyhearted or not, renouncing its transmissibility. Kafka's genius lay in the fact that he tried something altogether new: he gave up truth so that he could hold on to its transmissibility . . . His works are by nature parables. But their poverty and their beauty consist in their need to be *more* than parables. (*SW* III, 326)

Here, Benjamin sees Kafka in mad pursuit of pure transmissibility (which speaks suggestively to the uncanny, senseless architecture of interconnected corridors and doors in Kafka's novels, and his fascination with networked technologies like the telephone and telegraph). The typical "heroes" that occupy Kafka's texts – talking animals, madmen, fools, hybrid creatures – appear to Benjamin to signify precisely the opposite of the idea of a psychoanalytically pregnant Kafka, haunted by incommunicable inner obsessions and anxieties. Rather, they represent pure transmissibility in the absence of any hidden inner content at all, which has evaporated in the forced heat of modernity:

> That is why, in Kafka, there is no longer any talk of wisdom. Only the products of its decomposition are left . . . First is rumor of the true things (a kind of whispered theological newspaper about the disreputable and the obsolete). The other product of this diathesis is folly, which, though it has entirely squandered the content of wisdom, retains the unruffled

complaisance that rumor utterly lacks . . . Of this much, Kafka was sure: first, that to help, one must be a fool; and, second, that only a fool's help is real help. (*SW* III, 326–7)

If Kafka is one major literary figure whose work, in Benjamin's view, revolves around this modern impoverishment of experience, the other most significant alternative example for him is the poet and art critic Charles Baudelaire, who is conventionally taken to be the first major figure of European literary modernism. It is in connection with his writing on Baudelaire, which became an autonomous book project spun out of his research on nineteenth-century Paris, that Benjamin gives his most theoretically elaborated account of the new psychological structure of experience and its implications for literary expression.

Although this is a multifarious theme in Benjamin's writings on Baudelaire, which span many years and hundreds of pages, the general framework is relatively consistent. Benjamin conceptually and historically elaborates a linguistic distinction available to him in German, which English and French do not make: between *Erfahrung* and *Erlebnis*, both typically translated as "experience." The verb *erfahren* and the noun *Erfahrung* carry connotation of a kind of knowledge through repeated action over time (as, for example, being an "experienced" swimmer or "work experience"); it also is used in sentences that refer to learning through oral discourse and narrative, as in the sense of such sentences as "Where did you hear that?" and "I heard all about it from Bill." For Benjamin, this concept of experience is connected to tradition, which passes on know-how through daily practice and face-to-face speech and storytelling. It is a mode of "experience" that is precisely not subjective and psychological, but rather *inter*-subjective, embedded in localized contexts, and reproduced through speech and embodied activity. By contrast, the verb *erleben* and the noun *Erlebnis* are closer to the modern, subjective, psychological conception of experience: i.e. "That trip to Berlin was one of the most exciting *experiences* of my life," or "I just had a terrible *experience* on the bus," or "If you want a real *experience*, go see that new movie." It has the implications of a highly singular intensity experienced by one individual, and its localization *within* the self or mind means that communicating its exact nature to anyone else becomes a problem. Indeed, the whole modernist reflection on the problems of communicating the inner content of an individual sensibility, and the corollary sense that the publically available forms of communication are alien, inauthentic falsifications of an inner richness emanates, in Benjamin's view, from the increasing evaporation of *Erfahrung* and the increasing dominance of *Erlebnis* in subjective life. It also leads to ever more attention being devoted to discovering or even producing certain (inner) experiences by means of surveys and tests, advertising, product design, and marketing. If, as some business theorists have postulated, the contemporary economy is increasingly an "experience economy," then the experience in question is an *Erlebnis* that has been designed, capitalized and sold.[2]

As Benjamin underscores, Baudelaire's poetry engages directly with the spaces, objects, and social characters of the metropolis, in which the transformation of experience and the dissolution of tradition is most stark. The buffeting flow of crowds, the desolate quiet of empty streets at night, the glimpse of prostitutes and strolling dandies, the peculiar solitude of atelier apartments, the calls of the ragpicker and the staggering drunkard are made, in Baudelaire's verse, into emblematic figures of a new type of experience. Benjamin suggests that typical urban experiences, which form the thematic repertoire of Baudelaire's poetry, are experienced by the individual as a violent source of sensation. They are experienced as a kind of *shock* that the inner self must attempt to cushion or parry. Baudelaire meets this flood of violent stimulation coming to him from outside with a heightened counterpressure of self-consciousness from within, an intensified intellectuality that the poetry expresses through its formalization of the chaotic urban sensations and its distantiating tone of irony. From this state of heightened consciousness, he develops a modern form of allegory, analogous to the allegory of the baroque period but adapted to the new urban content, which turns the living figures of the city into enigmatic emblems, ruins, and stony monuments – thus capturing the fleeting present of an encounter on the street in an eternal gesture or grimace. In doing so, Benjamin argues, Baudelaire offers a tableau of experiences of the mid-nineteenth-century metropolis that is of incomparable value for the later historian, who must approach Baudelaire's poetry like an interpreter puzzling over the confected hieroglyphics and riddles of a baroque emblem book. Here, however, rather than encrypting moral or philosophical meaning, the allegory leads us into the *social* secrets of a capitalist society that is reaching another decisive moment in its historical development.

Along with his essays on major modern literary figures, which he reads as indices of the changes in the structure of experience, Benjamin also made one major attempt to explain these changes causally, in his essay "The Work of Art in the Age of Its Technical Reproducibility." The motivating concern of the essay is the present-day tendency (in the 1930s) for art – or quasi-artistic images and productions – to become increasingly connected with collectivities, whether in organized mass political movements such as fascism and communism, or in the more fluid and formless collectives such as those that occupy tourist locales, places of mass leisure, shopping spaces, and urban street life. For Benjamin, this is a moment of great political danger, insofar as the reactionary forces of fascism have learned that such collective images can be manipulated as a potent force for concentrating and moving the masses. It is also, however, a chance to establish a new relation between the collective and art, which may hold liberatory possibilities as well. Benjamin thus poises his essay at a moment of decision, between the choice to aestheticize politics in the way of reactionary spectacles and mass media manipulation, or to politicize art and use it consciously as an instrument of collective liberation.

The moment of decision that Benjamin evokes is the outcome of a historical process in which both the art object and the experience connected to it have been radically transformed by the introduction of new technologies for multiplying the visual and aural image: engraving and lithography, followed by photography and cinema. Benjamin suggests that the archaic form of the artwork, essentially preserved up to the full emergence of modern industrial capitalism in the nineteenth century, is based on the cultic use of images and relics. A highly unique, valuable, rare object is kept in a special place and is available to see only at times appointed by the ritual calendar – for example, images of the virgin Mary that are unveiled and carried in religious processions, accompanied by the recitation of liturgical texts. Such images are not simply "pictures" of the virgin, they manifest her sacred presence under these special conditions of reception. Benjamin calls the sacredness attached to such ritually situated images "aura": a sort of halo around the work that evokes a spiritual realm foreign to that of work and everyday life. Already during the baroque, with its courtly works of art, and the eighteenth century with the emergence of the academies and salons, this sacredness has been progressively secularized: no longer "cultic" in the strictly religious sense, their "aura" is the weaker glow of specialness granted the artwork by putting it on display in settings such as galleries and salons. Visiting the museum, or the art show, or gazing over the works hung on the wall of a comfortable private living room become the secular correlates of withdrawing to a chapel to meditate and pray.

Technical means of reproducing and distributing artworks in cheap, portable form – photographs, posters, postcards, illustrated books, magazines and newspapers – decisively tear the artistic image out of these church-like spaces and introduce them into a wide range of new contexts: the streets, public transportation, movie houses, workplaces, cafés, and so on. The images, and the content they carry, now become free for use by new social agents – especially working-class people and women – who previously would have been excluded from access to the single works, or who might have seen them only under very controlled conditions, such as in the iconostasis of an Orthodox Christian Church. The possibility of possessing and using images brings them into an unprecedented nearness to everyday life, as they are incorporated into the newspapers we read, the design of the packaging of the products we consume, the advertising that convinces us to buy them, and the decoration of the environment in which we consume them. It is this condition of proximity to images that Benjamin refers to as the "dissolution of aura": the dispelling of the air of sacredness around the image and the apprehension of the image as an ordinary instrument of everyday modern life.

Benjamin sees a wide number of ramifications of this basic change. I will only mention two, closely related to the questions of modern experience already raised. The first is that the function of the image changes, from being predominantly a material vessel of a unique spiritual presence ("aura") to being largely a discursive vehicle for information and ideologies. The repeated, ritual contexts in which the traditional artwork appeared also made images important means of maintaining traditional ways of thinking and feeling; modern images, by contrast, more strongly emphasize novelty – new, exciting, surprising contents and feelings. Hence, in terms of the *Erfahrung / Erlebnis* distinction discussed earlier, we might say that the traditional, "auratic" work of art is bound to an order of experience strongly characterized by *Erfahrung*, the experience of repeated traditional actions and speech; whereas in contrast the technically reproducible, "non-auratic" image is an integral part of an order of experience in which *Erlebnis* predominates. The second point follows from the first. Just as Baudelaire's poetry transformed shock experience into allegorical poetic emblems, so too the snapshot, the photo-journalistic image, the newsreel, the photomontage, and other new image-forms represent ways of *positively* reappropriating shock experience and forging new forms of collective consciousness out of the resulting social allegories. Although, as suggested earlier, this possibility is available to the forces of reaction and of liberation, Benjamin believed that a conscious, revolutionary development of these modernist tools would be crucial for the progressive left in the coming historical crisis.

THOUGHT-IMAGES OF THE MODERN: ONE-WAY STREET

Although the exact ways in which Benjamin reflects his broadly modernist context has been hotly debated by a myriad of commentators, there is little doubt that Benjamin drank deeply at the well of the contemporary literary and artistic culture of his day, most notably from prestigious modernist writers (Marcel Proust, Paul Valéry, Hugo von Hofmannsthal, Stefan George, Hermann Hesse, Thomas Mann, Alfred Döblin, Franz Kafka), from various strains of the European avant-garde (expressionism, Dadaism, surrealism, futurism), and from political avant-gardes strongly influenced by communist politics (Bertolt Brecht, John Heartfield, Sergei Tretiakov, Sergei Eisenstein). In various ways, as critics have shown, Benjamin incorporated new compositional techniques, inspired by these modernist tendencies, into his own critical and theoretical works. Benjamin himself, for example, openly acknowledged the inspiration of Louis Aragon's hybrid surrealist prose text *Paris Peasant* in the genesis of his montage-text *One-Way Street* and his study of nineteenth-century Paris, *The Arcades Project*. Reading Aragon's work for the first time, he reports having to put the book down after only a few pages because his heart was palpitating so with excitement; years later he declared that his reading of Aragon's meandering philosophical novel stood at the very origin of his own research on the arcades, including, as we can see from the textual legacy, several early notes that seem strongly indebted to Aragon in style and approach. Among recent critics, Detlev Schöttker has used the term "constructive fragmentarism"[3] to describe Benjamin's idiosyncratic writing, tracing out in detail the parallelisms between the European avant-gardes and Benjamin in the deployment of key notions such as "construction," a buzzword of artists and critics alike under the influence of the leftist art tendencies in the early Soviet Union. Similarly, Frederic Schwartz has drawn attention to the parallels between the visual culture of the interwar avant-gardes and Benjamin's thinking about image and montage,[4] while Gerhard Richter has argued that the "thought-image" (*Denkbilder*) – a distinctive Frankfurt School subgenre related to but different than more traditional short prose forms such as the prose-poem, the parable, and the aphorism – offered Benjamin and associated thinkers such as Ernst Bloch and Theodor W. Adorno a characteristic vehicle for their cultural-theoretical meditations.[5]

Within Benjamin's larger investigation of cultural and social modernity, aesthetic modernism constitutes an intensive focus and a key source of examples, cases, and problems for his critical writing. Modernist forms and techniques, the fundamental modes of organizing material established in the early twentieth century by modernist artists and writers, also provide Benjamin with a repertoire of models for his critical and theoretical work, for a second-order, *reflexive* reuse of these techniques in an extra-artistic domain – or, better formulated, in an "in-between" domain that completes, through critical reflection, the cultural work that can only partially be accomplished by the modernist work of art. Before considering more closely Benjamin's specific engagements with modernist art, literature, and urbanism, therefore, I would like to place under the critical lens a key example of this "in-between" zone of critical-aesthetic investigation, Benjamin's 1928 collection of "thought-images," *One-Way Street*.

One-Way Street offers its reader a set of short texts, some as little as a few sentences long, others extending to a paragraph. Each bears a title, like a street sign, and within these sections some are further subdivided into named sections. Some titles refer to places one might find along a street, such as "Filling Station," "Optician," or "Polyclinic"; one simply asserts "Number 13" and another "Number 113," but then the latter moves through subtitled spaces such as "Cellar," "Vestibule," and "Dining Hall"; other sections seem to refer to posted signs such as "This Space for Rent," "Closed for Alterations," or "No Vagrants!" As Benjamin indicates from the outset, however, this peculiar street, which has numerous architectural by-ways and nested spaces along its apparently rectilinear route, is also a pathway into an emotional interior, a subjective passageway at the crossroads of eroticism and engineering. Thus, as its dedicatory epigraph to Benjamin's Latvian communist lover reads: "This street is named / Asja Lacis Street / after her who / as an engineer / cut it through the author" (*SW* I, 444). Utilizing, with admitted anachronism, a term from French Lettrist and Situationist theory after World War II, we might say that Benjamin's *One-Way Street* offers a *psychogeographical* mapping of urban space,[6] in which place, movement, and affectivity are bound together in a topological braid, in which inner and outer, subjective and objective elements become indiscernible.

Early in the book, in a section entitled "To the Public: Please Protect and Preserve These New Plantings," Benjamin spells out this reversibility of interior and exterior space, the projection of affect into objects and places and the occupation of these objective entities with highly personal thoughts and feelings:

> If the theory is correct that feeling is not located in the head, that we sentiently experience a window, a cloud, a tree not in our brains but rather in the place where we see it, then we are, in looking at our beloved, too, outside ourselves. But in a torment of tension and ravishment. Our feeling, dazzled, flutters like a flock of birds in the woman's radiance. And as birds seek refuge in the leafy recesses of a tree, feelings escape into the shaded wrinkles, the awkward movements and inconspicuous blemishes of the body we love, where they can lie low in safety. And no passer-by would guess that it is just here, in what is defective and censurable, that the fleeting darts of adoration nestle. (*SW* I, 449)

Benjamin suggests not simply that one can have a passionate experience of spaces and objects (insofar as they may become the stand-ins of one's lover or other emotionally charged human relationships), but also something further: that spatiality and passion are, as it were, inter-translatable and inter-communicable as such. Our passions are intrinsically bound to spaces and spatial dynamics, while the spaces of our lived experience are profoundly *passional*. Thus, in another section entitled "Ordnance," clearly referring to Benjamin's ill-fated love experience with Asja Lacis, he writes:

> I had arrived in Riga to visit a woman friend. Her house, her town, the language were unfamiliar to me. Nobody was expecting me; no one knew me. For two hours I walked the streets in solitude. Never again have I seen them so. From every gate a flame darted; each cornerstone sprayed sparks, and every streetcar came toward me like a fire engine. For she might have stepped out of the gateway, around the corner, been sitting in the streetcar. But of the two of us, I had to be, at any price, the first to see the other. For had she touched me with the match of her eyes, I would have gone up like a powder keg. (*SW* I, 461)

Benjamin suggests that it was not just his anticipation and desire that so charged his experience of Riga, a peripheral modern city that was the birthplace of Sergei Eisenstein and a treasury of art nouveau architecture, much of it built by Eisenstein's father Mikhail. It was also, rather, his solitude, his disorientation, and his unfamiliarity with Riga's ambiguous mixture of exotic and habitual decor that heightened his erotic expectation to an almost unbearable, explosive degree. The qualities of space, he implies, may enframe and inflame emotion just as much as, reciprocally, intense emotion may qualify the experience of space.

Benjamin found precedent for this view in the poetry of Charles Baudelaire, who, he believed, expressed a deep understanding of the subjective dimension of a new, modern urban experience in the burgeoning metropolis of Paris. In Baudelaire's famous poem "To A Passerby," which was one of Benjamin's most-cited examples, the poet experiences passionate desire for an anonymous passerby positioned exactly within an aperture opening up in the thronging crowd of the street, and thus becoming visible yet held at an unbridgeable distance from him:

> Amid the deafening traffic of the town,
> Tall, slender, in deep morning, with majesty,
> A woman passed, raising, with dignity
> In her poised hand, the flounces of her gown;
>
> Graceful, noble, with a statue's form.
> And I drank, trembling as a madman thrills,
> From her eyes, ashen sky where brooded storm,
> The softness that fascinates, the pleasure that kills.[7]

In another renowned modernist poem that expresses an analogous experience of metropolitan crowds, Ezra Pound's imagist manifesto-poem "In a Station of the Metro" (1913) registers:

> The apparition of these faces in the crowd;
> Petals on a wet, black bough.[8]

If Baudelaire concretely embodies his lyrical "apparition" as a woman who emerges from and disappears into the crowd, never again to be met until eternity, Pound, in contrast, represents it more abstractly, in the image of flowers blasted by a rainstorm. Yet both conjure forth an ephemeral beauty that surges up amidst the fluctuating spaces of the urban crowd. Each depicts a fleeting, "convulsive" beauty, to use André Breton's surrealist terminology,[9] tossed up out of the mobile constellations of bodies, urban space, and – importantly for Benjamin, as for poetic modernists such as Ezra Pound and Hart Crane in *The Bridge* – modern technologies such as the metropolitan subway. "Separation,"

Benjamin writes in a tacit commentary on this experience of beauty-in-passing, "penetrates the disappearing person like a pigment and steeps him in a gentle radiance" (*SW* I, 450). In a section entitled "Costume Wardrobe," Benjamin himself utilizes the everyday movement of crowds in and out of the Metro to explore the sentiment of eternity, the inverse-side of Baudelaire's and Pound's instant of lyric passion:

> Is there anyone who has not once been stunned, emerging from the Métro into the open air, to step into brilliant sunlight? And yet the sun shone just as brightly a few minutes earlier, when he went down. So quickly has he forgotten the weather of the upper world. And as quickly the world in its turn will forget him. For who can say more of his own existence than that it has passed through the lives of two or three others as gently and closely as the weather? (*SW* I, 484)

Benjamin's method of montage-construction in *One-Way Street* is illustrated well by the two sections that immediately follow his meditation on the exteriority of the feeling of love in "To the Public": "Construction Site" and "Minister of the Interior." If "To the Public" confounds publicness with the most private sentiment of desire, these next two sections interweave other subjective themes with modern technology and administration respectively. "Construction Site" focuses on children's relations to objects, their capacity, which is at least residual in adults as well, to repurpose the discarded material generated out of the processes of labor:

> The world is full of the most unrivaled objects for children's attention and use. And the most specific. For children are particularly fond of haunting any site where things are being visibly worked on. They are irresistibly drawn by the detritus generated by building, gardening, housework, tailoring, or carpentry. In waste products they recognize the face that the world of things turns directly and solely to them. In using these things, they do not so much imitate the works of adults as bring together, in the artifact produced in play, materials of widely differing kinds in a new, intuitive relationship. Children thus produce their own small world of things within the greater one. (*SW* I, 449–50)

As this passage suggests, children form Benjamin's model for a modernist montage-activity that can inspire the material things of the city with new, affectively infused meanings. In building their "small world of things within the greater one," they show the way to reverse a process that Benjamin diagnoses in "Imperial Panorama": "Warmth is ebbing from things. Objects of daily use gently but insistently repel us" (*SW* I, 453–4). Benjamin's modernistic child-engineer – corollary to the communist Latvian woman-engineer who has recalibrated the machinery of his heart, or alternatively, to a certain revolutionary

Latvian filmmaker who engineers cutting-room scraps into dialectical film-constructions – exhibits a unique combination of playful skill and fearlessness in handling the glass, scrap metal, rusty nails, and splintering wood of the construction site, making of it a place of empathy, invention, and imagination rather than danger and estrangement. Further avatars of this child-engineer appear later in *One-Way Street* in the section "Enlargements," which includes subsections on the "Child Reading," the "Pilfering Child," the "Child on the Carousel," the "Untidy Child," and the "Hiding Child" – as well as, one might add, Benjamin's own dreamy boyhood persona in his later autobiographical texts "A Berlin Chronicle" and *A Berlin Childhood Around 1900*.[10]

In addition to evoking new configurations – both actual and potential – between the public and private realms, between objective urban space and subjective urban experience, Benjamin also devotes a number of sections of *One-Way Street* to a related issue: the projection of writing beyond the confines of the printed page and, by implication, a change in writing's function as it comes to occupy new roles in the spaces of the modern city. It is not accidental, thus, that the very first section of the book, entitled "Filling Station," reflects on the nature of modern writing. As if the journey down his "one-way street" were to be powered by a new sort of high-energy literary petrol, Benjamin suggests that writing has become more a matter of precision mechanics operated on social machinery than a handicraft directly generating the product. He suggests, moreover, that the nature of literary activity is shifting towards the poles of documentation and agitation, away from more traditional forms of criticism and the expression of personal opinion:

> The construction of life is at present in the power far more of facts than of convictions, and of such facts as have scarcely ever become the basis of convictions. Under these circumstances, true literary activity cannot aspire to take place within a literary framework . . . Significant literary effectiveness can come into being only in a strict alternation between action and writing; it must nurture the inconspicuous forms that fit its influence in active communities better than does the pretentious, universal gesture of the book – in leaflets, brochures, articles, and placards. Only this prompt language shows itself actively equal to the moment. Opinions are to the vast apparatus of social existence what oil is to machines: one does not go up to a turbine and pour machine oil over it; one applies a little to hidden spindles and joints that one has to know. (*SW* I, 444)

Benjamin is suggesting that the modernistic forms his writing employs – fragmentary, hybrid genres rather than traditional literary, belle-lettristic, or academic forms – relate closely to the new functional relations he seeks to establish with his readership. Rather than the wholesale address of a large-scale work, for instance a book, to an anonymous and socially indeterminate readership – the equivalent of drenching the communicative apparatus with oil – he seeks to offer smaller, more precise shots of factual or ideological content to particular audiences. In this way, his writing can facilitate particular actions by particular social communities, or – in a new understanding of critique – may through precisely targeted acts of literary sabotage render key arguments and concepts inoperable by the enemy, as, for example, he claims in his essay "The Work of Art in the Age of Its Technical Reproducibility": "In what follows, the concepts which are introduced into the theory of art differ from those current in that they are completely useless for the purposes of fascism" (*SW* III, 102).

Throughout the late 1920s and '30s, especially under the growing influence of the poet and playwright Bertolt Brecht and left-wing Soviet writers such as Sergei Tretiakov, Benjamin would develop with ever-greater intensity the idea of a functional change in the forms, purposes, and media of writing – a theme that would culminate in the image of political tendency and collective, post-literary, "factographic" authorship in "The Author as Producer" and "The Work of Art in the Age of Its Technical Reproducibility" essays. In *One-Way Street*, however, Benjamin's stress falls on an increasingly documentary orientation of writing and, accompanying this, the growing role of technical and technological forms of language. Thus, for example, in the section entitled "Teaching Aid," Benjamin sardonically evokes the index as a "generic" model for a new sort of writing, in which the ideologies and beliefs of the day could be, as it were, cited and indexed, rather than passed off directly to be consumed:

> The typical work of modern scholarship is intended to be read like a catalogue. But when shall we actually write books like catalogues? If the deficient content were thus to determine the outward form, an excellent piece of writing would result, in which the value of opinions would be marked without their being thereby put on sale. (*SW* I, 457)

With less irony, in another section entitled "Attested Auditor of Books," Benjamin further develops this concept of the book as an ensemble of indexical references:

> The card index marks the conquest of three-dimensional writing, and so presents an astonishing counterpoint to the three-dimensionality of script in its original form as rune or knot notation. (And today the book is already, as the present mode of scholarly production demonstrates, an outdated mediation between two different filing systems. For everything that matters is to be found in the card box of the researcher who wrote it, and the scholar studying it assimilates it into his own card index.) (*SW* I, 456)

We can remark how Benjamin's future *Arcades Project*, which collected and catalogued into topical groups hundreds upon hundreds of quotations, extended this suggestion into an ambitious historiographic practice. With the exception of various essays, left in greater or lesser degrees of completion, we have inherited only Benjamin's teeming "card file" to his research into the Paris arcades, to make use of as we may for our own notes, further investigations, and subsequent citations.

Benjamin also, however, evokes a more direct connection of the fate of language in the city with the practice of the literary and artistic avant-garde. Through the growing technological mastery of typography, Benjamin suggests, a new set of picto-ideographic forms of language have become possible, both within books and ultimately beyond the confines of the book, in the technological media and in the lived spaces of the city – a practice that he could find exemplified by the posters and festival decorations of the early Soviet Union, or, in another way, in works that fused text, cinema, and city, like László Moholy-Nagy's unproduced film scenario "Dynamic of the Metropolis," which appeared first in the Hungarian avant-garde journal *MA* (Today) in 1924.[11] The typewriter, Benjamin believed, might allow a compositional precision making literature into a machine art rather than a handicraft (although the typewriter's presently rather primitive technology must be further refined for this to become reality): "The typewriter will alienate the hand of the man of letters from the pen only when the precision of typographic forms has directly entered the conception of his books. One might suppose that new systems with more variable typefaces would then be needed. They will replace the pliancy of the hand with the innervation of commanding fingers" (*SW* I, 457). In this vision of a machinic use of typography, Benjamin explicates the compositional role that visual arrangement would play for modernist poets such as Guillaume Apollinaire, Vincente Huidobro, Lajos Kássak, Jaroslav Seifert, Ezra Pound, William Carlos Williams, and Charles Olson, as well as later concrete poets including Eugen Gomringer, Max Bense, Friedrich Achleitner, Augusto and Haroldo de Campos, and Ian Hamilton Finlay.

The French symbolist poet Stéphane Mallarmé and, later, the Dadaist writers and artists, Benjamin suggests, were the first to draw the radical implications of this new technical horizon for the composition of poetry, bringing poetic language into a mimetic relation with the spatialized language of advertising and mass media. Mallarmé, he argues –

> was in the *Coup de dés* the first to incorporate the graphic tensions of the advertisement in the printed page. The typographic experiments later undertaken by the Dadaists stemmed, it is true, not from constructive principles but from the precise nervous reactions of these literati, and were therefore far less enduring than Mallarmé's, which grew out of the

inner nature of his style. But for this very reason they show the contemporary relevance of what Mallarmé, monadically, in his hermetic room, had discovered through a preestablished harmony with all the decisive events of our times in economics, technology, and public life. (*SW* I, 456)

Following Mallarmé's innovations, and accelerated by the progress of technical media, Benjamin suggests, script increasingly rises from the horizontal plane it occupied in print, to the vertical plane of display on walls, kiosks, and projection screens: "If centuries ago it began gradually to lie down, passing from the upright inscription to the manuscript resting on sloping desks before finally taking itself to bed in the printed book, it now begins just as slowly to rise again from the ground. The newspaper is read more in the vertical than in the horizontal plane, while film and advertisement force the printed word entirely into the dictatorial perpendicular" (*SW* I, 456).

In his most striking image of language merging with the material texture of urban space, Benjamin celebrates the light of advertisement, which reinvests the objects of urban life with the warmth that has, as he argues, ebbed from them: "What, in the end, makes advertisements so superior to criticism? Not what the moving red neon sign says – but the fiery pool reflecting it in the asphalt" (*SW* I, 476). The challenge to modernist writers, then, is to meet the power of advertisement on their own terms, at once registering contemporary urban reality mimetically and wielding it as a power to remake experience in new, unprecedented forms beyond business and administration:

> But it is quite beyond doubt that the development of writing will not indefinitely be bound by the claims to power of a chaotic academic and commercial activity; rather . . . writing, advancing ever more deeply into the graphic regions of its new eccentric figurativeness, will suddenly take possession of an adequate material content. In this picture-writing, poets, who will now as in earliest times be first and foremost experts in writing, will be able to participate only by mastering the fields in which (quite unobtrusively) it is being constructed: statistical and technical diagrams. With the founding of an international moving script, poets will renew their authority in the life of peoples, and find a role awaiting them in comparison to which all the innovative aspirations of rhetoric will reveal themselves as antiquated daydreams. (*SW* I, 456–7)

In his critical work following this prognostication of an expanded sort of modernist writing, Benjamin would find his views confirmed and elaborated in three key artistic instances : in developments in Soviet writing, in the utopian imaginings of the German expressionist Paul Scheerbart, and in the poetry and prose texts of the French surrealists.

Soviet Writing and the "Re-functioning" of Literature as a Space of Experience

In the writers and artists of the Soviet Union, Benjamin discovered not so much a direct model to be imitated – their social and political situation, he believed, was still too singular for that – but rather a telling example of the changing role that intellectuals might play within a new society under construction. Thus, for example, in his 1927 review of "The Political Groupings of Russian Writers," Benjamin surveys three main groupings, including writers advocating proletarian naturalism, a left avant-garde tendency, and a more mainstream "right" literary tendency. Although in later writings, such as "The Author as Producer," Benjamin would write affirmatively of left "tendency" writers such as Tretiakov (briefly mentioned in the 1927 review), here Benjamin takes a skeptical distance from the direct political content of all three trends, stressing instead the mass sociological transformation of *textual production* and *reading* in the Soviet Union over the cultural politics of writers:

> In our time, Russia's literature is – rightly – more important for statisticians than for aesthetes. Thousands of new authors and hundreds of thousands of new readers want above all to be counted and mobilized into the cadres of the new intellectual sharpshooters, who will be drilled for political command and whose munitions consist of the alphabet. In today's Russia, reading is more important than writing, reading newspapers is more important than reading books, and laboriously spelling out the words is more important than reading newspapers. (*SW* II, 9)

In his writings from his 1927 visit to Moscow, Benjamin would similarly give short shrift to the concerns of the "man of letters," while emphasizing the literal presence of pedagogical and propagandistic texts in classrooms, wall newspapers, and factories:

> Anyone entering a Russian classroom for the first time will stop short in surprise. The walls are crammed with pictures, drawings, and pasteboard models. They are temple walls to which the children daily donate their own work as gifts to the collective ... Wall newspapers are, for grown-ups, schemata of the same collective form of expression ... Every Lenin niche has its wall newspaper, which varies its style among factories and authors. The only thing common to all is the naïve cheerfulness: colorful pictures interspersed with prose and verses. (*SW* II, 40)

Even as late as his renowned essay "The Work of Art in the Age of Its Technical Reproducibility," thinking especially of developments in the Soviet Union, Benjamin would similarly argue above all for the importance of the mass social transformation of writing and reading in the present day:

The distinction between author and public is about to lose its axiomatic character. The difference becomes functional; it may vary from case to case. At any moment, the reader is ready to become a writer. As an expert – which he has had to become in any case in a highly specialized work process, even if only in some minor capacity – the reader gains access to authorship. Work itself is given a voice. And the ability to describe a job in words now forms part of the expertise needed to carry it out. Literary competence is no longer founded on specialized higher education but on polytechnic training, and thus is common property. (*SW* III, 114)

Despite this emphasis, however, Benjamin would draw two important conclusions from the Soviet literary debates, which, beyond any direct influence, decisively affected his sense of the new tasks and nature of contemporary writing. First, pondering the Soviet developments in parallel with modernistic tendencies in Western Europe, Benjamin would sharpen his view of literature as a kind of experimental "image-space" (a notion that would also decisively inform his reception of surrealism) in which current changes in experience could be imagined, enacted, tested, and communicated to others. The highly politicized nature of literary reception in the Soviet Union, where, Benjamin notes, "every important decision of the party confronts the writer with the most immediate challenge" (*SW* II, 6), foregrounds in a manner less mediated than in the capitalist West how literary ideas interact with ideological and experiential issues in society. Second, Benjamin believed that as contemporary writers ever more consciously confronted their task of furnishing the new image-space with appropriate content, thus building up the "construction site" in which the collective could playfully explore new modes of affectivity and solidarity, the forms and genres that had for centuries defined "literature" would also demand fresh innovation and change.

Thus, in an argument he set out in his 1929 essay "Program for a Proletarian Children's Theater," Benjamin embraces literature as a socially didactic instrument, but qualifies this didacticism in ways that differ from merely communicating an ideological or conceptual content. In an argument that refers back to the children's play with debris in *One-Way Street*'s "Construction Site," Benjamin argues that education should, first and foremost, create a play-space for practice and experiment, rather than emphasizing the communication of ideas. Accordingly, he conceives the children's theater as constituting a "dialectical site of education" in which the collective of children can explore gestures and signals related to concrete tasks, problems, and processes of making. The proletarian children's theater offers a defined space for "the radical unleashing of play" (*SW* II, 205), where children's activity can give shape to an ephemeral world that can be molded and reformed by imaginative learning processes set in motion within that space. In the space of play, a changeable future is being rehearsed, Benjamin suggests, investing each theatrical gesture performed there with a prefigurative character, like "a signal from another world, in which the child lives and commands" (SW II, 204). Extending this notion beyond Benjamin's immediate topic of children's theater, we might say that with his conception of prefigurative learning in theatrical play, Benjamin imagines an artistic "image-space" in which performative activity, whether individual or collective, productive or receptive, would provide imaginative and practical training for future experience.[12] Seen in this way, Benjamin's idiosyncratic, apparently contradictory embrace of both Brecht's literary didacticism and surrealism's imaginative flights makes better sense. Though stylistically and formally antithetical, these artistic extremes converge in his thinking on a new function of literature as a space of embodied encounter, as the prefigurative "training ground" for an anticipated, only partially visualizable future. The literary text is not the narrative, dramatic, or pictorial representation of this future, but rather its referring index: a "secret signal" to be interpreted and passed on to others in the community of (sign-) readers.

In his 1934 address, "The Author as Producer," Benjamin evinced the example of the Soviet "tendency" and reportage author, Sergei Tretiakov, whose literary ideas found echo among German writers, most notably with Bertolt Brecht. Benjamin calls especial attention in his lecture to Tretiakov's distinction between the "informing" writer and the "operating" writer. This distinction corresponds roughly to that which he himself had drawn, in his proletarian children's theater essay, between a pedagogy purveying ideas and a pedagogy furnishing a space for active, mimetic learning. As Benjamin suggests, the "operating" writer engages in action and defines his mission "in the account he gives of his own activity" (SW II, 770). From this new functional role of writing in relation to the tasks of political struggle and social construction, Benjamin draws far-reaching conclusions about the pressure placed on writing to evolve new forms and media that will allow it to transcend its current artistically defined bounds:

> The tasks that [Tretiakov] has performed, you will perhaps object, are those of a journalist or propagandist; all this has little to do with literature. But I cited the example of Tretiakov deliberately, in order to point out to you how comprehensive the horizon is within which we have to rethink our conceptions of literary forms or genres, in view of the technical factors affecting our present situation, if we are to identify the forms of expression that channel the literary energies of the present. There were not always novels in the past, and there will not always have to be; there have not always been tragedies or great epics. Not always were the forms of commentary, translation, indeed even so-called plagiarism playthings in the margins of literature . . . All this is to accustom you to the thought

that we are in the midst of a mighty recasting of literary forms, a melting down in which many of the opposites in which we have been used to think may lose their force. (*SW* II, 771)

Such developments in the Soviet Union, thus, were ultimately less important for the specific instances – such as Tretiakov's *China, Roar!,* mentioned in Benjamin's 1927 review, or *Commanders of the Field*, about the collectivization of agriculture, which Benjamin cites in "the Author as Producer" – than for their suggestion of new models of literary function. For Benjamin, the content of these works was, appropriately, situational and thus ephemeral, as the concerns of the day ebbed and flowed around current events. As he suggests, however, such works are crucial for their *exemplary* significance, and not just in the Soviet context: their ability "to induce other producers to produce" (*SW* II, 777) and "to put an improved apparatus at their disposal" (*SW* II, 777). They model for European writers a new sort of literary production, adumbrating forms and genres that can occupy new functions and open up new experiential territories. Over and above this, moreover, they lead to a different understanding of the present-day activity of complementary modernist and avant-garde writers in Western Europe, who, in their generic and formal experimentation, can now be understood to be playing an anticipatory role in relation to a new socio-cultural order in formation. Modernism, in this understanding, was through the imaginative arts already furnishing the not-yet fully awakened dream-images of a new social order. It was already manifesting a new communicative practice in a premature, anticipatory form.

EXPERIENCE AND POVERTY: PAUL SCHEERBART'S UTOPIA

A secret thread running through Benjamin's thinking about contemporary cultural politics, embracing both Western modernism and developments in the Soviet Union, is the concept of cultural "poverty," a culture of impoverished "experience" (*Erfahrung*), which for Benjamin carried a potentially positive sense of a culture liberated of traditional spiritual baggage and capable of travelling light into new experiential territory. In December 1933 – hence, not long after the accession of the National Socialists to power in Germany – he published an essay in Prague entitled "Experience and Poverty," in which he lent his thinking about cultural impoverishment a manifesto-like formulation (*SW* II, 731–5). The essay is notable in a number of respects. First, it shares a key passage with another of Benjamin's better-known essays, his 1936 essay on the nineteenth-century Russian short-story writer Nikolai Leskov, "The Storyteller." In both the 1933 and 1936 essays, in virtually identical words, Benjamin vividly evokes a mutation in experience that has occurred through the World War and its turbulent aftermath:

> No, this much is clear: experience has fallen in value, amid a generation which from 1914 to 1918 had to experience some of the most monstrous events in the history of the world . . . Wasn't it noticed at the time how many people returned from the front in silence? Not richer but poorer in communicable experience? And what poured out from the flood of war books ten years later was anything but the experience that passes from mouth to ear. No, there was nothing remarkable about that. For never has experience been contradicted more thoroughly: strategic experience has been contravened by positional warfare; economic experience, by the inflation; physical experience, by hunger; moral experiences, by the ruling powers. A generation that had gone to school in horse-drawn streetcars now stood in the open air, amid a landscape in which nothing was the same except the clouds and, at its center, in a force field of destructive torrents and explosions, the tiny, fragile human body. (*SW* II, 732)

But whereas in the later "The Storyteller" essay, Benjamin appears to linger nostalgically over the communal, traditional residues that still are discernable within the Russian writer's short stories, "Experience and Poverty" affirms, without ambiguity, the resolute liquidation of tradition and the barbaric condition of inventing anew on barren ground:

> Barbarism? Yes, indeed. We say this in order to introduce a new, positive concept of barbarism. For what does poverty of experience do for the barbarian? It forces him to start from scratch; to make a new start; to make a little go a long way; to begin with a little and build up further, looking neither left nor right. (*SW* II, 732)

As avatars of this new cultural poverty, Benjamin mentions several key figures of modern art, architecture, and popular culture: Paul Klee, Adolf Loos, Le Corbusier, Bertolt Brecht, Paul Scheerbart, and even – Mickey Mouse.[13] What unites them for Benjamin is their commitment to a desublimated, elemental production of cultural products, whether these take the form of stripped-down graphics, glass and ferro-concrete buildings, didactic poems and plays, science-fiction novels, or animated films. As Benjamin writes, "A complex artist like the painter Paul Klee and a programmatic one like Loos – both reject the traditional, solemn, noble image of man, festooned with all the sacrificial offerings of the past. They turn instead to the naked man of the contemporary world who lies screaming like a newborn babe in the dirty diapers of the present" (*SW* II, 733). Each in his own way, Benjamin suggests, takes on the condition of cultural poverty as their basis, to build upon rather than to disavow, cloak, or compensate with aesthetic "goods" or "values." Rather, they are preparing the "buildings, pictures, and stories," through which, if need be, "mankind is preparing to outlive culture" (*SW* II, 735).

Benjamin gives special attention to the science-fiction writer and modernist fantast Paul Scheerbart, who, along with the expressionist architect Bruno Taut, formulated a utopian program for the transformation of the planet through glass architecture. Just as Taut, in his anarcho-utopian treatise *Die Auflösung der Städte* (The Dissolution of the Cities) called for a resettlement of the earth on a new basis,[14] so too Scheerbart, in his 1914 treatise *Glass Architecture* – which also featured in Benjamin's exposé for the *Arcades Project* – had seen building in glass as the promised end of the industrial brick city as it had been constructed up to the present. Thus, in a section of *Glass Architecture* captioned "The transformation of the Earth's surface," Scheerbart struck a prophetic note:

> So many ideas constantly sound to us like a fairy-tale, when they are not really fantastic or utopian at all. Eighty years ago, the steam railway came, and undeniably transformed the face of the earth. From what has been said so far the earth's surface will once again be transformed, this time by glass architecture . . .
>
> The present brick "culture" of the city, which we all deplore, is due to the railway. Glass architecture will only come if the city as we know it goes. It is completely clear to all those who care about the future of our civilization that this dissolution must take place.[15]

Scheerbart was also, notably, the author of one of Benjamin's most treasured works of fiction, the "asteroid-novel" *Lesabéndio*,[16] given to him as a present by his friend Gershom Scholem. He drafted a review of the book in 1920, and, according to a letter of the same year, took it seriously enough to make it the focus of a projected philosophical critique and the basis of an exposition of his political views.[17] In his draft review, he signals the considerable interest of the book as a utopian image of technology's purest world-transfiguring manifestations, remarking:

> Art is not the forum of utopias. If it nevertheless appears that it is from this perspective that the decisive word about this book can be spoken, because it is full of humor, at the same time it is this humor that all the more securely transcends the region of art and makes the work a spiritual testimony. Its existence is not eternal and grounded solely in itself, but its testimony will be elevated by the higher things to which it gives witness. Of these higher things – the fulfillment of utopia – one cannot speak, only give witness.[18]

Although he did not realize his intention to further explore Scheerbart's utopia at that time, by 1933 his essay "Experience and Poverty" provides some hints of the direction in which he might have developed his thought, as does his conjunction in the *Arcades Project* of Scheerbart's visionary architecture with Fourier's utopian phalanstries.

Scheerbart's *Lesabéndio* narrates the activities of the residents of the aster-oid Pallas, which is traversed from pole to pole by two symmetrical cone-like craters connected by a communicating tunnel at its center. Its northern part is covered by thick, web-like clouds, which conceal that which lies above the asteroid and forms an obstacle to be overcome through a utopian building-project initiated by the title-character Lesabéndio. Not just Lesabéndio, however, but many of inhabitants of Pallas, whose flexible bodies, multiple limbs, and suction feet Scheerbart describes in ever-changing variations and with humorous panache, are animated by eccentrically specialized artistic, scientific, technical, and architectural passions that resonate with the experi-mental, utopian aspirations of the expressionist avant-garde of Scheerbart's day. For example, "Biba" is fascinated by the astronomical and philosophical implications of the sun; "Dex" performs construction work with a special sort of metallic material that forms long, strong beams and rays; "Labu" is an artist interested exclusively in curved forms; "Manesi" is an expert cultiva-tor of mushrooms and hanging plants; "Nuse" constructs numerous towers of light of varying sizes; "Peka" specializes in an art of right angles and flat surfaces, as well as crystalline forms; and "Sofanti" fabricates synthetic skins that resonate in Pallas's atmosphere with fantastic musical tones. Lesabéndio, however, outbids all these extraterrestrial expressionists in his combination of technical, artistic, and social ambition, with his utopian desire to build a hundred-mile high Tatlin-esque cosmic tower that could break through the enveloping web of clouds and afford a vision of what lies beyond the planetary limits of the Pallasian outlook. To succeed at this task, however, he must first organize a vast collective commitment on the part of the Pallasians, exercising his unbending will against the skepticism of his intellectual friends and rivals. In his discussions with the Pallasians, Lesabéndio speaks the language of mod-ernist architecture, spelling out the need for "concentration" and "planning":

> Then Lesabéndio said:
> "You're all so tired – but it's only because you don't concentrate your thoughts on a single, simple, good plan. Concentration of that sort is refreshing on its own, even when the plan's fulfillment is still far off. You let yourselves get bogged down."[19]

There are also technical, as well as political and moral, obstacles to Lesabéndio's plans: he must discover new sources of materials to allow the construction of this celestially ambitious construction; encourage a new fecundity, to increase the available stock of laborers for his project; and foster new sources of food to nourish the increased population on the asteroid. Eventually overcoming all obstacles as well as his own fear, Lesabéndio breaks through the clouds and reunites Pallas with the hidden, higher double asteroid to which it has always been, unsuspected by the Pallasians, paired. Atop his tower and gazing out into the cosmos, Lesabéndio undergoes a cosmic transformation – at once a painful death and a mystical translation – into a star, with the surrounding atmosphere becoming a new sensory organ for him, like a "colossal telescope"[20] through which he can communicate with the other asteroids and the green sun, which itself now seems to glow with new life.

Benjamin sees in Scheerbart's techno-cosmic, utopian fantasy the figurative means to meet the cultural impoverishment of the present on its own terms and turn it towards a radical exercise of utopian imagination. "No one," he writes, "has greeted this present with greater joy and hilarity than Paul Scheerbart" (*SW* II, 733). Scheerbart, he suggests, projects a new, playful interpenetration of humankind with modern technology such that both are transfigured by the encounter:

> Scheerbart is interested in inquiring how our telescopes, our airplanes, our rockets can transform human beings as they have been up to now into completely new, lovable, and interesting creatures. Moreover, these creatures talk in a completely new language. And what is crucial about this language is its arbitrary, constructed nature, in contrast to organic language. (*SW* II, 733)

Benjamin may have in mind the birth-scene that takes place early in the book, in which a new Pallasian reveals himself to be a spontaneous *zaum*-spouting futurist like Velimir Khlebnikov, a Hugo Ball- or Raoul Haussmann-like Dadaist sound poet, or a jazz scat-singer on a riff:

> The little Pallasian, who would grow to the size of the older Pallasians in a few days, rubbed his eyes for some time and eventually tried to talk. With great effort, he brought out the words, "Bom-bim-ba-ri-zapa- zulli-as-as!"[21]

Although the older Pallasians explain to the little one where and who he is and why he should speak the Pallasian language instead of his futuristic baby-talk, a trace of this act of radical, infantile linguistic innovation is preserved in Scheerbart's novel: in the child's name. Ever after, he will be called Bombimba, since, as Scheerbart explains, all Pallasians are named after their first words. In "Experience and Poverty," Benjamin underscores this techno-Adamic moment in Scheerbart, even going so far as to connect *Lesabéndio*'s reinvention of the language of names with the use of "dehumanized" technical names in the Soviet Union:

> This is the distinctive feature of the language of Scheerbart's human beings, or rather "people"; for humanlikeness – a principle of humanism – is something they reject. Even in their proper names: Peka, Labu, Sofanti, and the like are the names of the characters in the book

Lesabéndio, titled after its hero. The Russians, too, like to give their children "dehumanized" names: they call them "October," after the month of the Revolution; "Pyatiletka," after the Five-Year Plan; or "Aviakhim," after an airline. No technical renovation of language, but its mobilization in the service of struggle or work – at any rate, of changing reality instead of describing it. (*SW* II, 733)

Implicit in Benjamin's juxtaposition of Scheerbart's asteroid-utopia with recent Soviet construction is that what appeared the wildest outer-space fantasy in this science fiction novel of 1913 had become, only twenty years later, a diagnostic lens through which to discern real trends in the contemporary world: the emergence of post-humanist conceptions of personhood, and the invention of a performative nomenclature related to a collective politics organized by technology. As if we too had mounted Lesabéndio's tower to peer through our historical atmosphere with new sensory organs, a radically different, post-humanist world already confronts us on the horizon.[22]

Benjamin also remarked that the "art-form" through which Lesabéndio concentrated his utopian imagination and creative will was architecture (as might well be expected of a character created by the author of *Glass Architecture*). Scheerbart, Benjamin wrote, "place the greatest value on housing his 'people' – and following this model, his fellow citizens – in buildings befitting their station, in adjustable, movable glass-covered dwellings of the kind since built by Loos and Le Corbusier" (*SW* II, 733). Benjamin goes on to suggest that glass is a material that favors exposure over secrets and hence is the antithesis of the bourgeois interior as it was conceived in the nineteenth century. Glass opens the interior outward, evacuating it of "inwardness." In advocating a transparent, modernist glass architecture, thus, Scheerbart, Loos, and Le Corbusier together appear to Benjamin as the advance-guard "spokesmen of a new poverty" (*SW* II, 734).

In an unpublished short article written shortly before his death, Benjamin once again took up the topic of Scheerbart.[23] Here he associates Scheerbart with a concern that could be said to have constituted Benjamin's primary preoccupation in the last decade of his life: the danger, manifest in fascism and imperialist war, of a pathological relationship of human beings to technology, and in turn, the utopian possibility of a new humanity living in harmony with a technologically transfigured nature. Accordingly, he begins his article by quoting Scheerbart's sly response to World War I, which managed to slip past the censor and find publication in 1914: "Let me protest first against the expression 'world war.' I am sure that no heavenly body, however near, will involve itself in the affair in which we are embroiled. Everything leads me to believe that deep peace still reigns in interstellar space" (Scheerbart, quoted in *SW* IV, 386).[24] Benjamin comments on the cosmic and natural-historical perspective that Scheerbart takes on the events of human history:

> Scheerbart's books attracted hardly more attention from the public than these sentences did from the censor. That was only natural. This poet's work is imbued with an idea which could not have been more foreign to the notions then widespread. This idea – or rather, this image – was of a humanity which had deployed the full range of its technology and put it to humane use. To achieve this state of affairs, Scheerbart believed that two conditions were essential: first, people should discard the base and primitive belief that their task was to "exploit" the forces of nature; second, they should be true to the conviction that technology, by liberating human beings, would fraternally liberate the whole of creation. (*SW* IV, 386)

At the end of the article, Benjamin brings Scheerbart in conjunction with another favorite utopian author, the eighteenth-century French socialist Charles Fourier, who figured centrally in Benjamin's study of Paris's arcades. "In relating the great deeds of creation," Benjamin writes, Scheerbart

> sometimes seems like the twin brother of Fourier. In Fourier's extravagant fantasies about the world of the Harmonians, there is as much mockery of present-day humanity as there is faith in a humanity of the future. In the German poet we find these elements in the same proportions. It is unlikely that the German utopian knew the work of his French counterpart. But we can be sure that the image of the planet Mercury teaching the Harmonians their mother tongue would have delighted Paul Scheerbart. (*SW* IV, 387–8)

Benjamin's late essay on Scheerbart, in fact, stands in the closest relation with his last great work, the theses "On the Concept of History," and reveals how Benjamin's reading of this eccentric, marginal figure in modernist writing formed one of the major conceptual lenses through which he viewed the terrors of current history. Like Scheerbart, Benjamin employs in his theses such extra-human creatures as Wolfgang von Kempelen's chess-playing automaton[25] and Paul Klee's *Angelus Novus* – melancholy *semblables* of Scheerbart's joyful Lesabéndio – to imagine human history from a cosmic point of view. Scheerbart's figures asserted the possibility of "interstellar peace" and cosmic-utopian creativity even amidst the catastrophes of technological warfare. Benjamin's angel, as it were, turned Scheerbart's telescope around, seeing even in apparent "progress" in the human world only delusion and the rubble of continuous catastrophe. A kind of cosmic "spleen" sours the view of this profoundly Baudelairean poet-raptor. Yet through the figure of Fourier, the utopian note that Scheerbart sounded in *Lesabéndio*, the possibility of cosmic construction and a new consciousness of human beings' place among the stars, also marks Benjamin's final testament. In comparison to the exploitation of nature advocated in the visions of laboring humanity expounded by bourgeois and socialist thinkers alike, Benjamin writes –

> Fourier's fantasies, which have been so ridiculed, prove surprisingly sound. According to Fourier, cooperative labor would increase efficiency to such an extent that four moons would illuminate the sky at night, and the polar ice caps would recede, seawater would no longer taste salty, and beasts of prey would do man's bidding. All this illustrates a kind of labor which, far from exploiting nature, would help her give birth to the creations that now lie dormant in her womb. (*SW* IV, 394)

The Image-Space of Surrealism

Intriguingly – and on the face of it, rather improbably – the motif of glass architecture, which was key to Benjamin's reception of Scheerbart as well as a focus of his work on nineteenth- and twentieth-century urbanism, also constitutes an important axis of Benjamin's embrace of surrealism. Through the surrealists, Benjamin connected his expressionist and constructivist interest in glass architecture, coming from Scheerbart, Taut, Loos, and Corbusier, back towards the nineteenth-century ambiances of the Paris arcades, which would constitute the central topic of his researches throughout the 1930s.[26] Already in his 1929 essay, "Surrealism, the Last Snapshot of the European Intelligentsia," Benjamin anticipates the themes he treated in "Experience and Poverty," by stressing the impoverishment of the city environment that surrealism turned into its privileged object of lyric transfiguration. In his 1928 book *Nadja*, André Breton had utilized the metaphor of the glass house to celebrate the end of psychological literature and the advent of a new epoch of exposure in which the interior space of the psyche and the exterior space of the city would be indiscernibly intertwined in figures of desire and encounter. "I myself shall continue living in my glass house," Breton wrote, "where you can always see who comes to call; where everything hanging from the ceiling and on the walls stays where it is as if by magic, where I sleep nights in a glass bed, under glass sheets, where *who I am* will sooner or later appear etched by a diamond."[27] Similarly, ensconced in the glass of the soon-to-be-demolished Passage de l'Opéra, described in *Paris Peasant* as "a big glass coffin,"[28] Louis Aragon hyperbolically extolled the "transparency" with which he could observe the hidden, unawowed, but eagerly pursued desires of the arcade's denizens: "The secrets of each of you, like those of language and love, are revealed to me each night, and there are nights in broad daylight. You pass close to me, your clothes fly away, your account books open at the page where the dissimulations and the frauds are to be found, the intimacies of your bedroom are revealed, and your heart!"[29] Similarly, later in his exploration of the Passage, Aragon would suggest the pornographic theater, with its "truly modern dramaturgy free of all fakery,"[30] as a model for the avant-garde: an art of exposed bodies transparently expounding sexual desires for all to see. With the echo of Scheerbart in his ear, Benjamin would pick up on the architectural, as well as the moral overtones of Breton's and Aragon's metaphors of transparency and visual exposure. "To live in a glass house," Benjamin commented, "is a revolutionary virtue par excellence. It is also an intoxication, a moral exhibitionism, that we badly need. Discretion concerning one's own existence, once an aristocratic virtue, has become more an more an affair of petty-bourgeois parvenus" (*SW* II, 209).

Just as Benjamin, in *One-Way Street*, had employed the subjective energies of love and erotic desire as a compass to estrange his path through a familiar city (or to guide him through an actually unknown city, like Riga, where he sought his lover Asja Lacis), so too Breton in *Nadja* utilizes erotic errancy to open up the space of Paris to surrealist illumination. Breton, Benjamin writes –

> can boast an extraordinary discovery: he was the first to perceive the revolutionary energies that appear in the "outmoded" . . . The relation of these things to revolution – no one can have a more exact concept of it than these authors. No one before these visionaries and augurs perceived how destitution – not only social but architectonic, the poverty of interiors, enslaved and enslaving objects – can be suddenly transformed into revolutionary nihilism. (*SW* II, 210)

In fact, as Benjamin describes it, the precise innovation of the surrealists would be to draw social and collective – hence, political – implications from the subjective experience that Baudelaire called "spleen," reflecting the sense of nausea before the clutter of goods that have lost their freshness for the buyer who once seized them with desire:

> I have more memories than if I had lived a thousand years.
>
> Even a bureau crammed with souvenirs,
> Old bills, love letters, photographs, receipts,
> Court depositions, locks of hair in plaits,
> Hides fewer secrets than my brain could yield.
> . . .
> I'm a stale boudoir where old-fashioned clothes
> Lie scattered among wilted fern and rose . . .[31]

For Baudelaire, if the new appears in the light of modern beauty, the poetic "ideal" flashing up out of the passing phenomena of the city, spleen is its shadow, which falls over the ideal already the moment after its instantaneous advent. Spleen is a temporal ambiguity as the heart of the new: the soon-will-be-stale that hollows it out from within, making constant refreshment both necessary and always, in advance, futile. As Benjamin succinctly summarizes in one of his notes on Baudelaire: "Spleen is the feeling that corresponds to catastrophe in permanence" (*SW* IV, 164). Though affectively and tonally quite different, the surrealists and Baudelaire, Benjamin suggests, ultimately draw from the same experiential infrastructure in the accelerated rhythms of the metropolitan life of Paris.

In his essay "The Philosophy of Toys," Baudelaire describes a similarly spleenful experience of the child, futilely seeking to get at the "soul" of his toy by prying, twisting, and digging in it. "At last," Baudelaire writes, "he opens it up, he is the stronger. But *where is the soul?* This is the beginning of melancholy and gloom."[32] Both the child's toy and the adult's commodity disappoint the desire to get beyond its surface and penetrate to its soul; it leaves the object, and by reflection, its owner as well, dispirited, disenchanted. Yet in an anticipation of Benjamin's evocation of surrealism's "revolutionary nihilism," Baudelaire ends his essay enigmatically with the child who suddenly breaks the toy in his hand. Ironically, Baudelaire notes, "I must admit that I do not understand the mysterious motive which causes their action. Are they in a superstitious passion against these tiny objects which imitate humanity, or are they perhaps forcing them to undergo a kind of Masonic initiation before introducing them into nursery life? – *Puzzling question!*"[33] With this latter evocation of the Masons, a conspiratorial secret society associated with Jacobin revolutionary violence, Baudelaire suggests that this childish destructiveness, though vented against the toy, is in the end no mere child's play. As Benjamin notes, "Baudelaire's violent temper goes hand in hand with his destructive animus" (*SW* IV, 174). That such "destructive animus" could have a critical, even revolutionary function, is suggested by a passage in which Benjamin appears to explicate the "puzzling question" with which Baudelaire concludes his essay:

> The course of history, seen in terms of the concept of catastrophe, can actually claim no more attention from thinkers than a child's kaleidoscope, which with every turn of the hand dissolves the established order into a new array . . . The concepts of the ruling class have always been the mirrors that enabled an image of "order" to prevail. – The kaleidoscope must be smashed. (*SW* IV, 164)

Experienced in a "spleenful" way, the kaleidoscopic spectacle of urban life reveals its melancholy impoverishment. Surrealism, Benjamin suggests, leads even further and more systematically into the "destructive animus" of Baudelaire, still instinctive and childish, unleashing a "revolutionary nihilism" capable of charging the vacant spaces of the city with explosive tension. As Benjamin writes,

At the center of this world of things stands the most dreamed-about of their objects: the city of Paris itself. But only revolt completely exposes its Surrealist face (deserted streets in which whistles and shots dictate the outcome). And no face is surrealistic to the same degree as the true face of a city. No picture by de Chirico or Max Ernst can match the sharp elevations of the city's inner strongholds, which one must overrun and occupy in order to master their fate and – in their fate, in the fate of the masses – one's own. (*SW* II, 211)

FROM SURREALISM TO ANTHROPOLOGICAL MATERIALISM

At the conclusion of his 1929 "Surrealism" essay, Benjamin introduced a concept that would be crucial to his understanding of modernism's role in developing a new "image-space" in which rapid changes of experience, influenced especially by technology and mass politics, could be modeled, tested, and worked through. This was the concept of "anthropological materialism." In the concluding paragraph of his essay, Benjamin alluded to a new, surrealist image-space "in which political materialism and physical creaturliness share the inner man, the psyche, the individual, or whatever else we wish to throw to them, with dialectical justice, so that no limb remains untorn" (*SW* II, 217). This space, in which human and non-human material, bodies and things, emotions and concepts, words and images mingled to create new constellations of experience, could not be adequately explained by the mechanical materialism of positivistic science or the economistic Marxism still informing the official communist and social democratic movements. It required a new "anthropological" materialism in which, on the one hand, humanity's place in natural history would be comprehended, and on the other hand, human projects, emotions, activities, and technologies would be seen to be integral to the movements and forms of the material world.

One source of inspiration for Benjamin's anthropological materialism was, clearly, the erotic poetry of surrealism, which Benjamin compared to medieval "dolce stil novo" and Provençal troubadour poetry in bestowing a kind of mystical illumination of the world in which the beloved dwells, including the spaces she inhabits and the ordinary things she has touched. Indeed, under the pressure of an almost explosively heightened sense of lyric desire, André Breton, Louis Aragon, and Paul Eluard pressed the traditional blazons of medieval love poetry towards a promiscuous interpenetration of bodies and things, often blending in an ecstasy of surreal figuration the human with non-human world and the individual with the social:

> My wife her match-thin wrists
> Whose fingers are chance and the ace of hearts
> Whose fingers are mowed hay

My love with marten and beechnut beneath her arms
Midsummer night
Of privet and the nests of angel fish
Whose arms are seafoam and river locks
And the mingling of wheat and mill
Whose legs are Roman candles
Moving like clockwork and despair[34]

Similarly in Benjamin's favorite prose-works of surrealism, Breton's *Nadja* or Aragon's *Paris Peasant*, eroticism becomes the occasion for the subject's capillary permeation of the material world. Thus, for example, the ecstatic paean to blondness set off by Aragon's glimpse of a lock of hair in the Passage de l'Opéra, which I quote here in its full, extravagant extent:

So one day, in the Passage de l'Opéra, I found myself contemplating the pure, lazy coils of a python of blondness. And suddenly, for the first time in my life, the idea struck me that men have discovered only one term of comparison for what is blond: *flaxen*, and have left it at that. Flax, poor wretches, have you never looked at ferns? I have spent months on end nibbling fern hair. I have known hair that was pure resin, topaz hair, hair pulsing with hysteria. Blond as hysteria, blond as the sky, blond as tiredness, blond as a kiss. My palette of blondnesses would include the elegance of motorcars, the odour of sainfoin, the silence of mornings, the perplexities of waiting, the ravages of glancing touches. How blond is the sound of the rain, how blond the song of mirrors! From the perfume of gloves to the cry of the own, from the beating of the murderer's heart to the flower-flames of the laburnum, from the first nibble to the last song, how many blondnesses from how many eyelids: blondness of roofs, blondness of winds, blondness of tables or palm trees, there are whole days of blondness, blond's department stores, arcades for desire, arsenals of orangeade powder. Blond everywhere: I surrender myself to this pitch pine of the senses, to this concept of a blondness which is not so much a colour as a sort of spirit of colour blended with the accents of love. From white to red through yellow, blond keeps its mystery intact. Blond resembles the stammerings of ecstasy, the piracies of lips, the tremors of limpid waters. Blond takes flight from definitions down a wayward path where flowers and seashells greet my eyes. It is woman glinting upon stones, a paradoxical shadow of caresses in space, a breath of dishevelment of reason. Blond as the reign of passionate embraces, these tresses were dissolving, then, in the shop in the passage, and as for me, I had been slowly dying there for the past fifteen minutes or so.[35]

It would be easy to see in this passage a mere fetishistic fancy, and unquestionably Aragon is taking a kind of theatricalized, hyperbolic auto-erotic pleasure in the sheer boundlessness of his verbal invention on the motif of blondness. But Benjamin discerned more than just subjective enjoyment in such passages. In fact, as Aragon's evocation of "slowly dying there for the past fifteen minutes or so," his hymn to blondness is as much a mystical suspension or cancellation of subjectivity, which in turn allows him to experience, at the height of intensity, what Benjamin would call, in his discussion of fashion in his 1935 exposé for the *Arcades Project*, "the sex appeal of the inorganic" (*AP*, 19). In the revised exposé of 1939 (drawing from the *Arcades Project* notes), Benjamin appends a quote from Guillaume Apollinaire's 1916 novel *The Poet Assassinated*, which, with an extravagance comparable to the materialist metaphors of surrealist poetry, presents fashion as a commingling of women's bodies with various materials and things:

> Any material from nature's domain can now be introduced into the composition of women's clothes. I saw a charming dress made of corks ... A major designer is thinking about launching tailor-made outfits made of old bookbindings done in calf ... Fish bones are being worn a lot on hats ... Steel, wool, sandstone, and files have suddenly entered the vestementary arts ... Feathers now decorate not only hats but shoes and gloves; and next year they'll be on umbrellas. They're doing shoes in Venetian glass and hats in Baccarat crystal ... I forgot to tell you that last Wednesday I saw on the boulevards an old dowager dressed in mirrors stuck to fabric. The effect was sumptuous in the sunlight. You'd have thought it was a gold mine out for a walk. Later it started raining and the lady looked like a silver mine ...[36]

In the fetishistic extravagances of fashion that Apollinaire wittily satirized, as in the metaphorical erotic excesses of surrealism – and both of these already anticipated by Baudelaire's famous "praise of cosmetics" in "The Painter of Modern Life" – Benjamin discerned a common affective impulse leading empathetically into the interior of things and their material qualities:

> In fetishism, sex does away with the boundaries separating the organic world from the inorganic. Clothing and jewelry are its allies. It is as much at home with what is dead as it is with living flesh. The latter, moreover, shows it the way to establish itself in the former. Hair is a frontier region lying between the two kingdoms of *sexus*. Something different is disclosed in the drunkenness of passion: the landscapes of the body ... These landscapes are traversed by paths which lead sexuality into the world of the inorganic. Fashion itself is only another medium enticing it still more deeply into the universe of matter. (*AP* [B3, 8] 69–70)

Corbusier, Modern Urbanism, and Architectural Modernism

As a final consideration in our discussion of Benjamin and modernism, I will touch upon his relation to modernist architecture, which, as already noted, he read through the twin prisms of the nineteenth-century arcades (via surrealism) and through the utopian fantasies of Paul Scheerbart. Yet, as he writes in a note in the *Arcades Project*, if one were to seek a pendant to the contribution of the surrealists, it would have be found in the urbanism and modernist architecture of Le Corbusier: "To encompass both Breton and Le Corbusier – that would mean drawing the spirit of contemporary France like a bow, with which knowledge shoots the moment in the heart" (*AP* [N1a, 5] 459). Benjamin, like many of his contemporaries – as Manfredo Tafuri argues in his path-breaking study *Architecture and Utopia* – viewed urbanistic planning and modernist architecture as the summa of the previous work of the artistic avant-garde, the collective realization of avant-garde art in a rationalized, liberated city-space. As Tafuri suggests, the artistic object is transcended in urban design, while at the same time the artistic impulse purports to have remolded social experience itself:

> it was no longer objects that were offered to judgment, but a process to be lived and used as such . . . Since new forms were no longer meant to be absolute values but instead proposals for the organization of collective life . . . architecture summoned the public to participate in its work of design. Thus through architecture the ideology of the public took a great step forward.[37]

Benjamin reflects this general fascination of the avant-garde with architecture and urbanism, in, for example, his celebratory association of film and architecture as canons of new forms of mass reception. Both, he argues, are taken in collectively through use, through bodily habituation in a state of distraction. "Under certain circumstances," like today, he implies, "this form of reception shaped by architecture acquires canonical value. For the tasks which face the human apparatus of perception at historical turning points cannot be performed solely by optical means – that is, by way of contemplation. They are mastered gradually – taking their cue from tactile reception – through habit" (*SW* III, 120).

What Benjamin expresses here with somewhat obscure indirection can be formulated more clearly: At this historical juncture in which a new collectivist system, fascist or communist, is about to establish its hegemony, the reception of architecture constitutes the model for the contemporary arts more generally. The arts must become, in analogy to modern architecture, functional, rational, public, and practical in their orientation. Adhering to the example of architecture, the modern arts – especially technical, popular arts like cinema – offer the masses a training-ground for new experience, shaped by habitual use, necessary to thrive in the coming social order.

In his thinking about architecture, Benjamin drew especial sustenance from the Swiss architectural historian Sigfried Giedion's treatise and manifesto of architectural modernity, *Building in France, Building in Iron, Building in Ferro-Concrete*. Giedion, whom scholars have dubbed "the apologist-in-chief"[38] and the "ghostwriter"[39] of the Modern Movement in architecture, was the secretary of CIAM (Congrès Internationaux d'Architecture Moderne) and the author of one of the most influential works of architectural theory of the twentieth-century, *Space, Time, and Architecture*, based on Giedion's 1938 lectures at Harvard University and published in 1941. His subsequent book, *Mechanization Takes Command* (1948), is a landmark work in the history of technology, and his methodological claim in this study to be writing the "anonymous history" of the twentieth century bears close comparison to Benjamin's focus on the anonymous, collective dissemination of the arcade as a nineteenth-century architectural and cultural space.[40] Other focal points of Benjamin's investigations of architecture include: the creation of city "perspectives" in the Haussmannisation of Paris; the architectural reorganization of social time implicit in the glass and iron constructions of the Universal Exhibitions; and the reconstellation of interior and exterior space, of city and dwelling place, effected by the new building materials and architectural forms.

Architecture as an instance of art and of everyday culture necessarily entails both collective production and collective reception. It has an explicit relation to publicness, even when it offers refuge in domestic spaces such as the family home or ambiguous escape in liminal spaces such as the arcade. Its reception nearly always involves a large component of practical, embodied activity by those passing through or dwelling in built spaces. Methodologically and rhetorically, then, it also facilitates a metaphorical movement typical of Benjamin's writing, a shuttling between specific description and theoretical generalization and an analogous projection of mass phenomena out of Benjamin's single perspective as observer and interpreter. A note from Convolute M ["The Flâneur"], typical of passages also found in Benjamin's impressionistic "city portraits" of Naples, Marseilles, Berlin, or Moscow, illustrates well this metaphorical translation and projection from a singular to collective scale:

> Streets are the dwelling place of the collective. The collective is an eternally unquiet, eternally agitated being that – in the space between the building fronts – experiences, learns, understands, and invents as much as individuals do within the privacy of their own four walls. For this collective, glossy enameled shop signs are a wall decoration as good as, if not better than, an oil painting in the drawing room of a bourgeois; walls with their "Post No Bills" are its writing desk, newspaper stands its

libraries, mailboxes its bronze busts, benches its bedroom furniture, and the café terrace is the balcony from which it looks down on its household. The section of railing where road workers hang their jackets is the vestibule, and the gateway which leads from the row of courtyards out into the open is the long corridor that daunts the bourgeois, being for the courtyards the entry to the chambers of the city. Among these latter, the arcade was the drawing room. More than anywhere else, the street reveals itself in the arcade as the furnished and familiar interior of the masses. (*AP* [M3a,4] 423)

Passages such as this render the field of single social facts and experience permeable to figural representation, a surplus in signs over and above its capacity to signify, an effect of what Benjamin would elsewhere refer to as the "mimetic faculty." Methodically subjecting historical facts to figural associations, Benjamin sought to discover critical "constellations" immanent but hidden in the material, thus disclosing inapparent connections between seemingly unconnected entities or phenomena.

As a built structure, architecture also poses in a particularly ostentatious way the everyday presence of differential rhythms of time: rhythms of physical emergence and decay, rhythms of social and ideological change, rhythms of valuation and devaluation, rhythms of fashion and obsolescence. Methodologically, architecture stands as the extreme "constructive" pole of Benjamin's historiography, which explores precisely the temporal polarization and tension that exists in the field of cultural artifacts. Yet these pure extremes – represented, as I have noted, by the surrealist embrace of the obsolete and Le Corbusier's emphatic modernity – are but points of reference against which the typical historical artifact reveals its dream-like ambiguity of forward- and backward-looking elements. In the case of architecture, the most regressive and anti-constructive legacy of the nineteenth century was, according to both Giedion and Benjamin, the *house*. As Giedion wrote (and as Benjamin quotes, in Convolute L ["Dream House, Museum, Spa"]): "The house has always shown itself 'barely receptive to new formulations'" (*AP* [L1, 8] 406). The latter part of Giedion's book prognosticates solutions to the problem of human dwelling through the constructive possibilities of ferro-concrete in housing. The modernist Corbusier is the hero of this latter section, being the architect who, through the removal of supporting walls and an innovative use of glass, disintegrated the opposition of space and plasticity in building, creating "the eternally open house."[41] Analogously, Benjamin observes that "Le Corbusier's work seems to stand at the terminus of the mythological figuration 'house'" (*AP* [L1a, 4] 407).[42]

As the Venice School historians Manfredo Tafuri and Francesco Dal Co have pointed out, modern architecture was closely tied to the enormous transformations of twentieth-century capitalism and the corporate state and thus forms a pivotal point for understanding the change in the nature and function of intellectual labor in modern society.[43] In his own reflections on intellectual labor, Benjamin gave greater consideration to the changing role of writers and visual artists in the age of reportage and cinema and never developed, like Tafuri and Dal Co many years later, a detailed disciplinary critique of architecture. Yet Benjamin's essayistic remarks on the "refunctioning" of intellectual work may apply even more appropriately to architecture than to the artistic disciplines he treated in, for example, "The Author as Producer" and "The Work of Art in the Age of Its Technical Reproducibility." In the *Arcades Project*, for example, Benjamin hints that architecture, even more than photography, may have exposed the limits of the concept of art in the nineteenth century:

> architecture was historically the earliest field to outgrow the concept of art, or, better, . . . it tolerated least well being contemplated as "art" – a category which the nineteenth century, to a previously unimagined extent but with hardly more justification at bottom, imposed on the creations of intellectual productivity. (*AP* [F3, 1] 155)

In any case, the strong methodological centrality of architecture in the *Arcades Project* implies that Benjamin intuited its importance as a site for further reflection in his evolving critique of traditional intellectual labor.

A crucial motif of Giedion's celebration of glass and iron and ferro-concrete building is the way in which these materials allow an increasing openness of architectural structure and, correlatively, an intensified continuity and interpenetration of architecture and urban context. Thus, for example, Giedion relates Mart Stam's superstructure of the Rokin Dam in Amsterdam (1926) to the Eiffel Tower (1889), juxtaposing a sketch of the Dutch structure to a sharply angled photograph of suspended stairs in the Eiffel Tower. His caption to the Stam image reads:

> Only now do the seeds that lie in structures such as the Eiffel Tower come to full fruition. The affinity with a building such as the Eiffel Tower lies not merely in the connection and interpenetration by suspended transportation or free-hanging stations; one reaches the conclusion viewing both buildings: ARCHITECTURE NO LONGER HAS RIGID BOUNDARIES.[44]

By the second half of the book, dedicated to ferro-concrete, Giedion rises to a hymn of praise for the new post-monumental openness of Corbusier's houses:

> The solid volume is opened up wherever possible by cubes of air, strip windows, immediate transition to the sky. The new architecture shatters the original conceptual polarity: space or plasticity. The new situation can no longer be understood with these old terms!

> Corbusier's houses are neither spatial nor plastic: air flows through them! Air becomes a constituent factor! Neither space nor plastic form counts, only RELATION and INTERPENETRATION! There is only a single, indivisible space. The shells fall away between interior and exterior.[45]

As Georgiadis points out, Giedion places *the observer* at the center of his investigations, for whom the visual field of the city is increasingly a floating field of objects in space.[46] Besides allowing a dematerialization of support and the enclosure of greater continuous volumes within the building, iron and glass lattices extend the *observer's* eye horizontally beyond the building's boundaries as well. It draws together in a common visual framework objects at different points in depth, projecting them, as it were, onto a flattened plane of perception in which perspectival depth cues have been replaced by complex "cubistic" interrelations within an indefinitely extended space.

Benjamin, similarly, picks up this idea of intensified interconnection between elements of the urban environment and the interpenetration of interior and exterior spaces. Echoing imagery in Breton's *Nadja*, he asserts in his "Surrealism" essay that "To live in a glass house is a revolutionary virtue *par excellence*," and praises Corbusier's liquidation of the dwelling's monumentality. Benjamin stresses the dialectical tensions within particular buildings or particular instances of architectural discourse between emergent technical features and regressive forms, between the stifled hints of a modern, disenchanted horizontality of space and the residues of a premodern, mythic, hierarchical topology of place. One of the most important instances in the *Arcades Project* of the ambiguity that results from flawed, partial attempts to assimilate technological change was the "Haussmannization" of Paris that began in the Second Empire and lasted long enough to leave its final, decadent traces in Aragon's *Paris Peasant*, set in an arcade destined to fall victim to the dregs of the long-late Baron's reconstruction plan.[47] ("Surrealism was born in an arcade" (*AP* [C1,2] 82) Benjamin notes.) Benjamin's main thematic motif in the notes devoted to Haussmannization is that of "perspectives," Haussmann's reorganization of city space around the visual perspectives allowed by long, wide boulevards that converge on key monuments. He notes a "remarkable propensity for structures that convey and connect – as, of course, the arcades do. And this connecting or mediating function has a literal and spatial as well as a figurative and stylistic bearing" (*AP* [E2a, 4] 124).

Along with this apparent allusion to Giedion's emphasis on spatial continuity and visual extension, Benjamin also quotes Corbusier's admiring remarks about Haussmann's radical "surgical experiments" with meager, mechanical implements, which are pictured in Corbusier's 1925 book *Urbanisme* (see Benjamin's note at AP [E5a, 6] 133). However, far from germinally anticipating Giedion's free horizontality, for Benjamin urban reconstruction under the sign of "perspective" was a means of containing and controlling modernity within the bounds of aesthetics. It was, to put it otherwise, an early instance of "the aestheticizing of politics," in which the masses are allowed to "express themselves" rather than "represent themselves." [48] Thus, Benjamin writes, "Haussmann's predilection for perspectives, for long open vistas, represents an attempt to dictate art forms to technology (the technology of city planning). This always results in kitsch" (*AP* [E2a, 7] 126). And, as in the artwork essay of 1935, Benjamin does not fail to see the contemporary telos of this kitsch of aestheticized politics as being fascism and technological warfare. He concludes by linking the nineteenth-century struggle for the city to the current war against fascism, which like the Paris Commune of 1871 would end in repression, bloodshed, and defeat: "Haussmann's work is accomplished today, as the Spanish war makes clear, by quite other means" (*AP* [E13, 2] 147).

NOTES

1. Key works of criticism that illuminate different facets of Benjamin's concept of experience include: Howard Caygill, *Walter Benjamin: The Colour of Experience* (London: Routledge, 1998); Esther Leslie, *Walter Benjamin: Overpowering Conformism* (London: Pluto Press, 2000); and Miriam Bratu Hansen, *Cinema and Experience: Siegfried Kracauer, Walter Benjamin, and Theodor W. Adorno* (Berkeley and Los Angeles: University of California Press, 2012). For a broad intellectual-historical consideration of the concept of experience, see the study by the eminent historian of the Frankfurt School, Martin Jay, *Songs of Experience: Modern American and European Variations on a Universal Theme* (Berkeley and Los Angeles: University of California Press, 2006).
2. B. Joseph Pine II and James H. Gilmore, *The Experience Economy: Work is Theater and Every Business a Stage* (Cambridge, MA: Harvard Business School Press, 1999).
3. Detlev Schöttker, *Konstruktiver Fragmentarismus: Form und Rezeption der Schriften Walter Benjamins* (Frankfurt a/M: Suhrkamp Verlag, 1999).
4. Frederic J. Schwartz, "The Eye of the Expert: Walter Benjamin and the Avant-Garde," *Art History* 24/3 (2001), pp. 401–44; and Schwartz, *Blind Spots: Critical Theory and the History of Art in Twentieth-Century Germany* (New Haven: Yale University Press, 2005).
5. Gerhard Richter, *Thought-Images: Frankfurt School Writers' Reflections from Damaged Life* (Stanford: Stanford University Press, 2007).
6. For a useful discussion of the Situationist conception of urbanism, see Simon Sadler, *The Situationist City* (Cambridge, MA: The MIT Press, 1998), and more recently, David Pinder, *Visions of the City: Utopianism, Power, and Politics in Twentieth-Century Urbanism* (Edinburgh: Edinburgh University Press, 2005).
7. Charles Baudelaire, "To A Passer-By," trans. C.F. MacIntyre, in *Flowers of Evil*, ed. Marthiel and Jackson Matthews (New York: New Directions, 1989), p. 118.
8. Ezra Pound, "In a Station of the Metro," in *Personae: The Shorter Poems*, ed. Lea Baechler (New York: New Directions, 1990), p. 111.
9. André Breton, *Mad Love*, trans. Mary Ann Caws (Lincoln, NB: Bison Books, 1988).
10. For a broader discussion of the figure of the child as an operator of historical

change, see my article, "The Burning Babe: Children, Film Narrative, and the Figures of Historical Witness," in *Witness and Memory: The Discourse of Trauma*, ed. Ana Douglass and Thomas A. Vogler (New York: Routledge, 2003), pp. 207–33.

11. László Moholy-Nagy, "Filmváz: A Nagyváros dinamikája" [Film Scenario: Dynamic of the Metropolis], *MA*, Music and Theater Special Number (15 September 1924): no pagination.

12. For more on the concept of "image-space," see Sigrid Weigel, *Body- and Image-Space: Re-reading Walter Benjamin* (London: Routledge, 1996).

13. Esther Leslie and Miriam Bratu Hansen have explicated the importance of Walt Disney's animation, especially its signature figure, Mickey Mouse. See Esther Leslie, *Hollywood Flatland: Animation, Critical Theory and the Avant-Garde* (London: Verso, 2002); Miriam Bratu Hansen, "Of Mice and Ducks: Benjamin and Adorno on Disney," *South Atlantic Quarterly* 92/1 (1993), pp. 27–61; and Hansen, *Cinema and Experience*.

14. Bruno Taut, *Die Auflösung der Städte* (Hagen: Folkwang Verlag, 1920).

15. Paul Scheerbart, *Glass Architecture*, ed. Dennis Sharp, trans. James Palmes (with Bruno Taut, *Alpine Architecture*) (New York: Praeger Publishers, 1972), p. 71.

16. Paul Scheerbart, *Lesabéndio: Ein Asteroiden-Roman* (Frankfurt a/M: Suhrkamp Verlag, 1986); English translation: *Lesabéndio: An Asteroid Novel*, trans. Christina Svendsen (Cambridge, MA: Wakefield Press, 2012).

17. Letter of Walter Benjamin to Gershom Scholem, ca. 1 December 1920, in *The Correspondence of Walter Benjamin, 1910–1940*, ed. Gershom Scholem and Theodor W. Adorno, trans. Manfred R. and Evelyn M. Jacobson (Chicago: University of Chicago Press, 1994), p. 168.

18. Walter Benjamin, "Paul Scheerbart: Lesabéndio," in *Gesammelte Schriften* II, 2, ed. Rolf Tiedemann and Hermann Schweppenhäuser (Frankfurt a/M: Suhrkamp Verlag, 1977), pp. 619–20; translation mine.

19. Scheerbart, *Lesabéndio*, p. 33.

20. Scheerbart, *Lesabéndio*, p. 221.

21. Scheerbart, *Lesabéndio*, p. 53.

22. On Benjamin's non-human dimensions, see Beatrice Hanssen, *Walter Benjamin's Other History: Of Stones, Animals, Human Beings, and Angels* (Berkeley and Los Angeles: University of California Press, 2000); and Sigrid Weigel, *Walter Benjamin: Images, the Creaturely, and the Holy* (Stanford: Stanford University Press, 2013).

23. Benjamin, "On Scheerbart," *SW* IV, pp. 386–8.

24. In this regard, Scheerbart's cosmic pacifism is the exact complementary antithesis to that of another of Benjamin's favorite authors, Karl Kraus. In Kraus's anti-war drama *Last Days of Mankind*, Martians annihilate the Earth's population after viewing the spectacle of the World War and concluding that there is no intelligent life on the planet.

25. For historical background on Kempelen and contemporary artworks inspired by his automata, see the exhibition catalogue *Kempelen – Man in the Machine* (Budapest: Műcsarnok / Kunsthalle, 2007).

26. For detailed discussion of Benjamin's relation to surrealism, see Margaret Cohen, *Profane Illumination: Walter Benjamin and the Paris of Surrealist Revolution* (Berkeley and Los Angeles: University of California Press, 1995).

27. André Breton, *Nadja*, trans. Richard Howard (New York: Grove Press, 1960), p. 18.

28. Louis Aragon, *Paris Peasant*, trans. Simon Watson Taylor (London: Picador, 1971), p. 47.

29. Aragon, *Paris Peasant*, p. 99.
30. Aragon, *Paris Peasant*, p. 120.
31. Charles Baudelaire, "Spleen," trans. Anthony Hecht, in *Flowers of Evil*, p. 91.
32. Charles Baudelaire, "The Philosophy of Toys," in Charles Baudelaire, *The Painter of Modern Life and Other Essays*, ed. and trans. Jonathan Mayne (London: Phaidon Press, 1964), p. 204.
33. Baudelaire, "The Philosophy of Toys," p. 204.
34. André Breton, "Free Union," in *Poems of André Breton*, ed. and trans. Jean-Pierre Cauvin and Mary Ann Caws (Boston: Black Widow Press, 2006), p. 93; translation modified.
35. Aragon, *Paris Peasant*, pp. 52–3.
36. Guillaume Apollinaire, quoted in *AP* [B3a, 1], 70. Hereafter I cite Benjamin's notebook and entry number in the text enclosed in brackets followed by the page number, as in this note.
37. Manfredo Tafuri, *Architecture and Utopia: Design and Capitalist Development*, trans. Barbara Luigia La Penta (Cambridge, MA: The MIT Press, 1976), p. 101.
38. Iain Boyd White, "Introduction" to Socratis Georgiadis, *Sigfried Giedion: An Intellectual Biography*, trans. Colin Hall (Edinburgh: Edinburgh University Press, 1993), p. vii.
39. Hilde Heynen, *Architecture and Modernity: A Critique* (Cambridge, MA: The MIT Press, 1999), p. 4.
40. The "elective affinities" between Benjamin and Giedion are notable. Nearly the same age, they both critically adopted to the study of art and culture the methodologies of the art historians Heinrich Wöfflin and especially Alois Riegl; both were involved in literary work, including, in both cases, as minor playwrights; both occupied themselves early in their careers with revising previous low estimates of baroque art and culture and with critiques of Romanticism; both self-consciously adopted methods of montage and construction for the writing of history; both saw the politics and concerns of the present as a necessary horizon for historical writing; both aligned themselves with the politicized avant-garde, and in architecture specifically with Le Corbusier and functionalism. As with Giedion's participation in the CIAM, Benjamin had practical contacts with the architectural avant-garde through the journal *G*, which had at its head the abstract filmmaker Hans Richter and the architect Mies van der Rohe (see Detlef Mertins, "The Threatening and Enticing Face of Prehistory: Walter Benjamin and the Utopia of Glass," *Assemblage* 29 [1996], pp. 7–23; see pp. 13ff). Following the publication of Giedion's *Bauen in Frankreich* in 1928, Benjamin wrote him an appreciative letter, reprinted in Sigfried Giedion, *Building in France. Building in Iron. Building in Ferro-Concrete*, trans. J. Duncan Berry (Santa Monica: The Getty Center for the History of Art and the Humanities, 1995).
41. Giedion, *Building in France*, p. 168.
42. See, however, Karel Teige's criticisms of Le Corbusier, which center upon the residues of received geometrical forms and "cosmically" justified proportions and orientations in such projects as his proposal for the League of Nations complex in Geneva. Interestingly, in light of Benjamin's association of individualistic interiority and the domestic interior, Teige especially focuses on what he sees as Corbusier's illegitimate equation of house and public building. Karel Teige, "Anti-Corbusier" (collected articles from 1929–31), in Teige, *Arte e ideologia, 1922–1933*, ed. Sergio Corduas, trans. Sergio Corduas, Antonella D'Amelia, and Barbara Zane (Turin: Einaudi, 1982), pp. 203–48.
43. On this problem, see Tafuri's *Architecture and Utopia*; also: Manfredo Tafuri, *Theories and History of Architecture* (New York: Harper & Row, 1976);

Manfredo Tafuri, *The Sphere and the Labyrinth: Avant-Gardes and Architecture from Piranesi to the 1970s*, trans. Pellegrino d'Acierno and Robert Connolly (Cambridge, MA: The MIT Press, 1987); Manfredo Tafuri and Francesco Dal Co, *Modern Architecture* (2 Vols), trans. Robert Erich Wolf (New York: Rizzoli, 1976); Francesco Dal Co, *Figures of Architecture and Thought: German Architecture Culture, 1880–1920* (New York: Rizzoli, 1990).

44. Giedion, *Building in France*, p. 145.
45. Giedion, *Building in France*, p. 169.
46. Georgiadis, "Introduction" to Giedion, *Building in France*, pp. 42–3.
47. For historical background on nineteenth-century Paris and its urbanist transformations, see Patrice Higonnet, *Paris: Capital of the World*, trans. Arthur Goldhammer (Cambridge, MA: The Belknap Press of Harvard University Press, 2002); and David Harvey, *Paris, Capital of Modernity* (New York: Routledge, 2006).
48. I am, of course, freely paraphrasing here from Benjamin's most famous essay, "The Work of Art in the Age of Its Technical Reproducibility." For a complementary account of Haussmannization as the constitution of an aesthetic "spectacle" (in Guy Debord's sense) of urban life, see T.J. Clark, *The Painting of Modern Life* (1984).

3

THEODOR ADORNO

Theodor W. Adorno was the youngest, but ultimately most influential major member of the Frankfurt School's organizational inner circle. Formally trained in both philosophy and music, and briefly active artistically as a follower of Arnold Schönberg's atonal composition and student of Alban Berg in Vienna, Adorno would make important contributions in a wide range of interdisciplinary research. Over the course of four decades, he would write and publish in the interdisciplinary fields of social philosophy, social psychology, sociology of music, sociological study of mass media, education theory, and sociological aesthetics, as well as in more disciplinarily focused areas such as philosophy, literary criticism, musical analysis, and empirical sociology. Adorno's published collected writings encompass thousands of pages, and new editions of drafted essays and studies, lectures, interviews, and correspondence have been appearing regularly up to the present.

Adorno lived primarily in Frankfurt and Vienna before Hitler's accession to power. In exile during most of the Nazi period, Adorno studied and worked as a researcher in Oxford, in New York, and in Los Angeles, where he coauthored with Max Horkheimer one of his most important works, *Dialectic of Enlightenment*. In Los Angeles he also played a notable supporting role in modernist literature as Thomas Mann's source of expert musical information for the novel *Doktor Faustus*, which in its development of the artist-protagonist

Adrian Leverkühn utilizes elements of Arnold Schönberg's compositional doctrine, as mediated and interpreted to Mann by Adorno. In tribute, Mann in turn gave Adorno a recognizable cameo appearance in the book as the elegant, ironic devil who offers the pact of tainted genius through sickness and madness to Mann's Leverkühn. In a broad allegory of modernism's aesthetic gambit in the age of imperialism, technological war, and spreading totalitarianism, Leverkühn will intentionally contract syphilis and renounce love, in return for twenty-four years of brilliant, inhumanly innovative artistic creativity.[1]

After World War II, on the invitation of his close collaborator Max Horkheimer, Adorno returned to the Federal Republic of Germany and took up a university post. In 1958, he replaced Horkheimer as the director of the Institute for Social Research. He was a key voice in the post-war discussions about a democratic, progressive post-Nazi German culture. Though frequently castigated for his elitist and mandarin traits, he was also a remarkably active public speaker about issues including the latest modernist musical developments in the New Music center of Darmstadt, the need to confront and work through the German organization of the Holocaust, the new tendencies in philosophy and social thought, and the dangers of the culture industry's growing monopolization of the various spheres of cultural life.

It was only with the rise of a radicalized student left in the later 1960s, parallel to second-generation criticisms and refinements of his thinking by younger followers such as Jürgen Habermas, Alfred Schmidt, Albrecht Wellmer, Alexander Kluge, and Oskar Negt, that Adorno's dense, reflective, often pessimistic thought was partially pushed aside as out of tune with the activist forces unleashed by the student movement. Yet forty years after Adorno's death in 1969, his writings have again taken on new relevance, finding a fresh wave of explication, reinterpretation, and application. In part, this may reflect a theoretical climate established by such heterogeneous tendencies as French philosophies of difference, feminist philosophy, deconstruction, and new forms of phenomenological thinking, which find resonance with Adorno's emphasis on granting philosophical voice to the "non-identical," as he sought to do in his most important philosophical works, *Negative Dialectics* and *Aesthetic Theory*. Like more recent post-structuralist theorists, and in part offering an analogous but alternative critical response to the legacies of German idealism, phenomenology, and modernist literature and art, Adorno explored the "heterological" margins of what had been taken as the legitimate object of mainstream philosophy. Though their specific approaches and conclusions are different, both post-structuralist thinkers and Adorno focus on that which precedes conceptualization or the residue left outside of conceptual frameworks; on that which deviates from legal and epistemological norms; on the sensual object of experience irreducible to discourse or thought, on all that which may only be communicated "aesthetically" through non-conceptual experiences of pleasure or suffering.[2] Recent social developments, however, have also contributed to Adorno's renewed relevance. The unprecedented concentration of mass media and entertainment in the hands of a few global companies has lent new interest to Adorno's hypothesized effects of a stratified, concentrated "culture industry" playing a crucial role in mediating between the present-day state of the economy, technology, and collective consciousness. Although some of Adorno's observations and judgments now seem exaggerated or dated, the central proposition of his writings on the culture industry has remained sound and even increased in urgency: that in the present moment of capitalist development, the Marxian theory of ideology needs to be developed beyond its "classical" form to comprehend the profound consciousness-shaping functions of industrially designed, produced, and disseminated culture.[3]

Along with the sheer quantity and range of his written production, Adorno was also an extraordinary, idiosyncratic prose stylist, employing a set of writing strategies that are inseparable from the content and major themes of his thought. In tune with his philosophical emphases on particularity, concreteness, micrological detail, and dialectical movement, Adorno evolved a writing style full of stylistic nuance, argumentative density, unusual words, sudden leaps of register and thought, hyperbolic similes, and ostentatious paradox – a style that has its most obvious correlates in the texts of literary modernists and avant-garde writers. Even his friends were occasionally perplexed by the convolutions of Adorno's style. It is reported that the composer Alban Berg and critic Willi Reich were listening to Adorno speak on the radio; after a moment in which the broadcast became inaudible, Berg quipped that they had likely missed the only straightforward sentence in the talk.[4]

Yet for a philosopher for whom generality was a sign of repression and untruth, "straightforward" meaning, easily reduced to formulae and stock phrases, was deeply suspicious. Adorno believed that philosophical truth must emerge from its performance in writing and its active experience by a reader. Justly compared at times to atonal music with its dissonant counterpoints and extreme leaps of interval and volume, Adorno's prose, like the literary complications of the modernists he admired, only reveals its meaning to a reader who is willing to struggle actively to follow its dialectic twists and turns, its reflexive reversals and reinscriptions of key terms and concepts. This was no mere stylistic quirk, however idiosyncratic Adorno's writing might appear. It was rather an intentional reflection, in the work of criticism and analysis, of the procedures, formal complications, and ambiguities seen in the primary works of literary, artistic, and musical modernism. By mimetically assuming features of the modernist artwork and reflecting them back with a critical difference, Adorno's writings sought to disclose their truth without, in turn, imposing an external, abstract concept upon them. For him the key task was less to formulate a concept of the modern artwork than to *assimilate* into the critical work as much as possible of the artwork's non-conceptual, non-reductive approach to differences and dissonances. No reader escapes the experience of frequent frustration, disorientation, resistance, and puzzlement as she progresses through the thicket of Adorno's sentences. Adorno seeks by design to provoke precisely these experiences of vertiginous loss of bearings and circuitous struggle towards the center of the dialectical knot of a problem; he strives in every sentence to unsettle easy understanding in order to educate the reader's sensibility and reflexively disclose the possibility of more individualized, still latent modes of thinking and feeling.

Although most of Adorno's writing took form in traditional genres such as the essay, lecture, and philosophical treatise, which Adorno nevertheless regularly disrupted with unconventional modes of style and argumentation, a few of his works might be said to involve direct modernist experimentation with the genres of critical thought and writing. Like Benjamin with *One-Way Street* or Ernst Bloch in his book *Traces*, which Adorno reviewed when it was reissued in the late 1950s,[5] his *Minima Moralia: Reflections from Damaged Life* (1951) experiments with the aphoristic legacy of German romanticism, taking inspiration from Nietzsche's radicalization of the aphoristic mode and from urban and cinematic montage to develop a brief mode of writing adequate to reflect on contemporary experience – in Adorno's case, the threshold years between 1944 and 1947, encompassing the end of World War II and the concluding years of his exile in the United States. Adorno's title plays off an allusion to the philosophical tradition, the *Magna Moralia* (Great Ethics) of Aristotle. It suggests that in his own times, the philosopher, exemplified by Adorno himself, of course, is only capable of a reduced ethics, a minimum necessary for survival; or perhaps that history itself has reduced the human capacity for ethics, and now one must search within the micrological detail of everyday life to understand how to evaluate action. In his opening dedication of the work to Max Horkheimer, Adorno further situates his text in relation to the philosophical past: "The melancholy science from which I make this offering to my friend relates to a region that from time immemorial was regarded as the true field of philosophy, but which, since the latter's conversion into method, has lapsed into intellectual neglect, sententious whimsy and finally oblivion: the teaching of the good life" (*MM*, 15). Thus Adorno wishes to take up the question that animated the classical philosophers, but also his aphoristic forerunner Friedrich Nietzsche, whose "gay science" has turned mournful in Adorno's more somber "melancholy science."

Adorno's book defies easy paraphrase or summary, which is precisely its exemplary point: to trace through highly concrete, often idiosyncratic and personal observations, memories, speculations, and reactions the complex interactions of the individual and the social whole. He wishes to expose those elements within individual behavior and affectivity that are damaged by or brought in conformity with repressive social norms. And vice versa, he hopes to find, even in highly conventional and ritualized behaviors, the possible deviations within which individuality still leaves its trace. This aphoristic procedure, however, corresponds to Adorno's theoretical insistence on the mediated interconnectedness of society and individual: "in an individualistic society, the general not only realizes itself through the interplay of particulars, but society is essentially the substance of the individual" (*MM*, 17).

This focus on the concrete allows Adorno, in contrast to, for instance, Hegel, to find an exemplary, even quasi-theoretical value in individual experiential detail, singularities of daily life that he handles more like the percussive scrapes, humming overtones, and sudden explosions of clashing notes in a modern musical composition than the hierarchically organized exposition of a philosophical system. Adorno presents this quotidian detail in a diary-like, paratactical form, explicitly not a synthetically systematic or narrative design, thus implicitly asserting the critical value of a singularly invented "modernistic" composition of thought over either positivistically amassed statistical data or abstract systems of formal concepts: "social analysis can learn incomparably more from individual experience than Hegel conceded, while conversely the large historical categories, after all that has meanwhile been perpetrated with their help, are no longer above suspicion of fraud" (*MM*, 17). The legacy of modernist music, along with hybrid literary-philosophical modes of writing from Schlegel, Kierkegaard, and Nietzsche to Benjamin and Bloch, provides Adorno with a paradigm for how this heterogeneous material might be organized to disclose this social-individual and individual-social truth.

MODERNISM AND THE CULTURE INDUSTRY

Adorno's views on modernism, to which he ascribes a critical function in present-day society, must be seen in the context of his theory of the "culture industry," which he understands as modernism's dialectical complement and secret sharer. His conception of the culture industry was formed in close critical dialogue with two of his most important interlocutors: Walter Benjamin and Max Horkheimer. Benjamin had given impetus to Adorno's thinking with a draft of his essay, "The Work of Art in the Age of Its Technical Reproducibility," in which Benjamin had welcomed the destructive influence of photographic and cinematic technology on traditional art forms and highlighted the political importance of mass art forms with technical reproducibility as an integral part of their productive means (especially such emergent media as photojournalism, documentary, animation, and entertainment film). Adorno, whose field of technical expertise was musical rather than visual art or literature, responded to Benjamin's theses with a much more negative assessment of the social effects of sound recording and related phenomena such as radio broadcasting of music. Adorno's response was articulated both in a long letter justifying the rejection of Benjamin's essay for publication in the journal of the Institute for Social Research and in an important essay of 1938 entitled "On the Fetish-Character in Music and the Regression of Listening."

Benjamin's essay was bold in its general conception and rich with a number of individual observations, which Adorno took up in his responses. However, the main lines of Benjamin's argument can be summarized in three propositions. First, the conception and function of art in modern society has undergone a crucial change, now that it is possible through technological means – especially photographic and cinematic – to circulate the work of art in multiple copies and multiple contexts rather than equating it with one unique, authentic artifact situated in a single context. The work, Benjamin argues, loses the "aura" of sacredness that originally lent itself to religious and exhibition functions, and it is increasingly drawn into a wide range of everyday, political, and social uses. Second, as the functions of these works change, bringing them into greater proximity with a wider range of social activities, so too the mode by which they are perceived and valued by the audience changes. Benjamin argues that rather than sacred awe or absorbed aesthetic contemplation, technically reproducible works – especially those, like film, for which the technology is an intrinsic part of the medium – are perceived in a "mode of distraction," as backgrounds or elements of other collectively performed activities. Third, this transformation of the function of art into a collective practice of perception linked to other social activities can be used for organizational, political ends by both reactionary forces and by progressive ones. Fascism has already shown an intuitive understanding of art's new potential for power, insofar as it has used spectacles and propaganda art for the "aestheticization of politics." Their communist opponents should respond by utilizing art in political ways, disenchanting the aesthetics of fascist power and mobilizing a revolutionary collective for action.

In his direct response to Benjamin, Adorno acknowledged their common interest in the "dialectical self-dissolution of myth," which Benjamin specified in his essay as "the disenchantment of art." Yet from the outset, Adorno rejects a central premise of Benjamin's argument: that the "magical," "mythical," "sacralizing" aspect of the work of art, that which could be summed up by the esoteric term "aura," was equal to its status as autonomous, and that in turn, eliminating artistic autonomy and integrating the artwork into social life would signify the elimination of its mythical character, the liquidation of its aura. Adorno argued that both autonomous art and non-autonomous art need to be treated as dialectically contradictory in themselves and that their valuation as regressive or progressive could only be made if the dialectical character of these categories was fully acknowledged:

What I would postulate is *more* dialectics. On the one hand, dialectical penetration of the "autonomous" work of art which is transcended by its own technique into a planned work; on the other, an even stronger dialecticization of utilitarian art in its negativity . . . You underestimate the technicality of autonomous art and overestimate that of dependent art.[6]

Adorno is particularly concerned to rescue the autonomous artwork from Benjamin's blanket dismissal of autonomy on political grounds, instead seeing within the autonomous work warring elements of reaction and liberation. "The centre of the autonomous work," Adorno wrote, "does not itself belong on the side of myth . . . but is inherently dialectical; within itself it juxtaposes the magical and the mark of freedom."[7]

Adorno's 1938 essay "On the Fetish-Character in Music and the Regression of Listening"[8] represents a further response to Benjamin's hypotheses about technical reproducible art. Here, however, Adorno takes up the effects of technology on musical listening, and contrary to Benjamin's prognoses of new collective skills in relation to technological art objects such as films, Adorno diagnoses a regression in collective listening capacities as the corollary of music's becoming ever more thing-like and commodified through recording and radio broadcast. Utilizing a psychoanalytic framework in conjunction with the Marxist notion of commodity fetishism and Lukács' reification concept – the perception of social relations as relations between things – he suggests that this technologically driven process leads to more and more formulaic products that require ever less of the listener's active knowledge and imagination. Music regresses into a kind of musical "child's language." Contrary to Benjamin's positive idea of the audience's perceiving the work in a critical "state of distraction," musical listening has tended to regress to a pre-individual, infantile activity lacking mental concentration and sustained attention; immediate gratification replaces the sublimated combination of pleasure and intellect that great music offers a fully competent listener. Yet the forces of society, as well as the more focused sphere of musical production and reproduction, pose systematic obstacles to the cultivation of such listening competence on any great scale, while at the same time, by mass-producing deficient products, it also mass-produces regressive listeners adapted to a formulaic culture. Several years before Adorno and Max Horkheimer coined the actual term, their underlying ideas about the "culture industry" and its effects can be read here in draft.

The term "culture industry" was introduced by Adorno and Horkheimer in a chapter of *Dialectic of Enlightenment* entitled "The Culture Industry: Enlightenment as Mass Deception," which accompanied one other chapter with contemporary scope, "Elements of Anti-Semitism: Limits of Enlightenment."[9] The conjunction is not accidental. Adorno and Horkheimer saw the culture industry and anti-Semitism, along with Stalinist totalitarianism, as analogous pathologies of modern society and as cases in which the instrumental means of modern rational social organization have been harnessed to substantively *irrational* ends, to the self-destruction of enlightenment on a mass scale. Viewed more geographically – since the culture industry theory was developed in large part in the American exile of the Frankfurt School during the 1940s – "culture industry" was intended to describe a softer, North American version of the totalitarianism being exercised by direct, violent means on the European continent and in the socialist East. If the profit motive could permeate the form and content of widely disseminated cultural goods, and if individual and collective consciousness could be trained to desire such goods and think within their prefabricated limits, then totalitarian domination might be effected even without the unwieldy apparatus of a police state and in ways that might ultimately prove even more efficacious, since apparently done with the full consent and cooperation of the subject population.

"Culture industry" also had a conceptual dimension that linked it to processes of commodification, division of labor, and planning typical of the industrial production of advanced capitalism. Moreover, it was distinct from other concepts that in Adorno and Horkheimer were inapplicable to the current phenomena they wished to describe, especially "popular culture" and "mass culture." As Adorno later wrote in his essay "Culture Industry Reconsidered" (1963),[10] they had originally used the term "mass culture" in drafting the chapter. But later they substituted that term with "culture industry," to avoid any implication that "it was a matter of something like a culture that arose spontaneously from the masses themselves," and also to reject from the outset any comparison to folk art. Neither was appropriate to the top-down, planned, commercial nature of culture industry products, nor to the corporately or state administered institutional framework into which all culture, high or low, artistic or entertainment, was being integrated. Adorno and Horkheimer also distinguished the products of the culture industry from the "light art" of a previous epoch. "Light art," they argue, "has been the shadow of autonomous art," a reminder that social conditions preclude autonomous art's being available and comprehensible to all. Thus the existence of light art betrays a truth that autonomous art cannot admit to: "The division itself is the truth: it does at least express the negativity of the culture which the different spheres constitute. Least of all can the antithesis be reconciled by absorbing light into serious art, or vice versa." The culture industry, in contrast to either serious or light art, blends the two together, sapping the truth-value of both: "the irreconcilable elements of culture, art and distraction, are subordinated to one end and subsumed under one false formula: the totality of the culture industry."[11]

Two other key concepts, which have broad application in Adorno's other work as well, are introduced in the culture industry chapter of *Dialectic of Enlightenment*: repetition and pseudo-individuation. Adorno associates repetition, paradoxically, with the demand for the new and with fashion (much of this analysis derives, ultimately, from Walter Benjamin's study of nineteenth-century Parisian culture, the "Arcades Project," which the Frankfurt School was supporting financially). Beneath the apparent changes of fashion and the ever-changing novelties of new consumer goods – all the new "stars," "hits," and "sensations" of the culture industry – is the repetition of the same abstract succession of newness and rapid obsolescence. Newness only appears as a function of this repetition, which brings "novelties" and "fashions" before the consumer with monotonous regularity. According to Adorno and Horkheimer, this conjunction of newness and repetition sinks into the structure of culture industry products themselves, which are formulaically designed and produced to be the latest "new thing." The more pressure on rapid changes of fashion and newness there is, the more intense the need to reach for hooks and clichés becomes, in order to guarantee the success of the cultural product. Innovation is limited to the profitable variation of time-tested formulae. If, however, the intrinsic structure of culture industry products becomes more and more formulaic, extrinsic aspects of style and publicity compensate, helping to create the spectacle of newness before the consuming public. This tendency Adorno and Horkheimer call pseudo-individuation. The star-system in general, and the use of mass media to publicize the eccentricities and scandals of star lifestyles, is an exemplary instance of these tendencies. Intrinsically, a pop star such as Britney Spears, Justin Bieber, or Miley Cyrus may be little more than an interchangeable embodiment of a design paradigm, or a name attached to a carefully designed set of culture industry "hits." Yet extrinsically, their publicity stylizes them in ways that either capture the public's imagination or imply, through reiteration and constant exposure, that the public should be interested in their banal antics and prefabricated opinions (today, preferably communicated in real time via Facebook and Twitter). Paradoxically, a designed, mass-produced product must be presented as a fascinating individual, and in turn this "pseudo-individual" may become a style paradigm, an object of fashionable imitation for thousands or even millions. Meanwhile, Adorno and Horkheimer imply, the more difficult work of giving shape to oneself as a genuine individual, resistant to conformism and enduring over time, is deflected into questions of consumer choice, fashion consciousness, and style. The concept of a stable individual withers, evacuated by repeated ascriptions of "individuality" to the confected, short-lived "sensations" of stardom and fashion.

Adorno subsequently applied the concept of culture industry and the related analysis of regression through stereotyped reception, repetition, and pseudo-individuation in a wide range of contexts; however, he deviated very little from the basic framework developed already in the 1930s and '40s. One specific problem he addressed with this framework is his analysis of "The Radio Symphony" (1941), in which he insightfully questions the cliché that the wider dissemination of classical music through the radio would lead to a broader, deeper acquaintance of the public with this music. He objected that this was by no means automatic and that, indeed, breadth of distribution may be counter-balanced by the homogenization of the acceptable canon of work and by erosion in the ability of the audience to listen effectively.

Far more problematic are his essays on jazz – see, for example, "On Jazz" (1936) and "Timeless Fashion: On Jazz" (1953) – in which Adorno could discern nothing but the stereotyping and pseudo-individuation of the most degraded "jazz" dance hits. In practice this meant that Adorno was incapable of appreciating the degree to which, from the 1940s on with the emergence of bebop, and into the 1960s with the upsurge of a fiery, politically conscious jazz avant-garde, jazz was a medium of modernist cultural contestation and political self-assertion by African-American artistic intellectuals. Moreover, Adorno's failure to discern the critical potential in jazz was not merely a lapse in cultural attention or taste. Adorno never came to terms theoretically with the existence of multiple functions and value-standards for music as an art form; he measured all music against the technical standards of Schönberg's innovations. The case of jazz thus highlights an important, fundamental shortcoming in Adorno's aesthetics: he tended to conceive of music within a restrictive, dichotomized framework, the critical canon epitomized by Schönberg versus all that which diverges from it, whether alternative traditions within classical music or non-classical alternatives within jazz or rock, which Adorno could not help but condemn wholesale as culture industry products. Any authentic work, in this dichotomizing framework, could only be a singular "non-identical" realization of a single critical standard set by Schönberg. Adorno never managed to formulate theoretically a more capacious conception of the "non-identical" that would have allowed him to evaluate a phenomenon like jazz adequately, or to recognize the possibility that critical functions – in a sense, alternative "modernisms" – might be realized in a variety of stylistic, technical, and formal modes. He thus was unable to grasp music as a *generically* and *culturally non-identical field*, with multiple functions and criteria of evaluation, and hence, diverse ways of giving rise to critical "modernisms" as well. In such a pluralistic framework, questions of a given work's technical and social progressiveness (or regressiveness) would need to be determined according to contextually situated, multiple, and comparative standards, metrics that would have to be more flexible and responsive to cultural differences than Adorno's rigorous but also rigid standards allowed.

MODERNIST PREMISES IN ADORNO'S *AESTHETIC THEORY*

Modernist artworks, especially musical, and the aesthetics that Adorno derived from them fulfill important *philosophical* imperatives in his thought, providing models and examples of alternative modes of experience, organization, and action with relevance to extra-artistic domains of life as well. Adorno's earliest philosophical training, in his teens, involved mentored reading of Immanuel Kant under the tutelage of Siegfried Kracauer, later renowed for his study of German expressionist cinema, *From Caligari to Hitler*, and his *Theory of Film*. The shadow of Kant's philosophical critiques hovered over Adorno's work throughout his career, up to and including his last, uncompleted work *Aesthetic Theory*. If *Negative Dialectics* represents, in a sense, Adorno's argument why a "critique of pure reason" is no longer possible for a present-day critical philosopher, and *Minima Moralia* is an analogous ethical reduction of a "critique of practical reason," then *Aesthetic Theory* might be construed as Adorno's attempt to answer Kant's *Critique of Judgment*. Despite its state of incompletion at his death, it is one of Adorno's most comprehensive books, combining the philosophical insights of his critical studies of the German idealist tradition with the philosophical anthropology established by *Dialectic of Enlightenment* and his practical criticism of key artists such as Samuel Beckett, Franz Kafka, Arnold Schönberg, and Bertolt Brecht. It is a dense, highly dialectical treatment of a few key themes such as the social content of art, the role of artistic form and illusion in mediating and qualifying this social content, the autonomy (or non-autonomy) of art, the relation of art to natural beauty, the role of technique and technology in the arts, the nature of artistic truth, and the functions of art as protest and utopian wish-image.

I can only discuss here two of the major topics among the myriad points that make up the whirling constellations of its arguments. The first of these is the problem of artistic illusion or "semblance," the artwork's fictionality, its removal of its content from the pragmatic world of immediate effectiveness or the epistemic world of concepts and arguments, in favor of a special existence as sensuous appearance. This special state of being is the corollary of the special social place occupied by autonomous art: art that primarily orients itself towards its own sphere of values, claiming value precisely as an *artistic* achievement, and not on the basis of the commercial, political, therapeutic, cultic, or other heteronomous functions that it might also, in a ancillary way, perform. For Adorno, aesthetic illusion is at once the "guilt" and the utopian possibility of art. It represents a "guilt," because the artwork necessarily suggests that those harmonies, intensities of experience, and alternative possibilities registered in its special media and forms are achievable in the present state of society. In a sense, they *are* achievable, but only *as art*, in "semblance": only insofar as we remain in the special space circumscribed by the frame of the painting, the opening of the book, the duration of the musical composition. As soon as we close the book and return to our office, to our family life, or to streets full of traffic and policemen and employees hurrying home, then we see that the "semblance" of the artwork was, in the pejorative sense, "just an illusion." The artistic image is falsely "universal" –

paradoxically only "universal" within its restricted sphere and, sociologically, only for that privileged minority who have sufficient leisure and education and financial resources to gain genuine access to the artistic worlds rising up out of works. Yet on the other hand, it is this very semblance – which renders art "ineffectual" – that also allows it a critical and even utopian distance from the objective "untruth" of a socially unjust world of everyday reality. Only in divergence from this world, rather than in adaptive conformity to it, can critical truth be disclosed in the *tension* between empirical and artistic reality. Therefore, though "illusory" and even "false" in one sense, the artwork's semblance is also dialectically inseparable from art's capacity for disclosing truth. If this dialectical aspect of semblance is to a greater or lesser extent a feature of all authentic art, the specifically modernist art that emerges in the twentieth century deepens both this guilty unreality and inefficaciousness of the artwork, as well as its potentially critical transcendence of our constrained, empirical world, by employing as artistic means various non-conventional forms and styles, significantly heightened difficulty and dissonance, and dense self-reflection on its own status as art. Adorno also draws the conclusion from this that the mediation of semblance (and its social corollary, artistic autonomy) is necessary to this truth-function of art. Any attempt to leap over semblance and make art directly effective – as with agitational art – or adapt it to immediate didactic, documentary, conceptual, or entertainment goals will betray the weak, but persistent power of autonomous art to say no to an unjust world and keep open a utopian alternative to it.

The other key aspect is the "logic of disintegration" that Adorno develops in *Aesthetic Theory*, which derives from his insistence that "non-identity" may most concretely be instanced only by advanced modern art. Modernist artists such as Beckett, Picasso, or Schönberg create their works through an analytic disintegration of their artistic material – breaking down into component elements, for example, theater's linguistic resources of dramatic speech, or painting's visual conventions of representing space, or music's tonal system. In Adorno's 1961 essay on Beckett's play *Endgame*, a study that informs his more occasional references to Beckett in *Aesthetic Theory*, he offers the following characterization of Beckett's use of disintegration as a means of avant-garde linguistic innovation:

> Instead of trying to liquidate the discursive element in language through pure sound, Beckett transforms it into an instrument of its own absurdity, following the ritual of the clown, whose babbling becomes nonsense by being presented as sense. The objective decay of language, that bilge of self-alienation, at once stereotyped and defective, which human beings' words and sentences have swollen up into within their own mouths, penetrates the aesthetic arcanum. The second language of those who

have fallen silent, an agglomeration of insolent phrases, pseudo-logical connections, and words galvanized into trademarks, the desolate echo of the world of the advertisement, is revamped to become the language of a literary work that negates language.[12]

Having disintegrated the artistic element down into its analytic components, Beckett, like Picasso and Schönberg, subsequently proceeds to construct larger-scale works from these elementary materials, lending the artwork an innovative, singular new form, organized through a mode of connection that is singular and unconventional, perhaps even unforeseen by the artist himself.

This is of interest for two reasons. First, it illustrates Adorno's consistent procedure of creating parallels and dialectical interactions between philosophical critique and critical, innovative art forms. Philosophy gives discursive and conceptual articulateness to artworks which, because of their innovativeness, resist easy reduction to paraphrase or discursive description. The artwork, in turn, lends flesh and sensual concreteness to the abstractions of the philosophical concept. Second, it suggests Adorno's ultimate sense of the function of artworks: as exempla and models of "non-identical," alternative modes of existence. These singular artistic instances mark the sheer possibility of difference in a situation in which greater and greater uniformity is the enforced norm, an important handhold against the abyss of despair and resignation in the face of dark days. They also provide actual experiences and concrete analogies that may be transferable, with conceptual elaboration and appropriate institutional arrangements and practice, to other social and intellectual domains. This possibility takes us back to the aforementioned problem of semblance, which cordons the artwork off from effective presence in the everyday social world. In a dialectical twist, Adorno suggests that modernist artworks, while not abolishing completely the special status of art that follows from its autonomy, nevertheless weaken it in key respects. Modernist artistic idioms and forms tend to dispel the fictionalizing spell of semblance, thus opening new channels of communicability, especially emotional and sensuous ones, between the artwork and the broader spheres of human life. Picasso, thus, hyperbolizes or mixes up the conventions that allow us, conventionally, to view a two-dimensional painted surface as a three-dimensional object or space; Schönberg asks us to measure his dissonant combinations against the harmonic constructions of Mozart, Beethoven, and Brahms, to reveal the achievement of harmony as historically contingent; and Beckett never allows us for a moment to forget that his characters are purely creatures of the page or stage. Yet in so doing, these modernist artists also express their desire to find a line of flight that would carry them from the confines of artistic semblance into the fullness of effective life. Thus, for Adorno, the utopian divergence of the artwork may, in the end, prove to be the best training ground for us to learn to feel and act otherwise, to divert our course from the present-day state of injustice and from subjective resignation to it towards new utopian possibilities of experience and creation.

ADORNO'S MUSICAL MODERNISM I: *IN SEARCH OF WAGNER*

As a composer and theorist, Adorno was passionately committed to the compositional legacy of Arnold Schönberg and his two closest followers, Alban Berg and Anton Webern. More generally, his thinking about music was deeply entrenched in a Viennese-German canon of "classical" composers: a tradition beginning in the eighteenth century with Haydn and Mozart, reaching a nineteenth-century acme with Beethoven, passing through Romanticism to the next great technical innovation in the work of Richard Wagner, and finally, with Wagner and Gustav Mahler having provided an important solvent to the stability of the tonal system, achieving its final dissolution with Arnold Schönberg's atonal "liberation of dissonance." Key figures in this canon, especially Beethoven and Schönberg, served Adorno as the normative standard of composition against which he judged all other instances, whether the alternative modernism of Igor Stravinsky, Leoš Janáček, and Béla Bartók, the ambivalent modernisms of Richard Strauss and Paul Hindemith, the socialistically colored compositions of Dmitri Shostakovich and Sergei Prokofiev, post-Schönbergian experimental "new music" from composers such as Pierre Boulez and John Cage, or popular music such as jazz or pop songs.[13] He interpreted this compositional canon in parallel with the tradition of German classical and social philosophy from Kant and Hegel through Nietzsche, Marx, Weber, and Freud. Both music and philosophy, in Adorno's view, are mediated expressions of the historic situation of subjectivity in its confrontation with social and technological objectivities. By mediating subjective forces through the objective forms of art and thought, both art and philosophy render communicable latent dimensions of subjective life that would otherwise be lost in the stream of technical and social change. They also demonstrate how the world of objects can be permeated by subjective thought and feeling, thus modeling ways in which material things might be more richly experienced than simply as instruments of use or a supply of consumable goods. Methodologically, moreover, the analogical parallelism of music and philosophical thought is crucial for Adorno: philosophy lends music its articulate language of discourse and conceptuality, while music, in its irreducibility to complete discursive explanation and conceptual analysis, reveals the limits of the concept and restores philosophical knowledge to a state of embodied, sensual awareness.

Adorno wrote three book-length studies of individual composers – on Richard Wagner, Alban Berg, and Gustav Mahler. Both the Berg and the Mahler studies attempt, primarily, to offer a composite characterization – a "musical physiognomy," as Adorno subtitled his Mahler book – of these composers through analysis of characteristic features of their compositions. *In Search of Wagner*, written in London and New York between Autumn 1937 and Spring 1938, is in contrast more ambitious and more important as an early compendium of the methods and major themes of Adorno's later aesthetics. It is closely tied to the collective work of the Frankfurt School more generally and especially to the programmatic "anthropology of the bourgeois era" that Max Horkheimer had sketched in his 1936 essay, "Egoism and the Freedom Movement."[14] Arguably, the convergence of Horkheimer's intellectual history and Adorno's cultural-artistic criticism and social psychology already anticipates their collaborative argument in *Dialectic of Enlightenment* a few years later. In a series of ten topically arranged chapters, with titles such as "Social Character," "Gesture," "Phantasmagoria," and "Chimera," Adorno attempted to read both formal and thematic aspects of Wagner's production as allegorical images of social relations. This book is a composite and testing-ground of a number of hermeneutic and analytic frameworks that will be further elaborated in Adorno's subsequent work, so it is worth enumerating some of these.

First, there are the psychoanalytically tinged, social psychological diagnoses, in which Adorno attempts to read the trace of society in the comportment and gestures of individuals (a method that he would again turn to great effect in the aphorisms of *Minima Moralia*):

> In his role of beggar, Wagner violates the taboo of the bourgeois work-ethic, but his blessing redounds to the glory of his benefactors. He is an early example of the changing function of the bourgeois category of the individual. In his hopeless struggle with the power of society, the individual seeks to avert his own destruction by identifying with that power and then rationalizing the change of direction as authentic individual fulfillment. (*ISW*, 17)

Accompanying these diagnoses are social allegorizations of particular formal and stylistic features of the musical works, where Adorno tears at the mask of artistic appearance, rejoining the work's claims to artistic effect to more direct phenomena of social domination and submission:

> Faults of compositional technique in his music always stem from the fact that the musical logic, which is everywhere assumed by the material of his age, is softened up and replaced by a kind of gesticulation, rather in the way that agitators substitute linguistic gestures for the discursive exposition of their thoughts . . . Wagnerian gestures were from the outset translations onto the stage of the imagined reactions of the public – the murmurings of the people, applause, the triumph of self-confirmation, or waves of enthusiasm. (*ISW*, 35)

> The art of nuance in Wagner's orchestration represents the victory of rei-fication in instrumental practice. The contribution of the immediate sub-jective production of sound to the aesthetic totality has been displaced in favour of the objective sound available to the composer. (*ISW*, 82)

In another key critical motif, Adorno identifies the dialectical relation between Wagner's regression (in consciousness, individuation, and social meaning) and his notable advances in the technical rationalization of musical composition. This conjunction of regressive consciousness and technological rationalization is, as *Dialectic of Enlightenment* would later elaborate, the typically contradictory aspect of bourgeois culture and society, and it has its corollary in the inextricable mixture of splendor and mediocrity that is charac-teristic of Wagnerian musical drama:

> It is precisely the religious *Parsifal* that makes use of the film-like tech-nique of scene-transformation that marks the climax of this dialectic: the magic work of art dreams its complete antithesis, the mechanical work of art. The working methods of major composers have always contained elements of technical rationalization. We need only think of the ciphers and abbreviations in Beethoven's manuscripts. In his late works Wagner takes this practice to great length. Between the composition sketch and the full score a third form is inserted: the so-called orchestral sketch . . . The short interval between the two stages makes it possible to retain a grasp of the orchestral color that had been conceived in the original act of composition. This gives some indication of the ingenuity with which Wagner organized the division of labor . . . The magical effect is insepa-rable from the same rational process of production that it attempts to exorcize. (*ISW*, 109–10)

Adorno's critical formulations, in which technical progress and psychological regression, the rational and demonic, are complementary antithetical cul-tural functions, paralleled an important literary motif in several works of his friend Thomas Mann. In direct connection with Wagner's music, Mann's 1905 novella "The Blood of the Walsungs" ironically draws the twin children of a rich Jewish industrialist into a mimetic repetition of Wagnerian myth, when after attending a concert of *Die Walküre* they commit an act of incest mimicking that of Wagner's mythic twins Siegmund and Sieglinde, who sire the hero Siegfried in a passionate night of tragic, transgressive sibling love.[15] Mann would later, of course, associate musical rationality and demonic regres-sion even more directly in his monumental cultural-political allegory *Doktor Faustus*.

Adorno also reveals Wagner's failure to integrate the different sensory and generic components of musical drama, according to the theoretically stated ambitions of Wagnerian musical drama to realize the total work of art. This failure is not, however, a mere lapse on the artist's part, but his failure to see that the relations between the arts and between their communicative and signifying means are mediated by the whole social structure, not merely separated for arbitrary reasons or rejoinable by artistic fiat. The "reification" of the separate arts – their thing-like objectivity – in their distinct technical and institutional domains cannot be overcome by an act of artistic will, but only by changing the larger context and division of labor in which the life of the senses is structured and limited:

> The formal premises of an internal logic are replaced by a seamless external principle in which disparate procedures are simply aggregated in such a way as to make them appear collectively binding . . . The style becomes the sum of all the stimuli registered by the totality of his senses. The universe of perceptions at his disposal offers itself as a coherent totality of meaning, as the fullness of life: hence the fictive nature of the Wagnerian style. For in the contingent experience of individual bourgeois existence the separate senses do not unite to create a totality, a unified and guaranteed world of essences . . . The senses, which all have a different history, end up poles apart from each other, as a consequence of the growing reification of reality as well as of the division of labor. For this not only separates men from each other but also divides each man with himself. It is for this reason that the music drama proves unable to assign meaningful functions to the different arts. Its form, therefore, is that of a spurious identity. (*ISW*, 102)

Moreover, as Philippe Lacoue-Labarthe has emphasized in his insightful book *Musica Ficta (Figures of Wagner)*, this objection does not pertain solely to Wagner himself, but also to the much longer shadow his dream of the *Gesamtkunstwerk* casts over artistic modernism into the twentieth century, including James Joyce, for whom *Tristan and Isolde* was a touchbase in *Finnegans Wake*, and even the austere Schönberg treating the Old Testament ban on graven images in his uncompleted opera *Moses and Aron*. As Lacoue-Labarthe remarks, "It is as if, in the end, *Moses and Aron* were nothing other than the negative (in the photographic sense) of *Parsifal*, thus accomplishing, in a paradoxical manner, the project of the total work."[16] Like Adorno himself trying to write a modernist, anti-systematic, dissonant "aesthetic theory" as a negative image of the classical idealist aesthetics of Kant, Hegel, Schiller, and Schelling, so too Schönberg appears to Lacoue-Labarthe a modernist anti-Wagner, a relationship that remains a rigorous form of subordination-in-negation to the grand totalizing ambitions of Wagner's musical drama.

Finally, in a characteristic gesture of utopian hope that comes at the acme of one of Adorno's most devastating negative critiques, he also recovers a redemptive element in the tragic pessimism of Wagner's operas. Adorno here, as elsewhere in his critical writings, allegorizes the moments of tragic predicament and impasse as pointing beyond the closure of the historical moment, thus as preserving a utopian content:

> Even the masochistic capitulation of the ego is more than just masochistic. It is doubtless true that subjectivity surrenders its happiness to death; but by the same token it acknowledges a dawning realization that it does not wholly belong to itself. The monad is "sick," it is too impotent to enable its principle, that of isolated singularity, to prevail and to endure. It therefore surrenders itself. Its capitulation, however, does more than just help an evil society to victory over its own protest. Ultimately it also smashes through the foundations of the evil isolation of the individual himself. To die in love means also to become conscious of the limits imposed on the power of the property system over man. It means also to discover that the claims of pleasure, where they were followed through, would burst asunder that concept of the person as an autonomous, self-possessed being. (ISW, 154)

Refusing any reconciliation with the present, and hence foundering upon it – Adorno implies – the genuine artist, through his forms and characters, releases a spark of energies unbound by the limits of that present. It may hence light up a still-dark horizon of possible, better futures.

ADORNO'S MUSICAL MODERNISM II: *THE PHILOSOPHY OF THE NEW MUSIC*

The Philosophy of the New Music, published in 1948 and, as already noted, intimately intertwined with Mann's *Doktor Faustus*, is one of Adorno's most influential works of music criticism. Moving between a psychoanalytically tinged framework and an analysis of musical aspects, Adorno traces the fate of subjectivity in the work of the two greatest modern composers of the first half of the twentieth century: Arnold Schönberg and Igor Stravinsky. Schönberg's work, Adorno argues, represents the progressive tendency, insofar as his atonal "liberation of dissonance" allows the most elevated subjective expressiveness to emerge in the midst of the most technically advanced, rationalized environment of musical material. Seen dialectically from the reverse perspective, his compositions also invest the objectivity of the musical materials with a kind of quasi-subjective individuality, as if each constellation of tones had its own personality. In his artworks, thus, Schönberg performed two key functions that go well beyond simply musical importance.

First, his expressiveness preserves feelings, intensities, and contents of subjective experience that have been threatened by technological, scientific, and organizational developments of twentieth-century capitalism. Insofar as much of subjective experience has been supplanted by the forces of the market, by the impersonal mechanisms of technology, and by bureaucratic calculation, these artworks remind us of a fullness of subjective life that is worth holding onto in the future. Even where this subjective life communicated by the artwork is a painful or mournful one – figured, for instance, by Schönberg's harsh dissonances – it functions as the *negative* index of a happiness that cannot even be imagined if the twentieth-century liquidation of the subject is completed. Its negativity keeps an imaginative space open in which positive utopian contents may also develop.

Second, beyond this preservative function, Schönberg's artworks also have an exemplary value: they model a different kind of relation between subjectivity and technical rationality than that which is typical in either the sciences or in a market- and bureaucratically-organized society. Schönberg allows us to imagine and concretely experience, aesthetically, an ordered "world" in which the greatest individuality *follows from* the most thoroughgoing pursuit of technical rationality, and in which critical knowledge of the past (musical tradition from Bach to Mahler) is the *means* of the greatest innovative boldness. Schönberg's works would, then, represent a kind of "utopia now" that we can possess during the fleeting time of listening. Adorno, however, with characteristic dialectical subtlety, does not rest with this conclusion. For simply by being viewed or listened to, the artwork does not overcome our far-from-utopian society; it remains embedded in and conditioned by society's injustices and contradictions. Art's autonomy, which allows it space to imagine alternatives to the existing world, also consigns it to impotence in the face of society. Thus the modern artwork, in Adorno's view, not only models alternatives to contemporary society, but also registers, in the imperfections and dissonances that keep it from closing around the artistic fiction of a world, art's inability to actualize its utopian dreams under current historical conditions. The artwork may be utopian, but it is inevitably a mournful, wounded utopia. It mourns its own confinement to the "mere appearance" of the artwork, rather than being effective in the full domain of society and natural existence.

Adorno criticizes some of Schönberg's later compositions that employed the so-called "twelve-tone method," which varies preselected tone rows of all twelve notes of the chromatic scale according to quasi-mathematical patterns of permutation. Schönberg was attempting by this means to give composition a new rational basis once a tonal center had been eliminated, generating novel constellations of tone while maintaining rigor of construction. Adorno, however, believed that this newer method of achieving dissonance was actually a step back from Schönberg's previous accomplishments, since it substituted an arbitrary technical formula for the more intuitively expressive "free atonalism" of his earlier works – for Adorno, the unsurpassed standard of complex mediation of artistic material with subjective coloration and vice versa.

Adorno's criticisms of the later, "dodecaphonic" (twelve-tone) Schönberg are mild, however, compared to his vituperative attack on the work of Igor Stravinsky, who stands condemned of having given artistic voice – with a compositional brilliance that even Adorno cannot simply dismiss – to the baleful regression of subjectivity in the present-day. Adorno developed his critique around a set of basic motifs: Stravinsky's "objectivism," which dissolves the subject in favor of accepting as a given fact various reified social contents; his utilization of primitive myth and ritual as formal and thematic material; his conformation of music to dance, which subjects it to an "external" logic not intrinsic to the musical materials but rather to theatrical effect; his connection of musical innovation, especially in rhythm, to figures of mechanical compulsion, infantilism, and loss of subjectivity; and his "montage" of raw, disconnected elements to create a kind of "shock" effect, rather than the binding of expressive elements into a formally integrated whole. Moreover, Adorno saw his diagnosis confirmed in Stravinsky's rejection of Schönberg's rationalizing method and his choice, for a period, of a highly ironic neo-classicism, which returned to classical tonal forms, but emptied them of their original social and historical referentiality (in a kind of postmodernist citationality, *avant la lettre*).

Appreciating neither Stravinsky's irony nor the almost disdainful virtuosity with which he played tricks with the classical legacy, Adorno could discern nothing in this but sheer reaction. In this regard, Stravinsky would serve for him the role in his musical criticism that Heidegger did in his philosophical writings: in both Adorno perceived a dangerously mythic appeal to a primordially given state of being, utilizing the premise of authenticity to confirm the unchangeable nature of the world. Thus in the following passage, which concludes his critique of Stravinsky and the book as a whole, one can see Adorno attempting to wrest the "authentic" content of authenticity away from its false philosophical and artistic ideology:

> The echo of the immemorial, the memory of the primordial, from which every claim to aesthetic authenticity lives, is the trace of perpetuated injustice that this authenticity at the same time transcends in thought, but to which it nevertheless to this day exclusively owes its universality and its bindingness ... The falsification of myth documents an elective affinity with authentic myth.[17]

Adorno thus suggests a dialectical analysis of authenticity: the subjective longing for authenticity, and the concomitant theoretical overburdening of the idea of authenticity, whether in philosophy or art, has as its social precondition the structure of power that denies a nominal authenticity its real embodied, self-sufficient substantiality. Only were these conditions of power abolished – and with them the subjective desire for authenticity – could one assert that the artwork, or an individual existence, had truly attained a state of authenticity.

Until then, any positive appeal to authenticity will remain at once *empty* and ideologically *false* – hence in objective contradiction with its own concept and content, the concrete substantializing of truth.

A later work of importance in Adorno's musicological corpus is his 1962 lecture series *Introduction to the Sociology of Music*. It is notable for its synoptic scope, covering a wide range of topics from popular music and opera to symphonic and avant-garde music. It also is more casual and communicative in style, as it was originally intended for lecture and radio audiences. In editing it for publication, Adorno chose to leave it in its relatively extemporaneous form rather than burden its readers with his more typically challenging prose. Alongside many insightful individual comments and flashes of brilliant social interpretation, Adorno consistently considers the methodology, problem set, and limitations of the sociology of music, a relatively underdeveloped subdiscipline of musical studies even now. Offering at the outset a provisional typology of listeners, this book draws upon Adorno's work in the 1930s and '40s on the social conditions of listening, as well as on his experience with empirical radio research and psychological questionnaires.

Although Adorno could often be stubbornly partisan in his theoretical justification of the Schönberg tendency at the expense of his deeper appreciation of other innovative tendencies in modern music, he was too restless and engaged a thinker not to have qualified these more dogmatic extremes when faced with certain concrete problems and possibilities. One particularly surprising case is the book *Composing for the Films*, in which he collaborated with his fellow Schönberg-student and composer in exile Hanns Eisler, a communist and associate of Bertolt Brecht, whose relations with Adorno were mutually ambivalent at best. Moreover, film music explicitly faced Adorno with considering the composer's task in a manifestly *non*-autonomous creative situation: the effectiveness of the film, including its commercial success, necessarily took precedence over the composer's free invention or the immanent logic of his material.

Remarkably, many of the traits that Adorno criticized in Stravinsky – in his almost simultaneously written and published *Philosophy of the New Music* – receive a more positive treatment in *Composing for the Films*. These include: the use of montage to create auditory tension with other "media" components of the film's total structure; the employment of comic self-reflexivity, irony, parodic allusion as a compositional means; the consideration of structure in "segments" rather than as a more tightly integrated whole; and finally, the use of musical sounds to "affect" directly the senses and emotions of the viewer. In fact, with reference to this last point, Adorno and Eisler even refer explicitly to Stravinsky's achievements:

> The modern motion picture, in its most consistent productions, aims at unmetaphorical contents that are beyond the range of stylization. This

requires musical means that do not represent a stylized picture of pain, but rather its tonal record. This particular dimension of the new musical resources was made apparent by Stravinsky in his *Sacre du Printemps*.[18]

What was denounced as reified objectivism and false authenticity in *Philosophy of Modern Music* appears here, in the cinematic context, as a new musical resource for touching the nerves and hearts of viewers with unprecedented effectiveness.

Finally, two key essays from Adorno's post-World War II production can stand here for his hesitant updating of his positions in light of the very rapid changes in "new music" and the emergence of a number of theoretically articulate and technically gifted composers: Pierre Boulez, Karlheinz Stockhausen, John Cage, and György Ligeti first and foremost. "The Aging of the New Music" (1955) and "Vers une musique informelle" (1962) are characteristically dialectical: affirmative of the high ambitions of this younger generation of composers and relentlessly critical of their shortcomings – which are objectively as well as subjectively conditioned – in realizing these ambitions in innovative works of art. In the earlier of the two essays, Adorno diagnosed what he saw as the waning of the critical dimension of new music, its loss of "negativity" and its positive stabilization as just another administered cultural good of the post-war order, the stuff of official commissions, radio broadcasts, interviews, conferences, and festivals. Moreover, this social integration was not simply an extrinsic institutional tendency, it was reflected in the inner structure of musical works, as composers internalized these new conditions in facile, arbitrary, or scientist compositional procedures. While "Vers une musique informelle" echoes some of these criticisms, it nonetheless takes a more positive stance towards aspects of the new music that were untenable to Adorno in his earlier, more dogmatically Schönbergian position. In particular, Adorno for the first time admits that there may be alternative ways to organize musical material meaningfully than those of intervallic structure and counterpoint. Three possible alternatives he considers are the use of tone color as an organizing principle, the creation of form through shifting densities of interconnections, and chance as an organizational means. Adorno suggests that the kind of listening he always favored, "structural listening," which imaginatively mediates part and whole in the process of listening, may no longer be appropriate to these tendencies in composition.[19] But while structural listening may be appropriate to the tradition leading from Mozart and Beethoven to Schönberg and Webern, a new threshold may have been crossed with post-war new music:

> My reaction to most of these works is qualitatively different from my reaction to the whole tradition down to, and doubtlessly including, Webern's last works. My productive imagination does not reconstruct them all with equal success. I am not able to participate . . . in the process

of composing them as I listen . . . But what I am tempted at first to register as my own subjective inadequacy may turn out not to be that at all. It
may well prove to be the case that serial and post- serial music is founded
on a quite different mode of apperception . . . (*QUF*, 271)

In other words, the terrain of musical form and listening may have shifted from
that which had characterized it for a century and a half of European musical
history. Indeed, Adorno does not shy away from identifying precisely within
that which exceeds his imaginative capacities as a listener the utopian and
artistic core of the new music, which should be genuinely new, and not just
in the sense of bringing forth novelties: "The avant-garde therefore calls for
a music which takes the composer by surprise . . . In the future, experimental
music should not just confine itself to refusing to deal in the current coin; it
should also be music whose end cannot be foreseen in the course of production" (*QUF*, pp. 302–3).

Modernism and Masculinities

At the center of the Frankfurt School's theoretical account of artistic
modernism – above all, in the work of Walter Benjamin and Theodor Adorno
– was the question of modern temporal experience in the epoch of high capitalism and metropolitan urbanism. To what extent, they asked, did the artistic
innovations of the later nineteenth and early twentieth century, beginning with
Baudelaire and Wagner and continuing with futurist, expressionist, surrealist,
and constructivist avant-gardes, reflect a new social structuring of experienced
time? To what degree did this new time-sense confront artists and thinkers
with new problems of writing narrative, interpreting history, creating coherence in temporally developed form, or representing the interweaving of objective and subjective temporalities in a complex fabric of lived time? To what
extent does modernity, as a temporal complex, impact the ability of artworks
to refer to history, to serve as indices of "modern times"? And finally, is it
possible to see within modern artworks new models of temporal experience
or historical coherence that might serve as heuristics for new political, social,
even scientific practice?

Benjamin and Adorno, moreover, both consistently tied this concern with
modernism's temporal dimensions to social and historical questions of artistic
comportment and stance. Thus, for example, as expressions of the accelerating
tempo of modern urban life, Benjamin singled out Baudelaire's regular changes
of residence, his habit of writing in public places while standing up, his affirmation of the sudden *trouvé* snatched from the urban welter, and his self-reflexive
image of the poet as fencer parrying the shocks of the crowd. Deploying a new
rhetorical and thematic armature, Benjamin argued, Baudelaire translated into
specific poetic expressive means and types the rapidly changing rhythms of

fashion and obsolescence, the ebbs and flows of crowds in city streets, and the disintegration of enduring habits under the pressure of novelty and sensation. He observed the same consistent disintegration of temporal duration in the specifically sexual and gendered aspects of Baudelaire's modernity: his fascination with prostitutes and lesbians (as images of female sexuality separated from marriage and procreation), his sexual impotence, his insistent imagery of male submission and erotic damnation. Benjamin suggests that "infertility and impotence are the decisive factors" in Baudelaire's sexuality, and that they must be understood in their specifically negative relationship to the temporal durations established in the institution of the family.[20] Baudelaire's "erotology of the damned" is a strongly gender-marked comportment towards a more general fractured and accelerated temporality of the modern.

We see something analogous in the work of Benjamin's and Adorno's modernist contemporaries, for example in the collaborative musical dramas of Bertolt Brecht and Kurt Weill. In his 1930 "Songspiel" *The Rise and Fall of the City of Mahagonny*, for example, Brecht punctuates the satirically exaggerated cynical capitalism of his model city with a lover's duet between the lumberjack Jim and the prostitute Jenny. The song is focused on the image of two cranes conjoined in side-by-side flight, an image of a paradoxical stillness-in-motion that Brecht used to suggest love's temporary suspension of the cynical, profit-driven laws of Mahagonny. Moreover, both poetically and musically, the scene comes as a radical caesura in the action, accentuating its character as a stop in the order of time that the opera has established through its free-wheeling, cynical, episodic spectacle of man's (and woman's) beastliness. In contrast, the cranes are heartbreakingly different from the human menagerie they soar above. Like Jim and Jenny for a terribly brief instant, they dissolve their fixed gender roles of male customer and whore in a passionate yielding to durational stasis that floats free of objective time's fatal necessity:

JENNY: See there two cranes veer by one with another.
JIM: The clouds they pierce have been their lot together
JENNY: Since from their nest and by their lot escorted
JIM: From one life to a new life they departed
JENNY: At equal speed with equal miles below them
BOTH: And at each other's side alone we see them:
JENNY: That so the crane and cloud may share the lovely –
The lonely sky their passage heightens briefly;
JIM: That neither one may tarry back nor either
JENNY: Mark but the ceaseless lolling of the other
Upon the wind that goads them imprecisely
As on their bed of wind they lie more closely.
JIM: What though the wind into the void should lead them

While they live and let nothing yet divide them:
JENNY: So for that while no harm can touch their haven
JIM: So for that while they may be from all places driven
Where storms are lashing or the hunt beginning:
JENNY: So on through sun and moon's only too similar shining
In one another lost, they find their power
JIM: And fly from?
JENNY: Everyone.
JIM: And bound for where?
JENNY: For nowhere.
JIM: Do you know what time they have spent together?
JENNY: A short time.
JIM: And when will they veer asunder?
JENNY: Soon.
BOTH: So love to lovers keeps eternal noon.[21]

Their duet gives voice, of course, to the ephemerality of this rare suspension of the perception of time, to the miraculous synchronization of the speed of flight into stillness, and to the fact that both birds, both lovers, have achieved this oneness only through the brief alignment of two solitary trajectories that have come together and hence will come apart again dreadfully soon. It is the haunting awareness of this temporariness that intrudes on the utopia of passionate love, which seeks to find in the fleeting instant the image of eternity. It is no less that Baudelaire, in his famous paean to "The Painter of Modern Life," sought to formulate as the essence of "modernité" itself.

Intriguingly, the tragic temporality of flight also appears in one of Brecht's politically themed lyric allegories, his "Song of the Flocks of Starlings," which refers allegorically to the communists in China, who had recently suffered bloody defeat at the hands of the Nationalists:

1
We set out in the month of October
In the province of Suiyan
We flew fast in a southerly direction straight
Through four provinces, taking five days.
> Fly faster, the plains are waiting
> The cold increases and
> There it is warm.

2
We set out, eight thousand of us
From the province of Suiyan
We grew by thousands each day, the farther we came

> Through four provinces, taking five days.
>> Fly faster, the plains are waiting
>> The cold increases and
>> There it is warm.
>
> 3
>
> Now we are flying over the plain
> In the province of Hunan
> We see great nets beneath us and know
> Where we have flown to, taking five days:
>> The plains have waited
>> The warmth increases and
>> Our death is certain.[22]

Again, Brecht laments the tragic necessity that flight must soon end, and that the birds have flown into the nets where they face certain death. Yet their fatal end does not negate the extraordinary image of the flock in flight, both active and passive at once, and growing by thousands each day. Brecht's "bird song," like that in *Mahagonny*, is an image of a lyrical hiatus in time and its "necessity," a brief opening of a gap in history through which the new might enter the world: a temporal *u*-topia/*eu*-topia, which like Brecht's birds in flight, is dislocated from any fixity, "nowhere," yet pointing in anticipation and longing towards the "good place" where the hardships of the present will be overcome. "Song of the Flocks of Starlings" depicts this utopia as the paradoxical "indifference point" of revolutionary mobilization, where the passivity of following the migrating flock appears oddly indiscernible from the frantic activity of each bird individually striving forward on beating wings. For a few days, the "natural" laws of necessity that eventually return to the starlings' doom have been temporarily suspended, as the dark moving swarm blots out the sky and defies the earth's gravity.

Adorno, I would suggest, identified an analogously altered comportment – what could be characterized, paradoxically, as an actively "composed" passivity – as the complement of aesthetic modernity in musical works that he valued as the most significant in modern music: the compositions of Richard Wagner, Gustav Mahler, Arnold Schönberg, Igor Stravinsky, Alban Berg, Anton von Webern, Karlheinz Stockhausen, Pierre Boulez, and John Cage. Let us consider, for example, the following characterization in Adorno's essay of Webern's String Trio:

> The trio is constructed down to its very last note, but has nothing constructed about it: the power of the shaping spirit and the nonviolence of an ear that simply listens passively to its own composition while composing come together in a single identity. An irrepressible mistrust toward

the active intervention of the subject in his material, as a shaping presence, might well serve to define Webern's stance. (*SF*, 100)

Adorno revalues passivity as receptivity to sound and its shapes. He discerns in Webern a positive willingness to receive mimetic communication from the musical materials, to take on, as composing subject, the characteristics of the object rather than to impose subjective tastes, judgments, and meanings upon it. Moreover, in this passivity and stance of non-violence, Adorno sees a gendered defense against patriarchal authority in the art world, a willingness to set aside heroic masculinity in favor of an ethically motivated practice of relinquishing power:

> It is the stance implied in his motivic micro-work in the first miniatures: its aim was the defense against the arbitrary, against caprice. The need for security, a kind of wariness, is something he shared with his friend Berg. Possibly a response to the pressure exerted by Schönberg's authority, it brought both of them in opposition to the dominating, patriarchal manner of his music ... The authenticity of the impact he has made derives from such a lack of violence, from the absence of the composer as sovereign subject. (*SF*, 100–1)

With respect to Berg, Adorno goes still further, positively affirming the passive submission and receptivity to the material as a consistent compositional stance with implications for the formal principle of the musical works. Berg, he writes, "unlike Schönberg, had something passive about him" (*QUF*, 187). But he deployed this passivity to achieve internally coherent large-scale forms without the formal twelve-tone rows that Schönberg saw as a necessary means to this end. "The question of specific relevance to Berg," Adorno concludes, "is how it can be possible for an act of constant yielding, listening, a gesture of gliding, of not asserting himself, to culminate in something like a large-scale form" (*QUF*, 187). In his book-length study of Berg, Adorno similarly states that "Evanescence, the revocation of one's own existence, is for Berg not the stuff of expression, not music's allegorical theme, but rather the law to which music submits."[23]

Berg's passivity is not simply an aesthetic stance towards his materials; it is also an ethical disposition towards their social significance. This is evident when Berg, like Gustav Mahler before him, "carries along the lower, cast-off music, or rather reawakens it as subterranean folklore,"[24] as he does in *Wozzeck* in the lullaby that Marie sings to her child, in the military parade music, or in the tavern music that is incorporated in grotesque anamorphic projection. The social valence of Berg's passivity is even more manifest in relation to his *dramatis personae* such as Marie and Franz in *Wozzeck* or Lulu, Alwa, and Countess Geschwitz in *Lulu*. Here the passivity of the composer's listening ear is the first step to a social, even political passion for the oppressed, in which Adorno saw the redemptive possibility to disarm inexorable – seemingly cosmic, mythic – fate. He concludes his early essay on *Wozzeck*, published in 1929, with the following words:

> The entire third act skirts the abyss; the music contracts and counts the minutes until death. Then it throws itself into the orchestral epilogue and is reflected as distantly, in the children's scene of the conclusion, as the blue of the sky appears at the bottom of a well. This reflex alone indicates hope in *Wozzeck* . . . It illuminates the character of the opera softly, and late. Its character is *Passion*. The music does not suffer within the human being, does not, itself, participate in his actions and emotions. It suffers over him . . . The music lays the suffering that is dictated by the stars above bodily onto the shoulders of the human being, the individual, Wozzeck. In wrapping him in suffering so that it touches him wholly, it may hope that he will be absolved of that which threatens ineluctably in the rigid eternity of the stars.[25]

Adorno's comments on Berg are consistent with the more general philosophical orientation he would articulate in later writings such as *Negative Dialectics*, *Aesthetic Theory*, and related essays, in which the accent falls on a certain subjective passivity – a disposition to suspend subjective mastery, allowing oneself to be "affected" by the object, to experience it as a "passion." Thus, for example, in his late essay "Subject and Object," Adorno writes of a "fearless passivity" that is proper to the conduct of the negative dialectician:

> The preponderant exertion of knowledge is destruction of its usual exertion, that of using violence against the object. Approaching knowledge of the object is the act in which the subject rends the veil it is weaving around the object. It can do this only where, fearlessly passive, it entrusts itself to its own experience. In places where subjective reason scents subjective contingency, the primacy of the object is shimmering through – whatever in the object is not a subjective admixture. The subject is the object's agent, not its constituent.[26]

Adorno suggests that appropriate to the dialectical thinker's stance – or to the dialectical artist, as he implies Berg should be characterized – is a certain submissiveness and humble servitude towards the material world, of which he is the only the facilitating "agent" and not the originating creator. (One might also note here Adorno's deep appreciation and understanding of Samuel Beckett, whose imperative murmuring voices in the head are not only signs of schizophrenic dissociation, but also harkening recollections of the voice of Nature which, to the closed subjective reason of *Endgame*'s Hamm, is thought to have "forgotten us.")

In another essay on Berg, Adorno gives this stance of submission and servitude, this "fearless passivity," a specific erotic accent. He thus explicitly connects Berg's embrace of passivity as a compositional method to the highly charged gendering of the dramatic situations in his operas. Not just passivity, but male erotic submission, Adorno suggests, characterizes the composer's relation to his feminine love-objects in the operas *Wozzeck* and *Lulu*:

> The degenerate, addicted aspect of Berg's music is not a feature of his own ego. It does not aim at narcissistic self-glorification. Rather, it is an erotic enslavement, the object of which is nothing other than beauty and which calls to mind a nature that has been oppressed and degraded by the taboos of culture. The two great operas, *Wozzeck* and *Lulu*, contain nothing heroic, and in them spirit puts on no airs. Instead their enslaved and lethal love attaches itself to the lower depths, to lost souls, to the half-demented and at the same time helplessly self-sacrificing soldier, to his beloved whose instincts rebel against him and whom he destroys together with himself. Later that love attaches itself to Lulu . . . This music gives not alms, but total identification; without reservation it throws itself away for the sake of others. (*SF*, 72)

With this passage in mind, we can almost discern in the bondage of Odysseus, tied to the mast and tormented by the Sirens' female voices – a key episode for Adorno and Horkheimer in *Dialectic of Enlightenment* – an archaic anticipation of the "lower depths" of Frank Wedekind's human circus world or Bertolt Brecht's underworld characters. The erotic enslavement gripping *Wozzeck*'s Franz or *Lulu*'s Alwa and Countess Geschwitz, or the "*sexuelle Hörigkeit*" (sexual dependency) balladed by Mrs. Peachum in Brecht's *Threepenny Opera*, paradoxically appears in a redemptive light.

Male sexual servitude, Adorno suggests, is modernism's exacerbated figure of a still-latent, utopian masculinity, which, in sacrificing without reserve the last vestiges of heroic virility, discovers in submission a new expressive language of sympathy with the oppressed. Adorno renders the connection of Berg and Odysseus even more explicit, when he suggests that Berg is capable of listening with such sympathy to the voice of the past that he is able to open himself to the seductive affections of kitsch, without himself making kitsch of these emotions:

> Such a tone was always part of Berg's spiritualized music. Stylistic purists imagine themselves superior to such things and talk about kitsch when it shocks them. They hope to protect themselves against the shock of the parental world and against a seductiveness that they feel as strongly as Berg, but they lack the strength to expose themselves to it while retaining their self-control. Thanks to this strength, Berg has something of what

Wedekind, the author of *Lulu*, also possessed. Karl Kraus praised his *Pandora's Box* by saying that in it trashy poetry became the poetry of trash. (*SF*, 79)

Adorno speaks of "strength," but he means a specifically modern form of artistic *virtù* different from that possessed by the virile heroes of the past, or embodied by the brute muscularity of *Lulu*'s acrobat, Rodrigo Quast. He means a paradoxical strength to let go of power, a capacity for a sympathy that approaches a traditionally feminine-coded weakness and sentimentality – yet artistically meriting the characteristic that Adorno identified in Berg as "greatheartedness" (*SF*, 72).

Logics of Disintegration and the Redemption of Decadence

As I have suggested, Adorno links musical form, historico-anthropological time (myth, history, and utopia), and masculine erotic dispositions in a single critical constellation. This constellation comes into clear view in relation to Richard Wagner, who lies at the origin of Adorno's musicological corpus. Taking up an argument against Nietzsche's negative criticism of Wagner's decadence, Adorno revalues decadence as an estimable mode of passivity, a willed weakening of the artistic ego's domination of its material, which potentially facilitates a new alignment of the past with the future:

> There is not one decadent element in Wagner's work from which a productive mind could not extract the forces of the future. The weakening of the monad, which is no longer equal to its situation as monad and which therefore sinks back passively beneath the pressure of the totality, is not just representative of a doomed society. It also releases the forces that had previously grown up within itself . . . There is more of the social process in the limp individuality of Wagner's work than in aesthetic personas more equal to the challenge posed by society and hence more resolute in meeting it. (*ISW*, 153–4)

In ironic agreement with Nietzsche, who maliciously encapsulated the gendered implications of Wagner's decadence by arguing that the Ring operas and Flaubert's *Madame Bovary* were siblings of the same psychological impulse, Adorno likewise underscores the erotic aspect of decadence in Wagner, his masochism and resignation of heroic masculinity. But Adorno lends this ascription a positive accent:

> Even the masochistic capitulation of the ego is more than just masochistic. It is doubtless true that subjectivity surrenders its happiness to death; but by the same token it acknowledges a dawning realization that it does not wholly belong to itself. The monad is "sick," it is too impotent to enable its principle, that of isolated singularity, to prevail and to endure.

It therefore surrenders itself. Its capitulation, however, does more than just help an evil society to victory over its own protest. (*ISW*, 154)

In Adorno's view, the monadic individual – which we see in its formation with the Homeric hero Odysseus and in its dissolution amidst Wagner's "twilight" – is a formation of both social relations of production and gendered relations of reproduction. For Odysseus, his ear-stopped sailors and his faithfully waiting wife were mutually constitutive facets of his subjectivity; so too the enslaved Nibelungen and the familial palace of Walhalla, built from their pilfered gold, are fatally intertwined for the doomed characters of Wagner's Ring. Surrender of heroic masculinity and submission to pleasure, even unto death, represents Wagner's protest against a world-order in which love has been displaced by law, property, and contract and hence can only be experienced as fatal transgression:

> Ultimately, [capitulation] also smashes through the foundations of the evil isolation of the individual itself. To die in love means also to become conscious of the limits imposed on the power of the property system over man. It means also to discover that the claims of pleasure, where they were followed through, would burst asunder that concept of the person as an autonomous, self-possessed being that degrades its own life to that of a thing, and which deludes itself into believing that it will find pleasure in full possession of itself, whereas in reality that pleasure is frustrated by the act of self-possession. (*ISW*, 154)

Love-death yields to the fatal voice of myth, calling the human to regress back to the elements of earth and water. Yet recurrently, in ever-diminishing amplitude, it also holds consciousness upright against this regressive descent. Masculinity is therefore not so much abandoned in this process as refigured; it is torn asunder and resutured by the passionate intermittence of pleasure in the rhythmic fading of the subject. Wagnerian passion is thus not simply enjoyment of self-induced inanition of the present and regression to the archaic past, Adorno suggests. In their passion, Wagner's heroes also catch sight of a future in which the delusion of self-sufficient masculinity stands clarified in the light of death and the historical end of a fate-emprisoned world.

In compositional terms, Adorno suggests, the formal problem of how to handle recurrence and repetition also becomes an intensive point of ethical-erotic reflection on masculinity for the modernist composer. The mediating link is the question of time and its articulation by the organized recurrences of music. Thus, for example, Adorno discusses the reiterated gestural motifs that substitute in Wagner's operas, he argues, for genuine development:

> Sonata and symphony both make time their subject; through the substance they impart to it, they force it to manifest itself. If in the symphony

the passage of time is converted into a moment, then by contrast, Wagner's gesture is essentially immutable and atemporal. Impotently repeating itself, music abandons the struggle within the temporal framework it mastered in the symphony. (*ISW*, 37)

In his use of these compositional means, Adorno judges, Wagner remains a subjectivistic technician of repetition rather than a compositional agent of time's authentic coming to expression. Adorno perceives in Wagner's kaleidoscopic plethora of musical forms and colors an underlying sameness: "Whereas Wagner's music incessantly arouses the appearance, the expectation and the demand for novelty, strictly speaking nothing new takes place in it" (*ISW*, 42). Similarly, in an essay from 1963 on "Wagner's Relevance for Today," Adorno would reiterate this objection to Wagner, now further inflecting his judgment with the critique of identity thinking that he had advanced in *Negative Dialectics* and which, I have suggested, also implies the necessity of radical change in the nature of masculine subjectivity:

> In Wagner unceasing change ... ends in constant sameness ... For chromaticism – the principle par excellence of dynamics, of unceasing transition, of going further – is in itself nonqualitative, undifferentiated.
> One chromatic step resembles another. To this extent, chromatic music always has an affinity with identity.[27]

The incapacity to invite and actualize non-identity in musical composition is not simply a technical shortcoming, however; it is an ethical shortcoming in the creative comportment of the composer towards his materials, an index of insufficient strength to let go of masculine defenses and allow the voice of the other to manifest itself within his artistic process.

Even more than Wagner, however, Stravinsky most invites Adorno's charge of mechanical repetition and dissociative spatialization of musical time. In his notorious attack on Stravinsky in *Philosophy of New Music*, Adorno suggests that Stravinsky carried to exasperation Wagner's "suspension of musical time consciousness," which manifests the experience of a bourgeoisie, "which, no longer seeing anything in front of itself, denies the process of history itself and seeks its own utopia through the revocation of time in space."[28] In Stravinsky, Adorno suggests –

> Time is suspended, as if in a circus scene, and complexes of time are presented as if they were spatial. The trick surrenders power over the consciousness of duration, which emerges naked and heteronomous and gives the lie to the musical intention in the boredom that arises. Instead of carrying out the tension between music and time, Stravinsky merely makes a feint at the latter. For this reason, all of the forces shrivel that accrue to music when it absorbs time.[29]

In a later reconsideration of Stravinsky, Adorno would relate this dissociation of time to another characteristic aspect of Stravinsky's work, his penchant for musical parody. Adorno modulated his earlier critique into a subtle diagnosis of a self-directed violence unleashed by the problem of time for Stravinsky:

> He is beset by the crisis of the timeless products of a time-based art which constantly pose the question of how to repeat something without developing it and yet avoid monotony, or else to incorporate it integrally. The sections . . . may not be identical and yet may never be anything qualitatively different. This is why there is damage instead of development. The wounds are inflicted by time, something which identity finds offensive and which in truth does not allow identity to persist. This is the formal, unliterary significance of the parodic style in Stravinsky. The necessary damage to the form appears as mockery of it. What Stravinsky's music does to his stylistic models, it also does to itself. (*QUF*, 153–4)

By extension, then, Adorno suggests that a comportment that sets time apart as an alien otherness returns in the form of a self-directed destructive impulse.

The specifically gendered aspect of the violence remains mostly implicit in Adorno's account of Wagner and Stravinsky, but clearly enough it derives from defense of masculine creative sovereignty against the implication of temporal posteriority, thus defining one aspect of modernist aesthetics. Derivativeness conjures up the specter of sexual difference in the compositional field, as the myth of the male artist as modernist self-progenitor, forever "making it new," is brought up against the historical anteriority of musical styles. Unable wholly to repel or repress the feminine voice of temporal difference that sounds through musical history, Stravinsky's artistic masculinity recoils upon its own derivative constitution, registering the self-inflicted damage as an unsparing parodic deformation of traditional musical idioms. With Berg's *Lulu* (clearly indebted to its source in the scandalous Lulu dramas of Frank Wedekind[30]), the gendered dialectic of male artistry, sexual submission, female sexual difference, and sexualized violence comes to the fore in all its stark nakedness. In Wedekind's drama, Alwa Schön (schön = beautiful) is a playwright composing a play about Lulu that curiously resembles the play in which he is presently also taking part as a character, the one we are watching. Berg translates this detail into his own self-reflexive gesture, making Alwa a composer of musical spectacles. Alwa, then, is an internal figure of the composer of the opera *Lulu*, Alban Berg. The fate of the operatic characters "Lulu" and "Alwa" are closely tied to the creative process of composing *Lulu* (just as the dramatic character "Lulu" was a cipher for Wedekind's complex relation to his own drama). The rapidly changing trajectory of Lulu from wealth through lucky inheritance and speculative gain in the stock market to abject prostitution and death at the bloody hands of Jack the Ripper does not just naturalistically depict a social order in which individuals can be elevated to the heights of luxury or be cast down into the dregs of poverty in rapid, unmediated succession. It is also a comment on the increasingly problematic, destructive conditions that govern a traditionally male artistic creativity under modernism. As a corollary to Lulu's terrible fate, by the third act, Alwa, who has fled from Paris to London with Lulu, has contracted syphilis from her and is going mad. Like an absurd parody, *avant la lettre*, of Mann's Adrian Leverkühn, who receives the devil's allegorical gift of artistic genius in exchange for undergoing the passion of tertiary syphilis, Wedekind's and Berg's artist gets from his devil's bargain only sickness and sores. (As if, moreover, the character Lulu truly had to destroy everything she touched on her path towards her own violent death, Alban Berg himself died before completing his third act, from a spider bite that eventually caused his fatal blood-poisoning.)

I will conclude by suggesting two positive exemplars that Adorno affirms, indicating a future direction for composition in an historically unprecedented tolerance for "planned disorganization" and "informality." The first is given by Alban Berg, whom I have already discussed at length. However, it is notable that in his 1961 essay on Berg, Adorno identified Berg as a forerunner of a "musique informelle" that he saw as a way forward for a "new music" that was showing, by the 1950s, symptoms of "aging" and technical reification. With reference to Berg's "March" from Three Pieces for Orchestra, Opus 6, Adorno observed that Berg had discovered ways of composing "large-scale musical prose," one of the salient achievements of which was its ability to manage recurrence in a radical new fashion with respect to the flow of musical time. Referring back to an analysis he had already made of the piece in 1937, Adorno offers a self-corrective observation:

> I no longer think of the third, self-contained entry of the March as a reca-pitulation. In reality the piece simply moves forward inexorably, much as marches do, without looking back. It is as if Berg had been the first to explore from within a large-scale work the fact that the irreversibility of time is in profound contradiction to the recurrence of an identical being. (QUF, 190)

Notably, one could say as much of Gertrude Stein in the literary realm: her work, from *Three Lives* and *The Making of Americans* on, explored the tensions between recurrence and non-identity in time. Out of these temporal dimensions inherent to language, Stein unfolded her vast series of linguistic experiments in non-hierarchical, "prose informelle," organized around the structures of grammar and the pulse of recurrence rather than narrative, theme, or discursive order. We might, accordingly, put Stein and Berg together in another respect as well: as complementary instances of a new type of modernist gendered subjectivity, generating form from a passion for surrendering to time.

The other positive compositional exemplar is only sketchily given in another essay of 1961, whose title indicates its prospective nature: "Vers une musique informelle" (in *QUF*, 269–322). Although related to developments in the new compositions of Stockhausen, Boulez, and Cage that Adorno had been encountering at recent festivals and on the German radio, in the essay he is not willing to nominate any of these individuals as the new Odysseus who can apprehend authentically "informal" music. Instead, he offers his readers only the image of an anonymous ear, at once Beckettian in its reduced purity and Odyssean in its unreserved openness to the sound of the material world. To this ear, the composing subject's total control over the sonorous material would already have become indiscernible from total surrender to the murmur of material itself: "It must become the ear's form of reaction that passively appropriates what might be termed the tendency inherent in the material . . . It is comparable to the assertion that someone has mastered a language, an assertion which only possesses a meaning worthy of mankind if he has the strength to allow himself to be mastered by that language" (*QUF*, 319). The gender of this unnameable artistic master is likewise to date unknown, yet such ignorance with respect to its nominal identity and gender is not contingent but definitive of its utopian mastery, a mastery marked by its continuous abdication of sovereignty. For as Adorno concludes, "The aim of every artistic utopia today is to make things in ignorance of what they are" (*QUF*, 322). An emancipated humanity too would dwell within the powerless utopia that informal works adumbrate – learning to compose its experience collectively and freely, according to the example of uncoerced events of sound.

NOTES

1. For details of the Adorno–Mann relationship, see Thomas Mann, *Die Entstehung des Doktor Faustus* (The Genesis of Doctor Faustus) in *Doktor Faustus/Die Entstehung des Doktor Faustus* (Frankfurt a/M: S. Fischer Verlag, 1974), pp. 679–848; and Theodor W. Adorno and Thomas Mann, *Correspondence, 1943–1955*, ed. Christoph Gödde and Thomas Sprecher, trans. Nicholas Walker Gödde (Cambridge: Polity Press, 2006).
2. For further elaboration of this parallel, see Peter Dews, *Logics of Disintegration: Poststructuralist Thought and the Claims of Critical Theory* (London: Verso, 1987).
3. See Adorno's essays on the culture industry in Theodor W. Adorno, *The Culture Industry*, ed. J.M. Bernstein (New York: Routledge, 1991). For a recent revisiting of Adorno's culture industry theory with reference to contemporary examples, see Heinz Steinert, *Culture Industry*, trans. Sally-Ann Spencer (Cambridge: Polity Press, 2003).
4. Juliane Brand, "Translator's Introduction" to Adorno, *Alban Berg: Master of the Smallest Link* (Cambridge: Cambridge University Press, 1991), p. xi.
5. Theodor W. Adorno, "Ernst Bloch's *Spuren*," in *Notes to Literature* I, trans. Shierry Weber Nicholsen (New York: Columbia University Press, 1991), pp. 200–14.
6. Letter of Theodor W. Adorno to Walter Benjamin, 18 March 1936, in Adorno et al., *Aesthetics and Politics*, p. 124.

7. Adorno, *Aesthetics and Politics*, p. 121.
8. In *The Culture Industry*, pp. 29–60.
9. Max Horkheimer and Theodor W. Adorno, *Dialectic of Enlightenment*, trans. John Cumming (New York: Continuum, 1972), pp. 120–67 and 168–208.
10. Adorno, "Culture Industry Reconsidered," in *The Culture Industry*, pp. 98–106.
11. Horkheimer and Adorno, *Dialectic of Enlightenment*, pp. 135, 136.
12. Adorno, "Trying to Understand Endgame," in *Notes to Literature* I , p. 262.
13. Useful critical texts on Adorno's musicological writings include: Max Paddison, *Adorno's Aesthetics of Music* (Cambridge: Cambridge University Press, 1993); Max Paddison, *Adorno, Modernism, and Mass Culture: Essays on Critical Theory and Music* (London: Kahn and Averill, 1996); Robert W. Witkin, *Adorno on Music* (New York: Routledge, 1998); and *Mit den Ohren denken: Adornos Philosophie der Musik*, ed. Claus-Steffen Mahnkopf and Richard Klein (Frankfurt a/M: Suhrkamp Verlag, 1998).
14. In Horkheimer, *Between Philosophy and Social Science*, pp. 49–110.
15. Thomas Mann, "The Blood of the Walsungs," in *Death in Venice and Seven Other Stories* (New York: Vintage, 1963), pp. 289–316. In his 1933 essay "Suffering and Greatness of Richard Wagner," Mann noted the "indissoluble mingling of the daemonic and the bourgeois which is the essence of him," in Mann, *Essays*, trans. H.T. Lowe-Porter (New York: Vintage, 1957), p. 237. The perverse and regressive erotic dimensions of Wagner's life, work, and reception are documented in Laurence Dreyfus, *Wagner and the Erotic Impulse* (Cambridge, MA: Harvard University Press, 2010).
16. Philippe Lacoue-Labarthe, *Musica Ficta (Figures of Wagner)*, trans. Felicia McCarren (Stanford: Stanford University Press, 1994), p. 121.
17. Theodor W. Adorno, *The Philosophy of New Music*, trans. Robert Hullot-Kentor (Minneapolis: University of Minnesota Press, 2006), p. 158.
18. Theodor Adorno and Hanns Eisler, *Composing for the Films* (London: The Athlone Press, 1994), p. 38.
19. Rose Rosengard Subotnik offered an influential critique of Adorno's "structural listening" in her essay "Toward a Deconstruction of Structural Listening: A Critique of Schoenberg, Adorno, and Stravinsky," in *Deconstructive Variations: Music and Reason in Western Society* (Minneapolis: University of Minnesota, 1996). For further discussion of the structural listening paradigm, see the essays in *Beyond Structural Listening? Postmodern Modes of Hearing*, ed. Andrew Dell'Antonio (Berkeley and Los Angeles: University of California Press, 2004).
20. Benjamin, "J66a, 9," *AP*, 347.
21. Bertolt Brecht, *The Rise and Fall of the City of Mahagonny*, ed. John Willett and Ralph Manheim, trans. W.H. Auden and Chester Kallman (New York: Arcade Publishing, 1996), pp. 36–8.
22. Bertolt Brecht, "Song of the Flocks of Starlings," in *Poems 1913–1956*, eds. John Willett and Ralph Manheim (New York: Methuen, 1976), pp. 204–5.
23. Theodor W. Adorno, *Alban Berg: Master of the Smallest Link*, trans. Juliane Brand and Christopher Hailey (Cambridge: Cambridge University Press, 1994), p. 2.
24. Theodor W. Adorno, "The Opera *Wozzeck*," in Adorno, *Essays on Music*, ed. Richard Leppert (Berkeley and Los Angeles: University of California Press, 2002), p. 624.
25. Adorno, "The Opera *Wozzeck*," p. 625.
26. Theodor W. Adorno, "Subject and Object," in *The Essential Frankfurt School Reader*, ed. Andrew Arato and Eike Gebhardt (New York: Urizen Books, 1978), p. 504.
27. Adorno, "Wagner's Relevance for Today," in *Essays on Music*, p. 597.

28. Adorno, *Philosophy of New Music*, p. 140.
29. Adorno, *Philosophy of New Music*, pp. 142–3.
30. *Erdgeist* (Earth Spirit, 1895) and *Die Büchse der Pandora* (Pandora's Box, 1904). Besides Berg's opera *Lulu*, Wedekind's modernist dramas also inspired another major adaptation during the interwar Weimar period: G.W. Papst's silent masterpiece *Pandora's Box*, starring Louise Brooks as Lulu.

4

HERBERT MARCUSE

Herbert Marcuse's relation to modernism must be approached somewhat differently than that of Benjamin, who was intimately connected as translator, critic, and man of letters to several different modernist artistic currents in the Europe of his day, or that of Adorno, a trained composer and dedicated analyst of technically advanced modern music and literature. Aesthetics, it is true, was for Marcuse an important, enduring concern. As Morton Schoolman points out, "In every major work beginning with and subsequent to *Eros and Civilization*, Marcuse has devoted not less than an entire chapter to art and aesthetics,"[1] and this statement was written prior to the appearance of Marcuse's final work, *The Aesthetic Dimension*. Commentators as varied as Timothy Lukes,[2] Barry Katz,[3] Charles Reitz,[4] and Hermann Schweppenhäuser[5] have underscored the centrality of the aesthetic for Marcuse's thought, and Douglas Kellner devoted a full volume of his six-volume edition of the *Collected Papers* to Marcuse's essays, lectures, and interviews on "Art and Liberation."[6]

Despite this importance of art and aesthetics to Marcuse, however, his writings present a different set of issues in relation to modernism than do those of either Benjamin or Adorno. First, with the exception of his early thesis-work on the German artist-novel, Marcuse does not primarily present himself as a "critic" or specialized "analyst" of art or literature, as Benjamin and Adorno both clearly did. Although both, and especially Adorno, also produced works of general theory about art and aesthetics, in many cases a reader has to derive the more general ideas from their specific analyses of examples, such as Schönberg, Wagner, or Mahler in Adorno's case or Proust, Kafka, and Baudelaire in Benjamin's. The opposite is largely true for Marcuse: though artistic examples are regularly evinced, they tend to be made in passing, functioning illustratively for a more generic philosophical argument. As Kellner argues, Marcuse "eschewed interpretation, engaging more in formal, philosophical, and political analysis of art, than in the detailed reading of specific works," and he "never really situated his later aesthetic studies of surrealism, Proust, or lyric poetry in their historical contexts"[7] – which was a primary concern of, especially, Benjamin and to a significant extent Adorno as well.

Both Benjamin and Adorno, moreover, despite important differences, responded productively to the provocation of singular works of avant-garde art and literature in the formulation of their critical and theoretical concepts. Both were strongly oriented towards new works that were disturbingly innovative in form and function, thus calling in question received critical concepts and traditional receptive attitudes towards art. They developed their aesthetic thinking primarily out of their repeated attempts to meet the challenge that encounters with these works posed. Marcuse, in contrast, tended to stay on more steady ground, at least with respect to what he was willing to conceive the arts and aesthetics to be. In a much more conventional way than either Benjamin or Adorno, Marcuse took as his starting point the venerable tradition of German classical aesthetics – above all, the aesthetic thought of Kant, Schiller, and Hegel – and renewed this philosophical inheritance through an exciting metapsychological framework adopted from Freudian psychoanalysis. Although this could lead Marcuse's readers to draw radical artistic conclusions from his thought, Marcuse himself did not embrace modernist and avant-garde art as the necessary correlative of his aesthetic philosophy. On the contrary, though he was a richly cultivated man, and though his interests did extend to modernists such as Beckett, Proust, and Aragon, his artistic tastes were more conservative than those of Benjamin and Adorno, who each in their own way took up residence on an extreme margin in the territory of the arts. We can look at this difference from two perspectives, a medium-perspective and an historical one. As Charles Reitz points out, Marcuse was much more strongly grounded in literature than in other arts;[8] in contrast, though both were also steeped in literature, Adorno had expert technical knowledge of modern musical technique and theory, and Benjamin embraced new developments not just in a kind of writing that stretched traditional definitions of literature to the breaking point, but also in architecture, photography, film, and performance. Viewed in a historical perspective, when the word "art" appears in Marcuse's writings, it is far more likely to have as its referent works of the European historical tradition, the "classics" of Western civilization rather than the leading edge of the avant-garde. Hence, the music of Beethoven, the poems of Goethe, the dramas of Shakespeare, or the paintings of Michelangelo are preferred points of reference over analogous modernist works of, say, Alban Berg, Ivan Goll, Vsevolod Meyerhold, or Otto Dix – much less those disquietingly vanguard innovators at the borders of media such as Dziga Vertov, Hannah Höch, László Moholy-Nagy, Joseph Cornell, Edgard Varèse, John Cage, Merce Cunningham, Jean-Luc Godard, Andy Warhol, Robert Smithson, Joseph Beuys, Pier Paolo Pasolini, or Alexander Kluge (just to indicate something of the range of twentieth-century progressive artists Marcuse might have engaged with during his long, intellectually capacious career).

Benjamin and Adorno each took up very strong, consistent perspectives on the autonomy of the artwork and its social significance in modern society. In fact, their positions are typically seen as antithetical rivals in a dialectical tug of war between the two thinkers. Benjamin, as we saw, strongly affirmed the new roles and spaces of art that he found emerging in his time, a broad shift he characterized as the eclipse of the aesthetic function of art in favor of a "political" one – by which he meant such alternative, manifestly collective functions as documentation, pedagogy, organization, and experimentation with mass experiential effects. Adorno, in contrast, radically affirmed the special status of singular, highly refined, critical works of art, which could retain the fine grain of concrete difference in a society tending ever more strongly towards administrative homogenization and commodified abstraction. Adorno's aesthetics envisage individuals engaging with critical artworks in order to preserve and heighten their individuation in an increasingly threatened social situation. Marcuse's position, it might be argued, is more equivocal, oscillating from work to work between, as Reitz has put it, a view of art-as-alienation (and hence something to be criticized or even overcome) and of art-against-alienation (and hence to be affirmed and sustained). Moreover, with respect to the problem of modern and contemporary art, Marcuse's equivocalness can be even more perplexing, for at times he excepts avant-garde art from the characteristics he ascribes to art in general. Avant-garde art may, he suggests, perversely deny itself the imaginative resources that traditional art draws upon, and hence his affirmative philosophical arguments about art may nonetheless stop short at the border of so-called "living art," "anti-art," or "politicized art," as was typified in various ways by Dadaist collage, constructivist design, readymades, documentary, monochrome painting, minimalist sculpture, aleatoric performance, procedural composition, multimedia happenings, conceptualism, underground film, and protest art – that is to say, by many of the defining modernist trends of the twentieth century.

In an exchange of views with his younger Frankfurt School colleague Jürgen Habermas in 1977, Marcuse specified his relations to modernism, as well as the limits of his willingness to entertain the provocations of the contemporary

avant-garde. I reproduce the exchange at length, because the density and speci-
ficity of reference to artistic and literary figures is relatively rare in Marcuse's
often generalizing writings on aesthetics:

> HABERMAS: Herbert, how does it happen that in your aesthetic writ-
> ings you haven't made avant-garde art, which perhaps one could see as
> beginning with symbolism, with Baudelaire and Mallarmé, an explicit
> theme? The system of historical references with which you exemplify, let
> us say, your aesthetic theses, reach, also within literature, from classicism
> and romanticism to realism up to, let's say, Kafka and Brecht.
> MARCUSE: And Beckett.
> HABERMAS: I can't recall any place where you have specifically dis-
> cussed Beckett. Besides that you emphasize continuity, while Benjamin's
> and, above all, Adorno's theory of art in essence aimed at grasping that
> particular process of reflection in modern art . . . as modern art came to
> the fore: that it thematized its process of production, its media as such.
> This process that in painting perhaps begins with Kandinsky and today
> practically has led to a dissolution of the category of the artwork . . . This
> process was at the center of Adorno's theory. It has not been analyzed
> in yours.[9]

Concluding their discussion of the theme, Habermas presses Marcuse about
the potentially conservative dimensions of his rejection of the contemporary
avant-garde (comparing him, rather nastily, to the arch-conservative philosophical anthropologist Arnold Gehlen). Specifically, he challenges Marcuse's
insistence on the formal closure of the authentic artwork, which ensures its
tension, as a fictive heterocosmos, with existing reality. By the time of their
conversation in 1977, this formalism had been under an all-sided assault in
the art world by various tendencies of aleatorics, readymades and multiples,
documentary, improvisation, actionism, and conceptual art, which Marcuse
apparently dismisses out of hand:

> HABERMAS: From this perspective, you seem to offer a picture in which
> precisely the categories that were constitutive for modern art, the new,
> the experimental, the constructive, have led to a directly self-destructive
> process of the accelerated aging of the modern, which now peters out.
> On the feuilleton page of the *Frankfurter Allgemeine Zeitung*, but not
> only there, the formula of the end of the avant-garde is used. Would you
> agree?
> MARCUSE: I would agree, only to the degree that that which *this* avant-
> garde makes has nothing to do with art.
> HABERMAS: You stand together with Gehlen on this.
> MARCUSE: That doesn't bother me.[10]

Yet despite his rather paradoxical relation to much of what we think of as modern art and literature, and certainly to the avant-garde, Marcuse's work still remains crucial to any account of the Frankfurt School and modernism. To a substantial degree, he was influenced positively by the *earlier* historical moment of politicized avant-garde culture in Weimar Germany, with its heady confluence of expressionism, Dadaism, constructivism, and *Neue Sachlichkeit*; he rejects primarily "*this* avant-garde," the *neo*-avant-garde of the 1960s and early '70s. He also exerted an influence as a philosopher of the 1960s counter-culture and student revolt, which had many aesthetically experimental attributes as part of its defining politics of experience. But Marcuse is useful to consider here in another connection as well. Not primarily, as I have noted, an aesthetician or art critic, Marcuse nevertheless touched upon the social significance of the "aesthetic" in a fundamental sense and in ways that resonated with the most advanced tendencies in the arts (even those, perhaps especially those, that Marcuse himself rejected). On questions of artistic culture, Marcuse's taste may have somewhat constrained his thought; but about the full social domain of "aesthetic" sense and sensibility, about sensuous experience as both a collective and an individual structure, including that of eroticism, Marcuse made a galvanizing contribution. It is on the basis of the latter thematics in Marcuse's work that the art critic Gregory Battcock could, for example, explicitly claim him as *the* aesthetic theorist of the post-formalist artistic radicalism of later 1960s and early '70s: "just as Clement Greenberg became the major aesthetic definer of Abstract Expressionist and Minimal Art, we discover that a *political* philosopher, Herbert Marcuse, became the major *aesthetic* definer of a new kind of art."[11] Aside from Marcuse's widespread influence on counter-cultural thought in the student movements of both the United States and Europe, through the interest of critics such as Battcock and Ursula Meyer, among others, he also thus had some direct impact on New York-centered and European art scenes of the later 1960s.[12] Alex Alberro has noted, for example, that post-minimalist artist Dan Graham, in his celebrated magazine article / artwork *Homes for America* (in *Arts Magazine* 41, December 1966–January 1967) "adapted the analysis of 'one-dimensional society' articulated in the 1960s . . . by . . . Herbert Marcuse, and integrated certain key elements of that critique *tout court*."[13] Alberro goes on to qualify this statement with a retrospective quotation from Graham, which suggests how thoroughly Marcuse's ideas were part of the intellectual ambiance of the progressive art world, and might be absorbed even without direct reading and study: "I never read Marcuse, until the '80s . . . But I think the 'in the air' part is extremely important, as the influence of [his] ideas come through in the work."[14]

Finally, as Charles Reitz has argued, Marcuse emphatically linked his engagement with the arts to problems of aesthetic education. "I contend,"

Reitz states, "that Marcuse's contributions to a critical theory of art and critical theory of alienation only become fully intelligible on the basis of what he has to say about a critical theory of education. My point is that *educational* insights are the major purpose of his extensive analyses of art and alienation."[15] This means, however, that we can view Marcuse's aesthetics in light of the theory of social "learning processes" that derives from Jürgen Habermas's path-breaking work on public spheres and communicative practice, and has strongly informed the important work of the literary critic Peter Bürger, the third-generation Frankfurt School philosopher Albrecht Wellmer, and the filmmaker and writer Alexander Kluge (each discussed in my last chapter). Reitz has himself compared Marcuse to radical educational theorist Paolo Friere insofar as both develop a conception of education, including aesthetic education, as embodying a "disalienating, humanizing social philosophy-in-action."[16] Though Marcuse's conceptual apparatus remained wedded to classical mimetic and dialectical terminology, and though his tastes kept him from exploring more sympathetically some of the avant-garde tendencies of the day, in his emphasis on education, Marcuse perhaps comes closer than either Benjamin or Adorno to converging with this new stream of post-Habermasian Frankfurt School thought on art's contribution to social learning processes and the enrichment of intersubjective experience.

Overcoming Affirmative Culture

A landmark essay in Marcuse's oeuvre, justifiably still seen as one of the key works of the early Frankfurt School, is his 1937 essay "The Affirmative Character of Culture."[17] As Reitz describes it, Marcuse's essay is his "first statement of the new *aesthetic direction of the political* program of his middle period, that is, of *the practical value of the arts against alienation*."[18] This essay is worth dwelling on at some length, both for the details of its argument about the social functioning of art within the broader sphere of culture, and for what it reveals about the focus and limits of Marcuse's aesthetic thought at the time. "The Affirmative Character of Culture" is, we could say, a very forceful *critique* of art's "affirmative" cultural function, viewed against three key social backgrounds, those of antiquity, classic bourgeois society, and emerging post-bourgeois totalitarianism. What it is not, in contrast, is an explicit theory of *critical art* or of the form to be taken by a culture all but assumed in the essay but never openly formulated: a revolutionary *negative* culture, as a means of achieving, ultimately, a new, non-affirmative function for what was once "culture." This is another way of stating something already noted at the beginning of this chapter: Marcuse's reluctance, unlike Benjamin or Adorno in their different ways, to embrace the more radical, active negativity of avant-garde art as a specific form of socially critical practice.

Marcuse begins his essay with a discussion of Plato and Aristotle, in connection with the hierarchy of forms of knowledge in ancient philosophy. Knowledge of the necessities of everyday life is at the bottom of the hierarchy, while philosophical contemplation is at the top. In embracing this hierarchy, Marcuse asserts, Aristotle undermined his own intention to disclose the practical character of all sorts of knowledge. This is because the holistic nature of life, which includes both useful and necessary elements, as well as elements related to beauty, truth, and happiness, is sundered into distinct divisions. The former elements are given over to the life of the body, while the latter become the special preserve of the mind – and more importantly, even, the special preserve of those whose social privilege allows them to pursue the life of the mind at the expense of those who must toil with their bodies and attend to the bodily needs of the mind's representatives. Marcuse's view of this ancient idealism is, however, decidedly ambivalent. On the one hand, he argues, it recognized, in negative form, the inadequacy of the arrangement of the material order, which, in its facticity, could in no way be taken to be the standard of truth or beauty. In demanding the transcendence of the material order, then, ancient idealism formulated in compelling ways ideals that went beyond the given world. There is, however, on the other hand, a kind of "original sin" in this transcendence as well, since the ideal can become an end in itself, rather than a standard to which the material world should be approximated. Moreover, since the ontological and ethical hierarchies involved here express, as Marcuse explicitly states, "the badness of a social reality in which knowledge of the truth about human existence is no longer incorporated into practice" (AC, 84), making the ideal an end in itself implies a failure to transform, thus a guilty preservation, of the wretchedness of "mere" material life. "The history of idealism," Marcuse concludes, "is also the history of its coming to terms with the established order" (AC, 85).

This conclusion represents a crucial pivot in the essay, because with the slackening of the tension between the ideal and the material, which served a compromised, but nevertheless tangible critical function in ancient philosophy, idealism can evolve in bourgeois society into the "affirmative culture" that is properly Marcuse's object of scrutiny and critique in his essay. Marcuse defines this term as follows:

> By affirmative culture is meant that culture of the bourgeois epoch which led in the course of its own development to the segregation from civilization of the mental and spiritual world as an independent realm of value that is also considered superior to civilization. Its decisive characteristic is the assertion of a universally obligatory, eternally better and more valuable world that must be unconditionally affirmed: a world essentially different from the factual world of the daily struggle for existence, yet realizable by every individual for himself "from within," without any transformation of the state of fact. (AC, 85)

The function of affirmative culture is, for the bourgeoisie, to conjure away their dependence on a system of power, privilege, and material production. All these vulgar concerns are sublimated into the inner, ideal struggles to achieve true beauty, insight, and feeling in the realm of culture. Affirmative culture takes place in the sphere of consumption and circulation. Though Marcuse does not make the connection completely explicit, we might say that "culture," in this affirmative sense, has something of the same abstracting, idealizing properties as money, as Marx analyzed in *Capital* and Georg Simmel subsequently developed in connection with culture in *The Philosophy of Money*. Put bluntly, the moneyed classes – who are neither workers nor technical employees directly involved in production – can afford to forget the messy world of production and live in a ideal world of culture, as long as money continues to return its magical "interest." Even the capitalist directly involved in the problems of the factory – the facts and figures of supplies, the details of the production line, the managing of conflicts with labor, and so on – may come home and conjure away this uncharming world of charts, documents, clerks, and workers, by entering into a well-equipped library or attending (in a good subscription seat) a concert or performance.

Affirmative culture, then, is not just escapist, Marcuse implies. In its very inner fabric, it is also marked by class inequality and especially by the separation of manual and mental labor, production and circulation. In contrast to the cultural idealization that we saw in antiquity, where Marcuse highlighted a more strongly critical dimension in the ideals it put forward, affirmative culture in bourgeois society decisively tilts towards the apologetic, not so much measuring a bad reality against a set of ideals as simply rendering the bad reality invisible, like turning one's head away from the beggar on the steps of the opera house. Since affirmative culture is taken more and more as a "natural" acquisition of the bourgeoisie, part of a habitus taken on in largely tacit ways in the course of living a bourgeois lifestyle, it no longer even stands out how much time, effort, and resources it actually takes to know, say, "good" literature, music, dance, or other forms of high culture. To choose a modernist example not discussed by Marcuse, but relevant here as an illustration, the world of affirmative culture is that privileged bourgeois sphere to which Leonard Bast, the poor clerk in E.M. Forster's *Howard's End*, so desperately and maladroitly wants to gain entry. It is plausible to sense an element of snobbery in Forster's characterization of Bast's painful inability to achieve by sweaty effort that which bourgeois privilege allows the Schlegel sisters to have taken in by easy osmosis, through a lifetime of reading, concert-going, and intelligent discourse with other privileged members of the cultural elite (however much, at the same time, their gender also marginalizes them). Yet Forster also dramatizes with a sensitive eye the difficulty Bast faces in becoming "cultivated," taking on the lineaments of affirmative culture, by programmatic effort. He is painfully inept at performing the tacitly internalized social *gestures* of the cultured elite; he lacks proper orientation in what is tasteful or vulgar, what "everyone (who is anyone) knows." The exhaustion and lack of time that labor imposes on him sets him apart from those who can afford to cultivate their minds at leisure and over long periods of time; the margin of his income that can be devoted to books, concerts, and the other means of cultivation is extremely meager. In short, unlike for the Schlegels, Bast's world of labor, money, the hungers and discomforts of the body – all that affirmative culture is meant to bracket away and transcend – stubbornly keeps intruding itself on him, like the clunky boots with which, in a characteristic scene, he jars a table and knocks over a cheap photograph in a frame. We might observe that – as the epochal family shifts from business to culture in Thomas Mann's *Buddenbrooks* suggests, or as the intrusion of socially awkward lower-class intellectuals in the novels of Forster, Virginia Woolf, and (self-reflexively) James Joyce also illustrate – the nexus between social privilege and cultural acquisition was one of the major tensions that modernist fiction dramatized and sought through artistic culture to neutralize or resolve. The important question remains whether, in writing a work of literature in which one represents a character without the time or disposition to read the kind of work in which s/he appears, the contradictions of affirmative culture have not simply been exponentially heightened. Modernism, in any case, brings these cultural contradictions to the fore, revealing, through unresolved tensions in the narrative – in the dissonances released by bringing these conflicts into the open – that affirmative culture's closure is both illusory and, in a historical sense, threatened.

That was Marcuse's own conclusion in 1937, when he saw affirmative culture being given the lie by new totalitarian forces that were liquidating the old culture and integrating it more directly with ideology, mass politics, and industrial production. In a world in which culture, like the whole of society, was being subjected to "total mobilization" (the term introduced by the extreme right-wing writer Ernst Jünger)[19] and *Gleichschaltung* ("coordination," the National Socialist term for bringing all aspects of society and state under Nazi central control), there was simply no way to retreat into the idealities of literary, musical, artistic, or other cultural life. In Germany, art collections were being impounded and purged of modernist "degenerate art," while new artworks idealizing the Führer and Nazi ideology were being commissioned and displayed; books of suspect authors were being banned and burned; Jewish, left-wing, or otherwise suspect and unsympathetic intellectuals were fleeing the country or being removed from posts at universities and publishing houses. A poignant illustration of the illusions of "affirmative culture" is the Hungarian-Jewish author Istvan Örkény's "One Minute Story" based on his experience in wartime forced labor at the Russian front:

in memoriam dr. h.g.k.

"Hölderlin ist ihnen unbekannt?" [You are not familiar with Hölderlin?]
Dr. H.G.K. asked as he dug the pit for the horse's carcass.

"Who is that?" the German guard growled.

"The author of *Hyperion*," said Dr. H.G.K., who had a positive passion
for explanations. "The greatest figure of German Romanticism. How
about Heine?" he tried again.

"Who're them guys?" the guard growled, louder than before.

"Poets," Dr. H.G.K. said. "But Schiller. Surely you have heard of
Schiller?"

"That goes without saying," the German guard nodded.

"And Rilke?" Dr. H.G.K. insisted.

"Him, too," the German guard said and, turning the color of paprika,
shot Dr. H.G.K. in the back of the head.[20]

The dark humor of Örkény's story is, of course, that the German classics matter
only to the Jewish forced laborer, while his "true Aryan" guard couldn't give
a damn about them. Far from being engaged by this ludicrous attempt, in concentration camp conditions, to (in Forster's words) "only connect" through
culture, the guard is enraged by an upstart Jew bothering him with unknown
references to "his culture." Beneath the more evident ironies of this endpoint
of the dream of the Central European Jewish dream of assimilation through
culture, however, Örkény more subtly implies a second tension: that of class.
In a sense, with supreme unconsciousness about the class dimensions of the
affirmative culture he esteems, the urbane Dr. H.G.K. is unwisely lording over
an ignorant plebian the superiority of his cultural riches. Unfortunately, cultural capital counts for little when the brutish peasant is also an armed Nazi
camp guard and the member of the cultural elite is a Jewish forced laborer
being made to dig trenches for dead animals.

Marcuse, interestedly, offers a subtle estimation of the secret compact
between the affirmative culture represented by Örkény's hapless Dr. H.G.K.
and his barbaric guard. He notes that the abstract lack of recognition of social
differences that affirmative culture involves – Dr. H.G.K.'s sincere surprise
that his German guard doesn't know Hölderlin! – had a complementary, if
antithetical reflection in the new totalitarian forms of community in which
social difference was being forcibly resolved, including through the exclusion
and killing of those differences that cannot be assimilated (like the Jews for the
National Socialist "*Volksgemeinschaft*"):

> Affirmative culture had canceled social antagonisms in an abstract
> internal community. As persons, in their spiritual freedom and dignity,
> all men were considered of equal value. High above factual antitheses
> lay the realm of cultural solidarity. During the most recent period of

affirmative culture, this abstract internal community (abstract because it left the real antagonisms untouched) has turned into an equally abstract external community. The individual is inserted into a false collectivity (race, folk, blood, and soil). But this externalization has the same function as internalization: renunciation and subjection to the status quo, made bearable by the real appearance of gratification. (*AC*, 107)

In connection with Ernst Jünger, whose works "On Total Mobilization" and *The Worker*[21] were manifestos of a new, post-bourgeois culture of technology, political concentration, and power, Marcuse concludes that in bringing affirmative culture to a violent end, in absolutizing in the Nazi "community of fate" the affirmative culture's renunciation of material happiness in the social world, the new totalitarian culture actually represents affirmative culture's acme as well. What in bourgeois affirmative culture was a hidden implication of an idealizing culture becomes an openly affirmed fact under totalitarian culture – the affirmative of the world of a Darwinian struggle for survival, everyday violence, the reduction of political life to friend-enemy relationships, enslavement to technology, class domination, and war:

> Whereas formerly cultural exaltation was to satisfy the personal wish for happiness, now the individual's happiness is to disappear completely in the greatness of the folk. While culture formerly appeased the demand for happiness in real illusion, it is now to teach the individual that he may not advance such a claim at all . . . Demolishing culture in this way is thus an expression of the utmost intensification of tendencies fundamental to affirmative culture. (*AC*, 110)

Marcuse concludes his essay with a tantalizing gesture towards the dissolution of this bad complementarity of affirmative culture and the totalitarian culture that is, in a sense, both superseding it and realizing its delusory features to an exponential extreme. He argues: "Overcoming these tendencies in any real sense would lead not to demolishing culture as such but to abolishing its affirmative character" (*AC*, 111). This would entail overcoming affirmative culture's constitutive tendency to look away and separate from material life. A non-affirmative culture would, in turn, need to be "integrated" with material life, becoming in an integral component of a shared enjoyment of real, sensual, material happiness, not just for those with the privilege to be pure cultural consumers (in times of leisure at least), but also for those who bear the responsibility for producing and reproducing material life, from manual labor to domestic and child-bearing labor.

Marcuse even goes so far as to suggest that it is precisely the authoritarian state's liquidation of traditional, bourgeois, affirmative culture – in favor of agitational, pragmatic, productivist, ritualistic, or ideologically saturated

culture that has been centrally organized by the state – that allows us, dialectically, to imagine a non-affirmative culture as more than just a distant utopian
possibility. For negatively, the authoritarian state has made abundantly clear
that "today culture has become unnecessary" (*AC*, 111). "The authoritarian state's polemic against the cultural (*museal*) establishment contains an
element of correct knowledge" (*AC*, 111), as Marcuse amplifies. The problem,
however, is that in place of the old affirmative culture, the authoritarian state
substitutes a new, more all-embracing system of cultural illusion that more
emphatically and effectively obfuscates the problems of material life than did
its despised, weak-willed predecessor.

Marcuse concedes that the emergence of a genuinely integrated, non-
affirmative culture will not take place without a major mutation in what we
have, up till now, conceived culture to be: "Insofar as in Western thought
culture has meant affirmative culture, the abolition of its affirmative character will appear as the abolition of culture as such. To the extent that culture
has transmuted fulfillable, but factually unfulfilled, longings and instincts, it
will lose its object" (*AC*, 111). Suggesting his alignment with the aspirations
of the twentieth-century avant-gardes to abolish the traditional artwork and
utilize the field of everyday life and collective experience as the "medium" of
artistic activity, Marcuse writes: "Perhaps art as such will have no objects"
(*AC*, 111). He thus suggests that in the traditional conception of art, "art"
objects only ever appeared, and hence were only *identifiable* as such, sealed
off from much of the broader domain of life, confined within the *cordon
sanitaire* of affirmative culture. In one sense, overcoming affirmative culture
means the end of art – not, however, in the Hegelian sense that the home of
"spirit" passes to higher realms such as religion and the state, but rather that
art's place in the social division of labor, and hence in the social hierarchy of
production, will lose its special status and become, perhaps, indiscernible as
"art" in many of its manifestations. Marcuse is not, however, concerned that
this dissolution of the traditional conception of art will mean the disappearance of *culture*. Non-affirmative culture retains culture's "essence," once its
contingent, historical, affirmative form has been shaken off: the human activity
of imaginatively shaping images, figures, and forms to render our experience
sensually palpable, to allow us to play with new types and configurations of
experience, and to process experientially certain negative anthropological
constants such as sickness and grief, which will exist even after the historically contingent deformation of human experience, the monstrous quantum
of socially produced suffering, has been abolished from all memory. Marcuse
strikes an existentialist note, hearkening back to his early philosophical orientation towards Martin Heidegger and the *Lebensphilosophie* of Wilhelm
Dilthey:

As long as the world is mutable there will be enough conflict, sorrow, and suffering to destroy the idyllic picture. As long as there is a realm of necessity, there will be enough need. Even a non-affirmative culture will be burdened with mutability and necessity: dancing on the volcano, laughter in sorrow, flirtation with death. As long as this is true, the reproduction of life will still involve the reproduction of culture: the molding of unfulfilled longings and the purification of unfulfilled instincts. (*AC*, 112)

Non-affirmative culture will allow, Marcuse suggests, the true character of humans as finite beings to emerge in full for the first time. Re-conjoined to the senses and the realm of material fulfillment, non-affirmative culture promises to facilitate a more intense, more meaningful realization of the whole range of human experiences, whether pleasurable or painful.

This thought, of a thorough-going "aesthetic" fulfillment within material life, would remain fundamental to Marcuse for the following four decades of his work. How precisely the practice of art fits into this picture – art's relation to this "aesthetic state" or "aesthetic education of humanity" (to use Friedrich Schiller's terms) – was, however, a question that Marcuse answered in different ways over time, sometimes leaning towards the idea of art's dissolution as a special realm (his 1937 position), at other times insisting on art's special, even "permanent" character (as his 1977 book, *Die Permanenz der Kunst*, would forcefully argue). At times, Marcuse seemed to endorse the project of the radical artistic avant-gardes to create an interventive art that worked to directly shape individual and collective experience. At other moments, however, he explicitly precluded any identification with the actual practices of the avant-garde, whatever resonance there might have seemed to be between these and some of his theoretical positions.

In the discussion with Jürgen Habermas following the appearance of his last book, Marcuse explicitly measured the distance between his earlier and present positions, while drawing a sharp line between his aesthetic and that of the contemporary neo-avant-gardes: "If I had to write my essay from the 1930s today ["Affirmative Culture"] I would soften the affirmative character of art and emphasize more its critical communicative nature, and that is, in my opinion, precisely what has died out in the so-called avant-garde."[22] Arguably, this equivocation itself was characteristic of Marcuse's aesthetics, and, given the centrality of the aesthetic within his larger vision of human liberation, other elements of his theoretical work as well. Marcuse never came to a fully satisfactory formulation – satisfactory for either him or his readers – that reconciled his philosophical anthropology, his goal of emancipating human beings in their full rational and sensual capacities, with the empirical messiness of that special realm of practice known as art.

The Functions of Artistic Imagination

Marcuse's major theoretical works of the 1950s, '60s, and '70s – including *Eros and Civilization*, *One-Dimensional Man*, *An Essay on Liberation*, *Counterrevolution and Revolt*, and *The Aesthetic Dimension* – each sought to delineate the place of the aesthetic in the landscape of post-war, technological, industrial society, schismed between intensified, irrational repression and new possibilities for human liberation. These attempts by Marcuse had parallels in the art world of the later 1950s and the 1960s, and beyond the question of direct reciprocal influence, which certainly existed, one could also legitimately discern a broad cultural resonance that sounded in analogous ways in Marcuse's theory and the activities of many practitioners and critics in the contemporary arts. I will discuss these resonances, and Marcuse's particular expression of them, at greater length in the following sections. Prior to that, however, I wish to make brief reference to two texts that, though treating the aesthetic primarily in the context of other arguments, provide a crucial transition to the more elaborated arguments of other of Marcuse's books. These include the discussion of Soviet realism in Marcuse's 1959 study *Soviet Marxism* and the concept of "aesthetic reduction" in his 1964 book *One-Dimensional Man*.

Soviet Marxism is, today, one of Marcuse's lesser-read books, for the obvious reason that a critique of Soviet society, written in the midst of the Cold War, appears less relevant when Soviet society no longer exists. It also appears to be a less "theoretical" or philosophical work than other of his better-known writings. However, as the German student activist Rudi Dutschke noted in an interview, it was precisely this book that most attracted him to Marcuse's thought and which led him to invite Marcuse to Berlin to discuss contemporary issues with the radicalized students.[23] Not only, as Dutschke argued, did Marcuse offer a new, critical perspective on the deformation of socialism in the Soviet-bloc countries of Eastern and Central Europe, he laid out a broader perspective on the stabilization of the post-war international capitalist order and the necessary impact that entailed for Marxist theory and practice. We can summarize this impact, looking ahead, as a certain convergence between Western capitalist and Eastern socialist techno-industrial societies and an increasing closure, on both sides of the Iron Curtain, of thought and imagination in favor of "one-dimensionality."

In the Soviet Union, this was dramatically demonstrated in the position of the arts, which are traditionally the haven of imaginative dimensions not reducible to the limits of given, factual reality. Marcuse's discussion of art in *Soviet Marxism* appears, notably, in the chapter devoted to a much-debate topic in Marxist theory, the relation of base and superstructure in society. This topic had taken on new relevance in the Soviet Union in the early 1950s, when Stalin, a few years before his death, pronounced on the unlikely problem of linguistics. Language, the Soviet leader argued, cannot be thought to be a superstructure like, say, literature or jurisprudence, because language does not change conjuncturally with changes in the society; it evolves much more slowly. Yet Stalin could not quite make up his mind exactly where language fits in the classic Marxist base / superstructure, forces of production / relations of production scheme, and offered a formulation that was more cryptic than illuminating, arguing that language was in a sense neither in the base nor in the superstructure but somehow in between. Given the political climate of the time, theorists and scholars whose work was rooted in language, from philosophers and philologists to historians and archeologists, had to adjust their positions to conform to this authoritative pronouncement. The problem was that, given the ambiguity of Stalin's statement, no one quite knew what the position was and substantial debates took place in the process. One possible implication, argued by some participants in the debates (for example, the politically threatened philosopher and literary critic Georg Lukács in Hungary), was that the extreme political instrumentalization of the arts characteristic of dogmatic socialist realism was contrary to "true" Marxist theory, which provided for a greater degree of autonomy of language-based culture from immediate, tactical conjunctures. While various sorts of stylistic and thematic changes in literary practice – "superstructural" in nature – were justified, literature's roots in the slowly evolving social domain of language argued for allowing socialist writers greater stability, rooted in literary traditions, beyond the constant tactical lurches and readjustments of official party literature under Stalin. Lukács (and others arguing along analogous lines) exploited the ambiguities of Stalin's pronouncements to reassert the autonomy of literature, while assuring its ultimate, mediated reference to social reality through its relation to the rooted traditions of the language, which originate in the people and are enriched by great writers of the people such as Tolstoy and Gorki. Lukács's argument pits a tradition of great nineteenth-century realism against the shallow schematism of present-day socialist realism. It does not, notably, argue for modernistic innovation, for the radical imaginative and expressive freedom of the literary avant-garde.

Marcuse's argument, in contrast, takes this step. As an insider and true believer looking for greater freedom of movement within the assumptions of Eastern European socialism, Lukács was seeking greater breathing room for literature and found just enough in the autonomy of "great realism," the realism of Balzac and Thomas Mann, rather than that of party writers like Alexander Fadayev, Nikolai Ostrovsky, and Valentin Katayev. Marcuse, on the contrary, is seeking a perspective of negation, from which the closure of the system can be criticized as a whole. He finds that perspective in art and philosophy, because it is not "realist" in the sense of conforming to rather than diverging from socially determined contents: "The more the base encroaches upon the ideology, manipulating and coordinating it with the established order, the more the ideological sphere which is remotest from the reality (art, philosophy), precisely because of its remoteness, becomes the last refuge for the opposition to this order" (*SM*, 125). The Soviet regime, he suggests, senses the danger represented by art and philosophy, which in their direct efficacy are relatively powerless, and seeks to restrict their capacities to transcend a bad reality by limiting them to one-dimensional reflection of that reality, a peculiar, impoverished brand of "realism." Philosophy, Marcuse suggests, had already effectively been neutralized by the party, though the construction of an official dialectical materialism. Only art remained a space of potential transcendence of Soviet reality: "With this negation of philosophy, the main ideological struggle then is directed against the transcendence in art. Soviet art must be 'realistic'" (*SM*, 128). The Soviet response was not to suppress art altogether, or to bring it to an end – as was projected both within Hegel's system and was advocated by leftist "proletarian culture" elements in the early Soviet Union. It was rather to preserve art in a neutralized condition, in a particular inflection of "affirmative culture": "Soviet art . . . insists on art, while outlawing the transcendence of art. It wants art that is not art, and it gets what it asks for" (*SM*, 131). Keenly aware of "the social function of art," Marcuse writes, Soviet aesthetics places "strong emphasis . . . on the cognitive function of art" (*SM*, 131), its ability to formulate and communicate ideological concepts and ideas. "The Soviet state by administrative decree," he continues, "prohibits the transcendence of art; it thus eliminates even the ideological reflex of freedom in an unfree society. Soviet realistic art, complying with the decree, becomes an instrument of social control in the last still nonconformist dimension of the human existence" (*SM*, 133).

To this hypertrophied ideological, "cognitive" function of official Soviet art, Marcuse counterposes what we might call the transcending, "utopian" function of free imaginative art, which operates not through conceptual ideas and ideologies, but through sensual "images of liberation." These images of liberation will, he argues, utilize an increasingly "irrealistic," modernistic and avant-garde idiom, the more restricted the other domains of social life become through administrative, political, and ideological reduction to a repressive common measure. Art only authentically performs its utopian function by refusing, as a whole, "the standards of the unfree reality" (*SM*, 132):

> The more totalitarian these standards become, the more reality controls all language and all communication, the more irrealistic and surrealistic will art tend to be, the more will it be driven from the concrete to the abstract, from harmony to dissonance, from content to form. Art is thus the refusal of everything that has been made part and parcel of reality.

> The works of the great "bourgeois" antirealists and "formalists" are far deeper committed to the idea of freedom than is socialist and Soviet realism. The irreality of their art expresses the irreality of freedom: art is as transcendental as its object. (*SM*, 132–3)

Consonant with other Stalin-period and Cold War defenses of modernism by leftist intellectuals, such as Clement Greenberg's 1939 essay "Avant-Garde and Kitsch" and Adorno's aesthetic writings, Marcuse here offers a "defensive" theory of modernism in the literature and art of the age of totalitarianism. In response to the narrowing range of social freedom, the arts respond by radicalizing their idiom and forms, risking incommunicability in order to preserve their exemplary otherness from an unfree social whole. He makes this defensive character of "formalism" even more explicit at the conclusion of his chapter on base and superstructure:

> The progressive elements in modern "bourgeois art" were precisely in those structures which preserved the "shock" character of art, that is, those expressing the catastrophic conflict. They represented the desperate attempt to break through the social standardization and falsification which had made the traditional artistic structures unusable for expressing the artistic content. The harmonious forms, in their realistic as well as classical and romantic development, had lost their transcendental, critical force; they stood no longer antagonistic to reality, but appeared as part and adornment of it – as instruments of adjustment . . . Under these circumstances, only their determinate negation could restore their content. (*SM*, 134)

Referring to arguments about music in the Soviet bloc in Adorno's 1948 essay "Die gegängelte Musik" (Constrained Music),[24] Marcuse concludes that Soviet art policy enforces conformity on the "per se nonconformistic artistic imagination" (*SM*, 134), both through repressive means and through the articulation of a constraining, one-dimensional aesthetic that from the outset dictates the limits of transcendence to the Soviet artist. Implicit in Marcuse's discussion, however, is that these broad tendencies towards one-dimensionality are also evident in Western societies: a point he would develop at length in *One-Dimensional Man*. If this is so, then the difference between the West and East in the aesthetic sphere may be crucial. If the East has imposed an official art policy designed to stamp out artistic transcendence, the absence of a single, totalitarian ideology of art in the West, despite the dangers of an increasingly concentrated culture industry, may be a salvational glimmer of hope. There, the still manifest possibilities of the modernist and avant-garde refusal of the existing unfree reality can still offer "images of liberation" that carry emancipatory force. Indeed, with the publication of *One-Dimensional Man*, Marcuse will suggest that all emancipation will follow the model of art's exemplary transcendence – an idea he generalized in that work under the notion of "aesthetic reduction" (*ODM*, 239–46).

In *One-Dimensional Man*, Marcuse concentrates especially on the expanding role that science and technology are playing in structuring contemporary social reality. This effective power exercised through science and technology is not just an outgrowth of their *application* to society, Marcuse argues, but something more fundamental: the socio-political implications of a civilization that in the very infrastructure of its thought is being shaped by techno-scientific values, goals, and methods. Thus, he concludes, any radical change in society will require – and entail as a consequence – a corollary upheaval in fundamental values and needs. But Marcuse introduces a dialectical twist here. He is not, he asserts, arguing for a romantic rejection of science and technology in favor of alternative ideals, such as beauty, community, virtue, and so on: that would be both futilely idealistic and, even were it realizable, regressive. Rather, he seeks to recognize in the advanced development of science and technology, which could relieve human beings of many of the pains and fears they suffer in their struggle to survive, the potential *vehicles* of an alternative ensemble of human values. Marcuse describes this dialectic as one of *translation*, which he expounds, it becomes clear, as the actualization, in the "idiom" of technical pragmatics, of the wishes, hopes, and dreams that human beings formulate in the arts of imagination:

> Industrial society possesses the instrumentalities for transforming the metaphysical into the physical, the inner into the outer, the adventures of the mind into adventures of technology . . . In this process, the relation between the material and intellectual faculties and needs undergoes a fundamental change. The free play of thought and imagination assumes a rational and directing function in the realization of a pacified existence of man and nature. (*ODM*, 234)

He goes on from here to suggest that art, in relation to this potential for a technological "translation" from "metaphysical" imagination to physical reality, has an exemplary role to play, because of a "specific *rationality* of art" (*ODM*, 238).

On the one hand, this rationality is dialectically instantiated by art's negative relation to an irrational social reality: "The powerless, illusory truth of art . . . testifies to the validity of its images. The more blatantly irrational the society becomes, the greater the rationality of the artistic universe" (*ODM*, 239). On the other hand, this particular rationality derives from what Hegel called "aesthetic reduction," the characteristic selectiveness of artworks with respect to a represented reality, which grants them a free autonomy from their context, in which contingency and a lack of freedom prevails. This allows the artwork to exist as if establishing its own world and to set for itself the governing "rules" of that world. "Such transformation is reduction," Marcuse explains,

> because the contingent situation suffers requirements which are external, and which stand in the way of its free realization. These requirements constitute an "apparatus" inasmuch as they are not merely natural but rather subject to free, rational change and development. Thus, the artistic transformation violates the natural object, but the violated is itself oppressive; thus the aesthetic transformation is liberation. (*ODM*, 240)

The art object transgresses the logic and reason of given reality. But insofar as this reality is itself traversed by contingency, violence, and irrationality, the aesthetic "reduction" is not a sin against reason, but rather an assertion of reason against reality's insufficiency.

Two implications follow from this concept of aesthetic reduction. First is that the artwork sets a model for *other* social domains and practices in asserting the transgressive imagination against an irrationally insufficient reality. The "aesthetic reduction" is not confined to art, though it emanates from art and is most clearly – and almost exclusively – exemplified by art in present-day society. Yet not only art, but other social practices can carry out an aesthetic reduction by focusing on the goal of giving "free play" to the whole range of human faculties, which is how Kant and Schiller understood the defining characteristic of the aesthetic. Of course, thinking about urban planning, technical design, or education in these terms would require a radical reorientation, but this is precisely Marcuse's point. To reorient such practices through aesthetic reduction and realize them through technical means would require both radical imagination and revolutionary social change. As he concludes about this extension of aesthetic reduction beyond the arts towards broader reaches of the social totality: "The aesthetic reduction appears in the technological transformation of Nature where and if it succeeds in linking mastery and liberation, directing mastery towards liberation" (*ODM*, 240).

Second, given the pessimistic diagnosis that most of *One-Dimensional Man* offers concerning the closure of thought in science, philosophy, and everyday life, Marcuse strongly implied that only a radically resistant, difficult *modernist* art and literature can now preserve art's exemplary function of negating present reality, modeling the aesthetic reduction, and lending impetus to "aesthetic education" in alternative ways of being and thinking. Even as current social developments push many areas of experience and possibility into the shadows of oblivion, restricting the means of expression so that they become unspeakable, art must resolutely attempt to speak the unspeakable, rescuing these repressed contents from inarticulateness:

> If the established society manages all normal communication, validating or invalidating it in accordance with social requirements, then the values

alien to these requirements may perhaps have no other medium of communication than the abnormal one of fiction. The aesthetic dimension still retains a freedom of expression which enables the writer and artist to call men and things by their name – to name the otherwise unnameable. (*ODM*, 247)

Authentic art, for Marcuse, invalidates a repressive reality by confronting it with the content that it sought to repress. It exemplifies, through aesthetic reduction, a world in which the contingent features of the present have been eliminated. Only insofar as it carries out these functions, in contrast to functions such as entertainment on the one hand and propagandistic communication on the other, may art genuinely encourage liberation in other domains of social practice.

Marcuse in the '60s and '70s: Ambivalence Towards the Avant-Garde

In the remaining portion of this chapter, I will consider a key topic in understanding Marcuse's relation to arts during the period of his maximum cultural impact, the 1960s and early '70s, in which his works found readers both in the radical student movements and in the increasingly politicized art world, where neo-avant-garde and activist artists seemed to be testing some of his ideas in practice. Specifically, Marcuse's liberationist revision of psychoanalysis seemed to find resonance among artists, such as Living Theatre founders Julian Beck and Judith Malina and painter and filmmaker Carolee Schneemann, influenced by a heterodox body of current anti-institutional, psychoanalytically and libidinally oriented thought, including Antonin Artaud, Paul Goodman, Wilhelm Reich, Norman O. Brown, and – Herbert Marcuse.

The 1960s in the United States saw an important convergence between two streams of "avant-garde" thought, both focused on bodily experience and the characteristics of the embodied sensorium. On the one hand, the progressive liberalization of sexual mores, the loosening of rigid gender roles, and a greater degree of social and legal tolerance for a range of erotic expression focused new attention on the sexual experiences of the body.[25] On the other hand, as a result of various new, phenomenologically undergirded artistic practices – among these, abstract expressionism (especially when conceived as "action painting"), performance and happenings, Cagean explorations of non-musical sound and silence, popular and elite uses of electronic technologies in music, and minimalist concerns with specific objects and spatial environments – awareness of sensuous bodily experience, of both artist and audience, as a key constituent of artistic activity increasingly commanded creative and critical attention. Accordingly, under the influence of a growing experimentalism in the arts, a social climate of affluence generating counter-cultural phenomena with accelerating speed, and an increasingly articulate body of theoretical works being read and discussed in artistic and counter-cultural circles, it was only a matter of time until bold new interests in sexual expression came to be conjoined with and articulated through the experimental genres of the artistic avant-garde.

Exemplary of this convergence is a single line that performance artist and filmmaker Carolee Schneemann wrote in her notebook in 1963:

> Sexual damming is expressive damning.[26]

In another entry Schneemann expounds a bit more, arguing that artistic expressivity and the capacity for a sort of emotional authenticity are, in her view, directly connected:

> Capacity for expressive life and for love are insolubly linked; that was my understanding when I taught; saw immediately facing the individuals in a class what their chance for expressive work was and its direct relationship to their social / sexual and emotional life.[27]

In one respect, this is hardly an original observation. It reiterates a view of expressive creativity that dates back to European romanticism, in which, in M.H. Abrams classic image, the artistic mind as the "mirror" of reality was supplanted by a new metaphor, the mind as a "lamp" that projects its illumination onto the artistic canvas or page. Of interest here, however, is the peculiar nature of that romantic lamp for a wide range of artists and aesthetic thinkers in the America of the 1960s (and of course, not just in the United States). It is a artistic lamp fueled by libidinal energy, in a desublimated and relatively direct form: a lamp of romantic expressivity shaped by Freudian and post-Freudian theories of the unconscious; touched by the newly disinhibited popular culture of the 1960s, including the youth counter-culture and the experience of rock music and possibly drug experimentation; and bearing traces of sexual liberationist thinking from heterodox intellectuals ranging from Reich and Goodman to Brown and Marcuse.

The dovetailing of transmedial avant-garde artistic practices with ideas of sexual liberation offered an emotionally charged way for artists to assert that their artistic work, in transcending the bounded artistic medium – especially painting – had opened onto a utopian threshold of a fully actual new sensibility wider than but also continuous with art.[28] In one respect, the task of this erotic anti-formalism was critical and iconoclastic: "I had to get that nude off the canvas, frozen flesh to art history's conjunction of perceptual erotics and an immobilizing social position" (Schneemann).[29] Yet it also projected a radical heightening and extension of the senses in ways that go beyond artistic experience as such, to adumbrate an erotic transformation of everyday social experience. Schneemann, for example, described this as a process of entering the image and being activated by it. Her formulation embraces both the popular culture images of the mass media as well as the artistic images she was painting, filming, performing, and installing as spatial-experiential environments: "We were being moved, we were being affected by images bringing information that was startling and taboo and terrible and made you convinced you had to do something. To enter the image itself! Activation as an intervention into the politics behind the revelatory images."[30] "Activation," in Schneemann's sense, entailed a new sort of image-mediated, aesthetic-political implication of the individual in the social, which was, however, already anticipated in the theoretical reflections of heterodox avant-garde theorists of the 1920s and '30s such as Walter Benjamin in his essay on surrealism and his cultural history of nineteenth-century Paris, the *Arcades Project*.[31]

The motif in Marcuse's work of an erotically transformed sensibility, a revolutionized and reembodied "aesthetic" of which artistic practice is a kind of anticipatory recollection, is closely tied to his revisionary reading of psychoanalysis in the mid-1950s in his book *Eros and Civilization*, especially with respect to Freud's speculations on culture and instinctual repression. In his speculative work of meta-psychology *Civilization and Its Discontents*, Freud had argued that social order and the capacity for labor depends upon a deferral of satisfaction of instinctual pleasure. Therefore, the more advanced a civilization becomes, the more ramified and complete becomes its means of repressing the unconscious forces that achieve satisfaction in sexual pleasure. Yet with greater repression, according to Freud, comes psychic conflict and neurosis. Civilization is thus haunted by two dangers: the temptation towards irrational, destructive irruptions of dammed-up instinctual forces (as Freud further expounded in his essay "Why War?") and the channeling of repressed instinctual satisfaction into pathological expressions (symptoms, anxieties, hysteria, etc.).

Marcuse, like his friend Norman O. Brown in his 1959 book *Life Against Death: The Psychoanalytic Meaning of History*, offered a powerful critique of Freud's pessimistic theory of civilization. While Marcuse and Brown accepted Freud's pessimism as essentially a clear-sighted view of present-day modern society, they drew critical and activist implications from this analysis rather than resignation. Thus, for example, Marcuse recapitulated in a philosophical explication of Freud's theory both the ontogenetic (individual) and phylogenetic (civilizational) implications of repression. His emphasis falls on the dialectical implication of the individual in the social constitution and, in turn, the continuity of individual psychic structures with the demands and contradictions of civilizational social formations. Thus, for example, he writes of sexuality that its organization

> reflects the basic features of the performance principle and its organization of society. Freud emphasizes the aspect of centralization. It is

especially operative in the "unification" of the various objects of the partial instincts into one libidinal object of the opposite sex, and in the establishment of genital supremacy. In both cases, the unifying process is repressive. (*EC*, 48)

Implicit in Marcuse's formulation is a view of capitalist modernity influenced by Marx and Weber, in which the centralization, integration, and rationalization of capitalist production leads to a coordinated, monopolistic organization of society as a whole. Marcuse implies that Freudian repression extends this centralizing tendency to the psychic economy, ultimately serving to adapt the individual subject to the social apparatus of production and domination. Like Brown, however, Marcuse challenged Freud's conservative conclusions about the *necessary* connections of civilization and repression, and hence also Freud's conclusion that the more cultured humanity becomes, the more civilization advances, the more prevalent neurotic illness and irrational outbreaks of violence and aggression become inevitable, such as had been witnessed in the two great European wars of the twentieth century. Marcuse and Brown viewed this connection of civilization and repression as "necessary" only in a historical sense. At a certain point in social development, they argued, repression was the historical means by which civilization had progressed, but under the emerging historical conditions of advanced technology and industrial abundance, the contingency of repression in the civilizing process was becoming ever more evident. In fact, by the mid-twentieth century, its progressive aspect had been eclipsed by its potential to release aggressiveness and occasion psychic damage. The major premise of Marcuse's *Eros and Civilization* was one that he shared with other Frankfurt School thinkers, especially Theodor W. Adorno, that the historical individual was a product not of an immutable nature, but rather of a particular configuration of social forces that were, in the middle decades of the twentieth century, increasingly in doubt.

Under the impact of the massive advances in modern technology as well as the forms of mass politics observable both in totalitarian societies such as the Stalinist Soviet Union and Nazi Germany and in democratic mass societies such as in the United States and Western Europe, this historical individual was increasingly a residual form of personal subjectivity. Marcuse drew this conclusion explicitly in connection with his critique of psychoanalysis: "As psychology tears the ideological veil and traces the construction of the personality, it is led to dissolve the individual: his autonomous personality appears as the *frozen* manifestation of the general repression of mankind" (*EC*, 57). Since psychoanalysis as articulated classically by Sigmund Freud and his followers took the individual person as its basic unit of theorization and of analysis, there was, however, a certain unsettling of classical psychoanalysis as well. In fact, Marcuse dedicated a 1963 essay to precisely this theme, bearing the telling title "The Obsolescence of the Freudian Concept of Man."[32] Nevertheless, this historical displacement of the individual unit of personhood from the focal point of psychoanalytic theory did not mean for Marcuse the abandonment of Freud's thought, but rather its revision in light of the new modes of socialization that he was seeing emerge at mid-century. In particular, Marcuse argued that the previous *psychological* focus of Freudian thought had to be rethought in *political categories* – or better put, that Freud's categories were already, in the present context, collective-political rather than individual-psychological concepts. He expounded:

> formerly autonomous and identifiable psychical processes are being absorbed by the function of the individual in the state – by his public existence. Psychological problems therefore turn into political problems: private disorder reflects more directly than before the disorder of the whole, and the cure of personal disorder depends more directly than before on the cure of the general disorder. (*EC*, xvii)

Utilizing this broad hypothesis about the socialization of the Freudian subject, and hence the corollary politicization of Freudian theoretical categories, Marcuse was able to envision forms of liberation that hovered ambiguously between literal and more figurative, analogical interpretations of what this might mean for political practice, for liberatory and revolutionary struggle. Changing the world, in the Marxian sense, meant liberating the person, understood in the Freudian sense, with its formative structure of instinctive drives, insistent demands for pleasure, and the repressions and sublimations that for Freud generate civilization, culture, morality – as well as neurotic illness. As Marcuse argued:

> Freud's correlation "instinctual repression – socially useful labor – civilization" can be meaningfully transformed into the correlation "instinctual liberation – socially useful work – civilization." We have suggested that the prevalent instinctual repression resulted, not so much from the necessity of labor, but from the specific social organization of labor imposed by the interest in domination – that repression was largely surplus-repression. Consequently, the elimination of surplus-repression would *per se* tend to eliminate, not labor, but the organization of the human existence into an instrument of labor. If this is true, the emergence of a non-repressive reality principle would alter rather than destroy the social organization of labor: the liberation of Eros could create new and durable work relations. (*EC*, 155)

What, however, was to be the precise nature of the praxis that could effect this dual change, revolutionizing society by liberating the subject and liberating the subject in the course of revolutionizing society? As it turns out, for Marcuse the "aesthetic" plays a key role in thinking through this question.

For Marcuse, the repression of sexual pleasure, as an instrument of the "civilizing process," the disciplining of the body and its powers for labor and social order, has a paradoxical result. In his view, sexual pleasure represents a positive, vital way in which human beings channel potentially destructive impulses and energies. Intensified sexual repression – narrowly genital sexuality as socially "useful" or "productive" sexuality, as well as the limitation of sexuality as such in the interest of the "performance principle" – leads in his view to the intensification of unresolved destructive forces. Therefore, increasing sexual repression, which Freud saw as necessary to the civilizing process itself, reaches its limits and undergoes a dialectical reversal. The civilizing process becomes anti-civilizational, turning in destructive ways against the civilized achievements it brought about. A similar thesis had been advanced by Marcuse's Frankfurt School colleagues Theodor Adorno and Max Horkheimer in *Dialectic of Enlightenment* in the late 1940s. Unlike the deeply pessimistic conclusions Adorno and Horkheimer drew from this Freudian anthropology, however, Marcuse emphasized the utopian project implicit in reversing this anti-civilizational tendency of a civilization based on domination and repression. If repression and domination were, in fact, the source of previous civilization, there was another way possible: to realize the potentials of a new civilizational dynamic based on overcoming repression, on gratification of the senses; a civilization rooted not in dominated labor and the domination of nature through labor, but upon the restructuring of labor as play in new forms of harmony with nature.

Marcuse explicitly called upon the German aesthetic tradition, particularly Friedrich Schiller's *On the Aesthetic Education of Man*, to suggest how aesthetics could be realized – realized in the sense of made real and effective – in the form of a society of free play and of enjoyment. In his famous twenty-seventh letter, Schiller introduced the notion of the "aesthetic state," in which the constraints of both physical and moral law have been lifted in favor of free play under the aegis of beauty. Although physical and moral necessity are crucial preconditions of society, only the aesthetic state makes society fully "real," Schiller stresses. This is because in Schiller's view only the forms of communication that are characteristic of the aesthetic – the apprehension of and participation in beauty – may authentically unite the free and autonomous individual with the substantive bonds of society: "It consummates the will of the whole through the nature of the individual. Though it may be his needs which drive man into society, and reason which implants within him the principles of social behavior, beauty alone can confer upon him a social character."[33] At the same time, however, Schiller equivocates about the "actuality" of the aesthetic state, which, he qualifies, may only exist on condition of its remaining "Schein": appearance, manifestation, semblance. In the very last paragraph of his text, he indicates both the possibility and rarity of an existent aesthetic state, since it exists largely as an inner spiritual need, while remaining almost unimaginable in the empirical world:

> But does such a State of Aesthetic Semblance really exist? And if so, where is it to be found? As a need, it exists in every finely attuned soul; as a realized fact, we are likely to find it, like the pure Church and the pure Republic, only in some few chosen circles, where conduct is governed, not by some soulless imitation of the manners and morals of others, but by the aesthetic nature we have made our own.[34]

In other words, in the current less-than-ideal situation of society, where physical and moral compulsion still predominate over freedom, the "aesthetic state" remains at best the sign of an educational ideal to be realized in the future, while presently only existent among a rarified, even possibly fictive elite.

As both Fredric Jameson and Josef Chytry have discussed,[35] Marcuse reworks Schiller's hypothesis of the aesthetic state in the form of a utopian overcoming of repression as the basis of the social organization of work. In his most optimistically utopian work, *An Essay on Liberation* from 1969, Marcuse put this explicitly in a formula in a chapter entitled "The New Sensibility," meaning the collective invention of a new sensory environment and new sensuous capacities: "The aesthetic as the possible Form of a free society."[36] Although he criticizes Schiller's failure to press his conception of the aesthetic state from a condition of inwardness to an external, "political" realization in external reality, Marcuse still ascribes an "explosive quality" to Schiller's conception. Whereas Schiller had diagnosed a conflict between a repressively formed reason and the order of sensuousness, in restoring the "right of sensuousness," Schiller nevertheless opened a literally revolutionary path to freedom:

> The reconciliation of the conflicting impulses would involve the removal of this tyranny . . . Freedom would have to be sought in the liberation of sensuousness rather than reason, and in the limitation of the "higher" faculties in favor of the "lower." In other words, the salvation of culture would involve the abolition of the repressive controls that civilization had imposed on sensuousness. And this is indeed the idea behind the *Aesthetic Education*. (EC, 190)

Marcuse goes on to spell out the socially transformative implications of this view. Not only do individual spiritual and psychological characteristics realize themselves in different ways, but also the objective social terrain of their realization must be restructured if the liberation of sensuousness is to succeed. "The additional release of sensuous energy," Marcuse writes, "must conform with the universal *order* of freedom . . . The free individual himself must bring about the harmony between individual and universal gratification . . . Order is freedom only if it is founded on and sustained by the free gratification of the individuals" (*EC*, 191).

Besides his more classically philosophical antecedents such as Schiller, Marcuse's subsequent call in the 1960s to break through the one-dimensional world of commodified experience and to liberate the senses in a new, utopian framework of collective and individual enjoyment was clearly indebted to his ideas of polymorphous perversity and the affirmation of Eros expounded in his earlier critique of Freud. Thus, for example, in his 1966 so-called "Political Preface" to his re-released *Eros and Civilization* (originally published in 1955), Marcuse reiterated his emphasis on the liberation of bodily needs, including the expression of previously repressed or frustrated forms of sexuality:

> "Polymorphous sexuality" was the term which I used to indicate that the new direction of progress would depend completely on the opportunity to activate repressed or arrested *organic*, biological needs: to make the human body an instrument of pleasure rather than labor. The old formula, the development of prevailing needs and faculties, seemed to be inadequate; the emergence of new, qualitatively different needs and faculties seemed to be the prerequisite, the content of liberation. (*EC*, xv)

If one were to ask how these could be actualized as play and just what this play might look like, however, we might easily conclude that Marcuse's ideas resonate with analogous utopian experiments explored throughout the 1960s by the artistic avant-garde, particularly in the sphere of theater, performance, and experimental film.

For example, Carolee Schneemann, quoted earlier, created a number of performance and film works in the mid-1960s that depicted, with a high degree of literal explicitness, acts of individual and group sex. These include, most famously, her performance-dance piece *Meat Joy* (1964) and her film *Fuses* (1965). As Schneemann explained –

> *Meat Joy* has the character of an erotic rite: excessive, indulgent, a celebration of flesh as material: raw fish, chicken, sausages, wet paint, transparent plastic, rope, brushes, paper scrap. Its propulsion is toward the ecstatic – shifting and turning between tenderness, wildness, precision, abandon: qualities which could at any moment be sensual, comic, joyous, repellent. Physical equivalences are enacted as a psychic and imagistic stream in which the layered elements mesh and gain intensity by the energy complement of the audience . . . Our proximity heightened the sense of communality, transgressing the polarity between performer and audience.[37]

Notably, Schneemann was also a highly politicized artist, especially engaged in protest against the Vietnam War in contemporaneous works such as her film *Viet Flakes* (1966) and her "kinetic theater" piece *Snows* (1967), both of which utilized atrocity photographs from the war in Indochina as image-materials. Just as *Meat Joy* encompassed the individual within an orgiastic mingling of bodies, so too *Snows* was immersive, but in a frightening and horrifying way:

> We were actually frightened in *Snows*. The experience was all-enveloping, making us aware of the audience as an extension of ourselves, but not of ourselves in self-conscious presentation. Walking the planks was dangerous, and the central imagery of *Viet Flakes*, once fully apparent as dire and agonizing, confounded our own pleasurable expectations and collaborations within the glistening white environment.[38]

One can think of these various works as representing complementary, if antithetical depictions of the individual female body as the pivot of collective suffering and pleasure, an enactment of critique of repression and violence on the one hand, and a positive utopian projection of a new, liberated social community on the other.[39] Moreover, if *Viet Flakes* and *Snows* exhibited the individualized, damaged body suffering the onslaught of military violence, *Meat Joy* and *Fuses* built up a collective image of liberation through the intensities of the body experiencing erotic pleasure:

> In the mid-sixties, when I began my film *Fuses* and the performance *Meat Joy*, I was thinking about "eroticizing my guilty culture." I saw a cultural task combined with a personal dilemma. My work was dependent on my sexuality – its satisfaction, integrity. I couldn't work without a coherent sexual relationship – that fueled my imagination, my energies. My mind works out of the knowledge of the body.[40]

Similar polarities between the suffering body in protest and the orgiastic body in erotic enjoyment also marked the influential performance works of Julian Beck and Judith Malina's Living Theatre.[41] Works such as *The Brig* (1963), set in a military prison, and *Frankenstein* (1966) subjected audiences to a visceral experience of contemporary culture's repressive sado-masochism. In contrast, *The Mysteries* (1964) and *Paradise Now* (1968) celebrated collective erotic revolt, inviting audiences to experience in a physically participatory way the company's "paradisal" celebration of bodies communing in sexual pleasure, a kind of radical schooling in the liberationist "aesthetic education" that Marcuse seemed to espouse. In a special issue of *The Drama Review* dedicated in 1969 to the return of the Living Theatre to the US after five years in Europe, critic Stefan Brecht explained the Living Theatre's project in terms of a psychoanalytically inflected ritual of inducing collective psychic crisis and reconstruction:

> The "ego" of the normal neurotic is to be destroyed, his natural spiritual powers to be liberated. Three schemata seem operative. A chain-reaction is expected from a direct attack on the ego. The destruction of inhibitions is to free creative functions, which then gather their own psychic energies. And/or: the audience's spontaneity is to be triggered, if necessary by provocation into antagonism or defense: the volitional energy mobilized might disintegrate the ego, might mobilize the natural spiritual powers. Or, finally, libido, imagination, love might be attacked directly, their stimulation resulting in de-inhibition and in a mobilization of autonomous energy. The Living Theatre seems to be trying a little of each, not just the last as some gentle admirers might have expected.[42]

Like Schneemann informed especially by a politicized, utopian reading of Antonin Artaud and Wilhelm Reich, the Living Theatre sought to constitute, through a theatricalized communication with their audiences, a new erotic free association of liberated individuals, adumbrating the experiences and forms of an anarchistically free society: at once a theatrical space, a pedagogical space of individual and collective learning, and an exemplar of anarchistic, communal living.

Interestingly, however, Marcuse consistently expressed his ambivalence towards those very artworks and artistic tendencies that would appear to have been lending his ideas a translation into actions and objects. Even in *An Essay on Liberation*, where he was calling for a utopian reinvention of society along aesthetic lines, he at the same time stubbornly defended the autonomy of art:

> The wild revolt of art has remained a short-lived shock, quickly absorbed in the art gallery, within the four walls, in the concert hall, by the market, and adorning the plazas and lobbies of the prospering business establishments . . . Transforming the intent of art is self-defeating – a self-defeat build into the very structure of art . . . The very Form of art contradicts the effort to do away with the segregation of art to a "second reality," to translate the truth of the productive imagination into the first reality.[43]

In a 1969 address at the Guggenheim Museum in New York entitled "Art as Form of Reality," Marcuse criticized "anti-art" tendencies and singled out the Living Theatre as a mode of art which, though intended to attack ideological illusion, ends up deepening it:

> The "living art," and especially the "living theatre" of today, does away with the Form of estrangement: in eliminating the distance between the actors, the audience, and the "outside," it establishes a familiarity and identification with the actors and their message which quickly draws the negation, the rebellion into the daily universe – as an enjoyable and

understandable element of this universe. The participation of the audience is spurious and the result of previous arrangements; the change in consciousness and behavior is itself part of the play – illusion is strengthened rather than destroyed.[44]

By 1972, his criticisms of the Living Theatre's liberationist spectacle would become even more pointed. Referencing Malina and Beck's "Collective Creation of the Living Theatre," *Paradise Now*, Marcuse wrote:

> The Living Theatre may serve as an example of self-defeating purpose. It makes a systematic attempt to unite the theater and the Revolution, the play and the battle, bodily and spiritual liberation, individual internal and social external change. But this union is shrouded in mysticism . . . The liberation of the body, the sexual revolution, becoming a ritual to be performed . . . loses its place in the political revolution: if sex is a voyage to God, it can be tolerated even in extreme forms . . . The radical desublimation which takes place in the theater, *as* theater, is organized, arranged, performed desublimation – it is close to turning into its opposite.[45]

Marcuse harbored a keen suspicion of the possibility that cultural radicalism might be co-opted to aesthetic ends, extreme revolutionary sentiments be ritualized as a pleasurable yet harmless transgression of bourgeois norms, and revolt get frozen in spectacular forms. For Marcuse by this time, in contrast to his anti-affirmative culture stance of the 1930s, autonomous art paradoxically seems an apotropaic protection against such aestheticization. Art, in its deployment of semblance and form, makes no disguise of its estrangement from reality and hence is less rather than more related to dialectical, critical or speculative (i.e. "two-dimensional") truth than "anti-art" or "living theater." For Marcuse, these latter modes of art, in collapsing the distinction between positive reality and artistic reality, lapse into the complementary errors of positivist immediacy and mysticism.

Above all in his late book *The Aesthetic Dimension* (1978) – or, in its even more striking German title, *Die Permanenz der Kunst* (1977) – Marcuse explicitly disavowed possible avant-garde implications of his own thought. In this work, he defends the capacity of art to allow us to imagine an alternative reality that exceeds the limits of actuality. Yet this capacity to create a heterocosmic image of another world depends on art's not being confused for something in the real world. In other words, for Marcuse, art must be autonomous to function in a critical-utopian fashion. Moreover, "anti-art," in relinquishing the ontological otherness of art's formed mimesis, only apparently disintegrates the repressive unities that it seeks to undo. In reality, it yields to another kind of mimesis, a compulsive imitation of administrative power, which can abstractly coordinate any content under schematic, blindly applied bureaucratic heuristics:

> The various phases and trends of anti-art or non-art share a common assumption – namely, that the modern period is characterized by a disintegration of reality which renders any self-enclosed form, any intention of meaning . . . untrue, if not impossible. The collage, or the juxtaposition of media, or the renunciation of any aesthetic mimesis are held to be adequate responses to given reality, which, disjoined and fragmented, militates against any aesthetic formation. This assumption is in flat contradiction to the actual state of affairs. We are experiencing, not the destruction of every whole, every unit or unity, every meaning, but rather the rule and power of the whole, the superimposed, administered unification. Not disintegration but reproduction and integration of that which is, is the catastrophe. And in the intellectual culture of our society, it is the aesthetic form which, by virtue of its otherness, can stand up against this integration.[46]

Art, in this view, must remain in ontological tension with our actual world and not seek to become realized within it. Marcuse thus gives a firm rejection to much of what was programmatic for both the avant-garde and for more agitational, activist forms of political art in the twentieth century.

NOTES

1. Morton Schoolman, "Marcuse's Aesthetics and the Displacement of Critical Theory," *New German Critique* 8 (1976), p. 79.
2. Timothy J. Lukes, *The Flight into Inwardness: An Exposition and Critique of Herbert Marcuse's Theory of Liberative Aesthetics* (Selingrove: Susquehanna University Press, 1985).
3. Barry Katz, *Herbert Marcuse and the Art of Liberation: An Intellectual Biography* (London: Verso, 1982).
4. Charles Reitz, *Art, Alienation, and the Humanities: A Critical Engagement with Herbert Marcuse* (Albany: State University of New York Press, 2000).
5. Gerhard Schweppenhäuser, "Art as Cognition and Rememberance: Autonomy and Transformation of Art in Herbert Marcuse's Aesthetics," Afterword to Herbert Marcuse, *Art and Liberation*, Collected Papers, Volume 4, ed. Douglas Kellner (New York: Routledge, 2007), pp. 237–56.
6. See preceding note.
7. Kellner in Marcuse, *Art and Liberation*, p. 67.
8. Reitz, *Art, Alienation, and the Humanities*, p. 16.
9. Herbert Marcuse, *Gespräche mit Herbert Marcuse* (Frankfurt a/M: Suhrkamp Verlag, 1978), p. 43.
10. Marcuse, *Gespräche mit Herbert Marcuse*, p. 49.
11. Gregory Battcock, "Herbert Marcuse," in *Why Art: Casual Notes on the Aesthetics of the Immediate Past* (New York: E.P. Dutton and Co., 1977), p. 36.
12. See, for example, Gregory Battcock, "Marcuse and Anti-Art," *Arts Magazine* 43/8 (1969), pp. 17–19, and Ursula Meyer, "De-Objectification of the Object,"

Arts Magazine 43/8 (1969), pp. 20–2. *Arts Magazine*, with which Battcock was a special correspondent, carried Herbert Marcuse's speech "Art in the One-Dimensional Society" as the cover page of its May 1967 issue.

13. Alex Alberro, "Reductivism in Reverse," in *Tracing Cultures: Art History, Criticism, Critical Fiction* (New York: Whitney Museum of American Art, 1994), p. 8.
14. Quoted in Alberro, "Reductivism in Reverse," p. 10.
15. Reitz, *Art, Alienation, and the Humanities*, p. 9.
16. Reitz, *Art, Alienation, and the Humanities*, pp. 248–9. For a collection that includes two lectures on education by Marcuse and several critical essays discussing educational aspects of Marcuse's work, see *Marcuse's Challenge to Education*, ed. Douglas Kellner et al. (Lanham, MD: Rowman and Littlefield, 2009).
17. Herbert Marcuse, "On the Affirmative Character of Culture," in *Art and Liberation*, pp. 81–112.
18. Reitz, *Art, Alienation, and the Humanities*, p. 84.
19. Ernst Jünger, "Total Mobilization," in *The Heidegger Controversy*, ed. Richard Wolin (Cambridge, MA: The MIT Press, 2005), pp. 119–39.
20. István Örkény, *One Minute Stories* (Budapest: Corvina, 1995).
21. Ernst Jünger, *Der Arbeiter: Herrschaft und Gestalt* (Stuttgart: Klett Cotta Verlag, 2013).
22. Marcuse, *Gespräche mit Herbert Marcuse*, p. 44.
23. Marcuse, *Gespräche mit Herbert Marcuse*, pp. 135–6.
24. Theodor W. Adorno, *Die gegängelte Musik: Bemerkungen über die Musikpolitik der Ostblockstaaten* (Frankfurt a/M: Eremiten-Presse, 1954).
25. See, for example, the cultural historical account of this process in David Allyn, *Make Love Not War: The Sexual Revolution: An Unfettered History* (New York: Routledge, 2001).
26. Carolee Schneemann, *More Than Meat Joy: Performance Works and Selected Writings*, ed. Bruce R. McPherson (Kingston, New York: Documentext, 1979/1997), p. 57.
27. Schneemann, *More Than Meat Joy*, p. 57.
28. See Sally Banes, *Greenwich Village 1963: Avant-Garde Performance and the Effervescent Body* (Durham, NC: Duke University Press, 1993), for a discussion of this tendency in 1960s American art.
29. Carolee Schneemann, "Interview with Kate Haug" (1979), reprinted in *Carolee Schneemann: Imagining Her Erotics* (Cambridge, MA: The MIT Press, 2002), p. 28.
30. Schneemann, *Carolee Schneemann: Imagining Her Erotics*, p. 37.
31. See on this point, Sigrid Weigel, "'Body- and Image Space': Traces Through Benjamin's Writings," in *Body- and Image-Space: Re-reading Walter Benjamin*, pp. 16–29.
32. Herbert Marcuse, *Five Lectures* (Boston: Beacon Press, 1970), pp. 44–61.
33. Friedrich Schiller, *On the Aesthetic Education of Man*, ed. Elizabeth M. Wilkinson and L.A. Willoughby (Oxford: Clarendon Press, 1967), p. 215.
34. Schiller, *On the Aesthetic Education of Man*, p. 219.
35. Fredric Jameson, *Marxism and Form: Twentieth-Century Dialectical Theories of Literature* (Princeton: Princeton University Press, 1974), pp. 83–115; Josef Chytry, *The Aesthetic State: A Quest in Modern German Thought* (Berkeley and Los Angeles: University of California Press, 1989).
36. Herbert Marcuse, *An Essay on Liberation* (Boston: Beacon Press, 1969), p. 25.
37. Schneemann, *More Than Meat Joy*, p. 68.
38. Schneemann, *Carolee Schneemann: Imagining Her Erotics*, p. 76.

39. For a more general treatment of this tendency towards experimental community in US art of the 1960s, see Banes, *Greenwich Village 1963: Avant-Garde Performance and the Effervescent Body*.
40. Schneemann, *Carolee Schneemann: Imagining Her Erotics*, p. 133.
41. On the Living Theatre, see John Tytell, *The Living Theatre: Art, Exile, and Outrage* (New York: Grove Press, 1995), and Pierre Biner, *The Living Theatre: A History Without Myths*, trans. Robert Meister (New York: Grove Press, 1972).
42. Stefan Brecht, "Revolution at the Brooklyn Academy of Music," *TDR: The Drama Review* 13/3 (1969), pp. 57.
43. Marcuse, *An Essay on Liberation*, p. 42.
44. Marcuse, "Art as Form of Reality," in *Art and Liberation*, p. 146.
45. Herbert Marcuse, *Counterrevolution and Revolt* (Boston: Beacon Press, 1972), p. 113.
46. Herbert Marcuse, *The Aesthetic Dimension: Toward a Critique of Marxist Aesthetics* (Boston: Beacon Press, 1978), pp. 49–50.

5

THE NEW WAVE: MODERNISM AND MODERNITY IN THE LATER FRANKFURT SCHOOL

The works of the early Frankfurt School thinkers discussed in the preceding chapters – Benjamin, Adorno, and Marcuse – have made an enduring impact on aesthetics and criticism across the arts, and, as I have argued, are particularly adapted to enrich our understanding of the twentieth-century modernist and avant-garde manifestations. They have been taken up repeatedly, debated, and reinterpreted in light of various emerging critical tendencies: the arguments around cultural politicization and media raised by the New Left and the student movement; cultural studies' reappraisal of popular and mass culture; the postmodernism debates of the 1980s and '90s; the "end of utopia" arguments that accompanied the collapse of actually existing socialism in 1989–91; the renewal of interest in the "culture industry" hypothesis with the unprecedented global media concentration and extension in the digital age; and so on. Moreover, these discussions have been enriched by an increasing availability of previously unedited, uncollected, or untranslated works, especially by Benjamin (the Harvard University Press collection of his writings and of the *Arcades Project* in English translation) and Adorno (both new volumes added to his *Gesammelte Schriften* and new translations of published works, lectures, and letters). New Modernist Studies in the United States and UK, represented by such key journals as *Modernism / Modernity* and *Modernist Cultures*, have been strongly influenced by this ongoing, steadily expanding appropriation of Frankfurt School thought by scholars of modernism.

In this chapter, however, I cannot even briefly survey this larger and longer-term reception and reinterpretation of the early Frankfurt School. I will instead focus on three German intellectuals who can be seen as direct heirs of the early Frankfurt School: the literary critic Peter Bürger, the philosopher Albrecht Wellmer, and the novelist, filmmaker, and cultural theorist Alexander Kluge. I have deliberately chosen these three examples of intellectuals working in heterogeneous, if interrelated areas of cultural production to suggest a range of perspectives and the critical reach that the Frankfurt School's interdisciplinary project has continued to have in later generations. Though I attempt to hint at the larger context of their thought and work, I will need to further restrict myself to discussing their specific intervention into the question of modernism and the avant-garde, via their critical reevaluations of the work of Benjamin, Adorno, and/or Marcuse.

Peter Bürger: The Avant-Garde's Critique of Artistic Autonomy

Peter Bürger's *Theory of the Avant-Garde*, which appeared in German in 1974 and in English in 1984, represents an extremely influential extension of the Frankfurt School's critical treatment of modernism. In this book and many related books and essays, Bürger fundamentally reframes discussions of modernism and the avant-garde through critiques of Frankfurt School thinkers such as Benjamin, Adorno, and Marcuse, as well as other Marxist literary theorists such as Lukács. Though his arguments have been contested from a number of perspectives for their reductiveness and lack of clear fit with the empirical histories of art and literature that they sought to encompass, the streamlined power of his conceptual framework also contributed to its importance for scholars of modernism and the avant-garde.

Bürger focuses on the function of art in bourgeois society, which is, in his view, to allow various social contents to be experienced *aesthetically*, with a sensuous vividness and at a distance from the realm of instrumental or cognitive purposiveness. Art's social "function" of representing that which is free from functionality historically depended, Bürger argues, on the development of an autonomous institution of art that quarantined it into special realms for its production and consumption: studios, academies, art exhibitions, salons, concerts, recitations, performances, and so on. These interrelated spaces and practices of art, along with criticism, artistic histories, and aesthetics that elaborated a specialized discourse around them, together constitute an institutionalized "art world" that supports the autonomy of art in its socially unique function. Of course, this autonomy is always, in any historical instance, more or less permeable to other social influences and functions, and even extreme art-for-art's-sake is inflected by the socially purposeful functions it actively refuses (i.e. *not*-communicating, *not*-instructing, *not*-representing national culture, *not*-being morally edifying, *not*-advocating for a political or social position). Yet for all its relativeness, artistic autonomy is effectively real in bourgeois society, which subsumes and further develops an elaborate ensemble of material spaces, objects, practices, and discourses of art. In the historical trajectory of autonomous art from the sixteenth to the early twentieth century, the more intensively that the institutional autonomy of art is developed, Bürger argues, the more art's purposeless purpose becomes troubling to artists and related cultural intellectuals. The emergence of the avant-gardes of the early twentieth century represents, he concludes, a backlash against this perceived purposelessness of art and an attack on the institutions of autonomy that undergird it. The artists and intellectuals of the avant-garde seek to restore social, political, moral, and existential efficacy to art, which had, in their view, been sapped from it by its delimitation, institutionally and discursively, to an increasingly narrow field of aesthetic experience. The avant-garde, thus, raises to a level of conscious reflection and advocacy the question of the existing and potential *functions* of art, which define its social character.

This general questioning of artistic autonomy gives rise to the early twentieth-century crisis of traditional art and literature and the experimental ferment as new forms and functions are explored. It is also significant historiographically: in questioning the functions of art and their institutional presuppositions, Bürger argues, the early twentieth-century avant-gardes allowed the whole of art and literary history to become legible in a new way. The prehistory and genesis, as well as various possible endings and afterlives, of a certain historical conception of art, once thought to represent Art in its totality, can be parsed for the first time. Through this powerful meta-narrative leading from the institution of autonomous art to the avant-garde break and beyond, Bürger thus evolves an institutional and functional theory of modern art that critically synthesizes various Hegelian-Marxist and Frankfurt School theoretical motifs.

With respect to the Frankfurt School critical legacy (and leaving out of consideration here other parts of his rich, highly condensed discussion in *Theory of the Avant-Garde*), Bürger considers various key theses from the modernist aesthetics of Benjamin, Adorno, and Marcuse, already discussed in detail in my preceding chapters. For example, early in his book, Bürger weighs and ultimately rejects Benjamin's celebrated theses about technical reproducibility as the driving force of the crisis of modern art, theses which played a key role in debates about the politicization of art in the late 1960s and early '70s in Germany and again in the postmodernist critical positions of art journals such as *October* in the 1980s.[1] Benjamin's technical reproducibility thesis is important for Bürger, however, not just because of its currency in the German left culture debates of the period. It also represents a strong alternative explanation of the very same phenomena Bürger himself considers as the central problem to address by means of a theory of the avant-garde. Benjamin acknowledged and offered a theoretical hypothesis about the general crisis of the arts in the interwar decades, positing that through the increasing role of technicity in the production and dissemination of art, its aesthetic function was being repurposed in favor of didactic, political (e.g. propaganda), and commercial (e.g. design, advertising, entertainment, etc.) goals. So too Bürger focuses on many of the same artistic manifestations, such as those associated with Dadaism, constructivism, and surrealism, but with an alternative explanation rooted in the avant-garde break with aestheticism and the avant-gardes' reimagining of the institutional spaces and functions of art. He suggests that despite intuitive insightfulness, Benjamin misidentifies the essence of the problem at hand – the rapid refunctioning of art, which leads to a general crisis of art in its traditional form – and instead retroactively constructs a hypothesis to explain that which, properly understood, is more the precipitating cause: "One cannot wholly resist the impression that Benjamin wanted to provide an *ex post facto* materialist foundation for a discovery he owed to his commerce with avant-gardiste art, the discovery of the loss of aura" (*TAG*, 29). Still, in a strong sense Benjamin sets the critical agenda for Bürger's theory, which is developed through critique: by revealing the degree and limits of validity of Benjamin's theory of technical reproducibility as an explanation of the interwar crisis of art and aesthetics.

Later in the book, Bürger adopts aspects of Benjamin's theory of allegory to interpret the change in the status of the modern art "work," its loss of wholeness and the prevalence of "montage" as its formal principle, its construction through a juxtaposition of parts without a larger synthetic form being presupposed. Benjamin himself developed his concept of allegory first in relation to northern baroque theater and visual art and later in connection with the commodity-world of nineteenth-century Paris, hence not directly in association with the art of the avant-garde. Yet there are ways in which his descriptions of the baroque allegory's heaping of up of disparate, fragmentary elements into mosaic-like, multi-semiotic compositions could just as easily apply to the Dadaistic Merz-collages of Kurt Schwitters or the "combines" of Robert Rauschenberg as to seventeenth-century emblem books. Bürger schematizes Benjamin's allegory concept into two pairs of hypotheses, the first pair having to do with the procedures of producing allegorical works and the latter pair involving the interpretation of these procedures. On the production side, Benjamin sees the overall fragmentary, incomplete nature of the work as definitive of the allegorical work of art. Along with this, he argues, the work's meaning is imposed upon conjoined, isolated fragments rather than residing in a more strongly synthetic formal totality. On the side of interpretation of these procedures, Benjamin argues, this essential incompleteness is viewed by the artwork's producer as an occasion of melancholy, which burgeons into a representation of history as a process of decline. Although in his study of German tragic drama Benjamin refers these characteristics to the artworks and the historical context of the northern European baroque, Bürger finds them suitable to the horizon of early twentieth-century culture and history as well. In fact, with hardly a hesitation, he directly appropriates Benjamin's allegory concept as a theoretical framework applicable to interpreting works of the avant-garde:

> The development of a concept of the non-organic work of art is a central task of the theory of the avant-garde. It can be undertaken by starting from Benjamin's concept of allegory ... Benjamin developed it as he was studying the literature of the Baroque, of course, but one may say that it is only in the avant-gardiste work that it finds its adequate object. Differently formulated, we may say that it was Benjamin's experience in dealing with works of the avant-garde that made possible both the development of the category and its application to the literature of the Baroque, and not the other way round. (*TAG*, 68)

As with his reframing of the notion of technical reproducibility as secondary to Benjamin's confrontation with the crisis of art precipitated by the avant-garde, Bürger suggests that the concept of baroque allegory is a hermeneutic lens shaped by Benjamin's experience of avant-garde art and turned backwards on an earlier historical period, rather than an application of a historical concept in the interpretation of the present.

As already mentioned, a pivot of Bürger's theory of the avant-garde is its attack on artistic autonomy, in its attempt to open out art to a holistic range of functions and experiences that exceeds the bounds of the aesthetic. In this respect, Bürger's "theory of the avant-garde" is directly and polemically opposed, as a dialectical negation, to Adorno's aesthetic theory, which is above all a theory and defense of artistic modernism. Though Bürger evaluates artistic autonomy differently than Adorno, he nevertheless borrows much from Adorno's fraught modernism in order to consider various alternatives to it – including the historical avant-garde's attack on artistic autonomy, the Brechtian poetics of engaged art, and postmodern artistic historicism and conventionalism. Bürger does not, in fact, rank Adorno fully on the side of either a modernist defense of autonomy or an avant-garde break with it, but rather diagnoses a contradictory equivocation between these positions, which leads to an ever-more attenuated field of actual works that can embody Adorno's aesthetic norms. On the one hand, Bürger argues, Adorno uncompromisingly embraced the inorganic work of art characteristic of the avant-garde and rejected any attempt to reinvest art with organic meaning as a regression, both psychically and politically. On the other hand, however, he insists on the limitation of this avant-garde dynamic to a principle of artistic production, of giving form to artworks, rather than carrying it over into the consideration of new ways that artworks might relate, functionally and representationally, to individual and collective experience. In a kind of Beckettian dilemma in aesthetic theory, Adorno thus entrenched himself in paradox: art retains an ever-thinner trace of its autonomy by making itself the witness of autonomy's disappearance in present-day society, which is unpropitious for the survival of art. "Artistic autonomy can't go on; it'll go on," he implicitly concludes in his *Aesthetic Theory*. Artistic form – however fractured, objective-mathematized, or residual – is the sole mediation that Adorno is willing to see as legitimate in relating artistic material and social content. He simply rules out of hand a range of extra-aesthetic communicative, cognitive, pedagogical, existential, and ideological functions that a post-avant-garde art might play – and in fact, has done in the hands of some of the most important artists of the twentieth century from Marcel Duchamp, Alexander Rodchenko, and André Breton to Constant Nieuwenhuys, Joseph Beuys, John Cage, Robert Smithson, and Jean-Luc Godard.

Moreover, Bürger suggests, Adorno fails to see that the avant-garde's challenge to the institution of art undermines the aesthetic norms that would allow one to choose on anything other than situational grounds between valid and invalid, or "authentic" and "inauthentic," works of art. Hierarchical or exclusive norms are supplanted, he argues, by differentiated functions of art, which can co-exist and relate to different spheres of value and experience, without contradiction. As Bürger and others (such as David Roberts[2]) have noted, this failure to acknowledge the loss of normative bases for validating art leads to notes of rigidity and decisionism in Adorno's aesthetics:

> As he sees only the twelve-tone technique as an advanced state of musical material, he is unable to appreciate either the avant-garde early Stravinsky of the *Histoire du Soldat* or the Neo-Classical composer. The decisionism at work in determining what material can be seen as advanced and which material may be defined as advanced is impossible to overlook – quite apart from the difficulties if we attempted to consider the twentieth-century narrators whom Adorno also canonized (Proust, Kafka, Joyce, and Beckett) as exponents of a single material tradition. Finally, it must be stressed that even in the "material aesthetic" the autonomy of normative discourses about art has not yet been acknowledged.[3]

This unacknowledged normativity in Adorno, which designates certain artistic materials as "advanced" and others as "regressive," takes place against an unmeasurable background in which aesthetic conventions and norms have been displaced or destroyed.

Necessarily, Adorno's normative judgments do not avoid an aspect of dogmatism or arbitrariness: at their best they appear subtle judgments of taste by a sensitive connoisseur, at worst a presumptuous magnification of individual aversions, prejudices, and blind spots into elaborate philosophical and social psychological arguments. His insensitivity to the rebellious aspects of jazz, for example, cannot help but seem today almost willfully obtuse. We might, in fact, see Adorno's "modernism" (and what Bürger characterizes as his "anti-avant-gardism") as residing precisely in his will to assert normative judgments in the absence of normative grounds, judgments "based" only on a contingent self-reflexivity that occasionally comes to temporary rest in a moment of sudden decision for or against a work or artist. This paradoxical aesthetic normativity without norms is the equivalent, in aesthetics, of Adorno's more general "negative dialectics": an ever-more fine-grained process of negative judgments eschewing any reductive synthesis, seeking to produce ever subtler grades of differentiation in the field of judgments and to approximate mimetically the inexhaustible concreteness of the pre-conceptualized object. Yet the contingency of aesthetic norms inaugurated by the avant-garde break, Bürger suggests, does not lead back to norms of validity or authenticity simply by its reflection in theory. Contingency infinitely reflected cannot be the salvation of aesthetic authenticity, contrary to Adorno's desperate hope in *Aesthetic Theory*. It rather turns into an ever-more exclusive pseudo-norm that ends up rejecting most of what was actually being done by artists from the 1950s on, and the social functions their works were actually performing. This is true to an even-greater extent if one considers the wider field of popular culture, counter-culture, mass media, and entertainment.

Herbert Marcuse's dialectical conception of art, as discussed in the previous chapter, also strongly influenced Bürger's theory of the avant-garde, even if the explicit references to Marcuse are relatively limited. Bürger does see in Marcuse's 1937 essay "The Affirmative Character of Culture" a precursor to his own functional theory of art. Marcuse, he argues,

> outlines the global determination of art's function in bourgeois society, which is a contradictory one: on the one hand it shows "forgotten truths" (thus it protests against a reality in which these truths have no validity); on the other, such truths are detached from reality through the medium of aesthetic semblance (*Schein*) – art thus stabilizes the very social conditions against which it protests. (*TAG*, 11)

Bürger picks up on Marcuse's skepticism about art's compensatory, "affirmative" role in bourgeois society, offering an ideal, "merely aesthetic" flight from the unhappy realities of an everyday life compromised by economic uncertainty, commercialized culture, inequality, and the frustration of happiness. He generalizes the function of bourgeois art, an instance of "affirmative culture," as being that of "neutralizing of impulses to change society" (*TAG*, 13), by channeling them into idealist, formalist aesthetic practices and discourses. Bürger also takes away a theoretical lesson from Marcuse's essay, a recasting of aesthetics in terms of *institution* and social *function*, a conception only deployed but not fully explicated in Marcuse's essay:

> The model provides the important theoretical insight that works of art are not received as single entities, but within institutional frameworks and conditions that largely determine the function of the works. When one speaks of the function of an individual work, one generally speaks figuratively; for the consequences that one may observe or infer are not primarily a function of its special qualities but rather of the manner which regulates the commerce with works of this kind in a given society or in certain strata or classes of a society. I have chosen the term "institution of art" to characterize such framing conditions. (*TAG*, 12)

Marcuse viewed the relative impotence of "affirmative culture" – in which, in the 1930s, he included much of art – as highlighted by the new horizon of totalitarianism, which was quickly liquidating "spirit" as an illusion, eliminating any privileged sphere of retreat from the ideologically and politically saturated field of culture. By contrast with Marcuse, however, Bürger lays greater emphasis on the inner field of artistic evolution than on the larger context of politico-social developments. He stresses the avant-garde break with autonomous art, which laid bare the increasing incommensurability between "art world" values and the realities of the larger social environment. Historically, this was exemplified in Duchamp's project to use a Rembrandt painting as an ironing board (a kind of reverse "readymade"), or, in a more politically charged example, by the Berlin Dadaists' sneering response to Oskar Kokoschka, who expressed concern that political street battles near a museum might threaten valuable paintings with stray bullets. The crucial point here is not whether artistic or political life is more important, but the disjuncture between the orders of value that would weigh the preservation of paintings against the success or failure of a revolutionary uprising. It points to the possible sidelining or eclipse of art's "aesthetic" and "affirmative" functions in favor of other positive functions integrated into the machinery of everyday social life under capitalism – from commercial mass entertainment and touristic attraction to pedagogical and propagandistic uses.

In works such as *Soviet Marxism*, *One-Dimensional Man*, *Counterrevolution and Revolt*, and *The Aesthetic Dimension* Marcuse stepped back from embracing the new, socially integrated functions of art in favor of preserving the "two-dimensional" imaginative capacities of art rooted in autonomy. So too Bürger expresses concern about the desirability of the goal of eliminating autonomy, which not only proved stubbornly persistent despite the avant-garde's assault, but which may also have benefits not to be surrendered lightly:

> Given the experience of the false sublation of autonomy, one will need to ask whether a sublation of the autonomy status can be desirable at all, whether the distance between art and the praxis of life is not requisite for

that free space within which alternatives to what exists become conceivable. (*TAG*, 54)

With the benefit of hindsight from another fifty years of historical experience after the avant-garde break of the early twentieth century, Bürger asks whether the utopian dreams of the avant-garde to sublate art and aesthetics into a transformed everyday life might in fact have been realized in a nightmarish way by the culture industry's engulfing stream of entertainment, mass media, design, advertisement, and kitsch. In Bürger's view, commodified culture industry, which does not even pretend to be autonomous from the dominant economic and political interests, represents the grotesque double of the avant-garde, insofar as culture industry short-circuits the gap between art and life by simply eliminating their dialectical tension. In this situation of generalized culture industry, then, artistic autonomy takes on a different contextual significance, as a resistance to reduction, neutralization, and depotentialization. When the heteronomy of culture industry has become the norm, Bürger suggests, artistic autonomy, however weak and compromised, may yet residually sustain values that we should not too hastily discard.

Within his *Theory of the Avant-Garde* this issue marks an unresolved contradiction in Bürger's conclusions about what happens after the failure of the historical avant-garde to realize its sublation of art into life. He offers no decisive conception of how aesthetic modernity, which led to the avant-garde break, might continue under weakened but persistent framing conditions that are at least partially autonomous, thus still confined to the aesthetic function of art. Yet the example of the work of Bertolt Brecht, whom he discusses briefly in *Theory of the Avant-Garde*, suggests how this contradiction might be resolved. Brecht's writing, Bürger argues, must be understood in the context of the twentieth-century avant-garde break that took place, but Brecht also diverges in crucial ways from the historical model of avant-gardism that Bürger sketches out. Rather than wishing "to destroy art as an institution," Bürger argues, Brecht "proposed to radically change it" (*TAG*, 88–9). Brecht focuses not on negating theater's institutional distinctiveness, but rather on modifying and potentiating its function within its autonomous institution. This change from within artistic autonomy includes furnishing theater with a greater range of political and pedagogical functions. Bürger suggests that the avant-garde's attack on the organic work of art and its introduction of the formal principle of montage is taken into the autonomous theatre by Brecht and used as a fulcrum to repurpose it for political engagement. Since the avant-garde allowed discrete elements to function as "individual signs" with significant independence from reference to some synthesizing form or global content, the semantic and formal range of autonomous theater could be opened up to contradictions, questions, ambiguities, and multiple versions – Brecht's typical method of revolving a moral or political question and inviting reflection and judgment rather than providing univocal answers. Yet while the avant-garde formally exemplifies its critical stance towards present-day society by attacking the idioms of art's sensemaking, Brecht's method allowed him to probe existing institutions, ideologies, and attitudes more analytically. As Bürger concludes, "the abolition of the dichotomy between 'pure' and 'political' art can take a different form" than the avant-garde's refusal to speak the language of existing society and confronting it, critically, with nonsense (e.g. Dada), alternative sense (futurist trans-sense language, surrealist automatism), or sublimity (expressionism, suprematism). "Instead of declaring the avant-gardiste structural principle of the nonorganic itself to be a political statement, it should be remembered that it enables political and nonpolitical motifs to exist side by side in a single work. On the basis of the nonorganic work, a new type of engaged art thus becomes possible" (*TAG*, 91).

Concluding my discussion of Bürger, I would note that in subsequent essays he addresses this problem in greater detail than in his brief discussion of Brecht in *Theory of the Avant-Garde*. In particular, in an essay entitled "The Decline of the Modern Age,"[4] through which Bürger intervened into the debates around so-called "postmodernism" in the 1980s, he reiterates in a more theoretically explicated form his argument for a critical mode within modernism that could be extended beyond the failure of the historical avant-garde. I cannot treat his argument at length here, but I will signal three salient points of his discussion. First, Bürger argues that modernism, the manifestation of aesthetic modernity in the twentieth century, must be understood in much broader, more inclusive terms than the various partisans of single positions were willing to entertain. Thus, for example, the dichotomy between progress and regression that Adorno established in his musical aesthetics, referring them respectively to the work of Schönberg and Stravinsky, must be grasped as complementary facets of modernism. Second, once this more pluralistic and internally differentiated concept of modernism is accepted, there are no principled grounds for excluding neo-classicism or realist elements, including various forms of politically engaged artistic discourses, from the aesthetic logic of modernism. "The longing for regression," Bürger writes, "is an eminently modern phenomenon, a reaction to the advancing rationalization process. It should not be tabooed, but worked out." What appears to be regressive may, in fact, be a means of refreshing and innovating within a seemingly petrified set of conventions: "What first seemed to be only a lack of culture could prove to be the starting point of a new way of dealing with works of art that overcomes the one-sided fixation on form and at the same time places the work back in relation to the experiences of the recipients" – Bürger has in mind here the Brechtian imperative to embrace the "bad new" rather than stick with the "good old," and to "vulgarize" consciously in order to raise questions of address and audience not visible within the well-formed work.[5] Finally, Bürger suggests that this late modernist continuation of modernism does not reject modernism's defining problematic of form, but relativizes it in light of art as a mode of communicative practice, which can carry out a number of different existential, ideological, pedagogical, and even ritual functions, without contradicting its distinctiveness. On the contrary, art is enriched by the complexity this focus on communicative practice brings. Bürger introduces the term "resemanticization of art" to describe this enrichment, a renewed emphasis on the "semantic dimension of art," its ability to figure, problematize, and communicate various social contents of importance to its multiple audiences.[6]

Albrecht Wellmer: Reconstructing Modernist Aesthetics After Habermas

As noted in my introductory chapter, the work of Jürgen Habermas had a decisive effect on the current of Frankfurt School thought, leading to a critique and even abandonment of a number of defining elements of its first-generation program and to an ongoing reconstruction of other elements in light of Habermas's "theory of communicative action." Here I will touch exclusively on one subset of the work of a key post-Habermasian thinker,[7] Albrecht Wellmer, who has published an important set of essays on aesthetics, particularly pertaining to the aesthetics of modern music.[8] Wellmer takes as his starting-point Adorno's strong association, in his *Aesthetic Theory*, of art's validity with both conceptual truth and social emancipation, and reconstructs these claims within a post-metaphysical philosophy influenced by Habermas, Ludwig Wittgenstein, Martin Heidegger, and Hans-Georg Gadamer. Within the post-Adorno Frankfurt School tendency, Wellmer represents the most outstanding attempt to articulate a set of specific claims about modernist art and aesthetics in a "critical" vein: critical in the philosophical sense of both establishing the range of ways in which modernism may have ethical, political, conceptual, and existential efficacy and the limits within which it exerts its possible effects.

To address Wellmer's approach to modernist artworks, I will begin with the more general frameworks of aesthetic reception that he formulates. Notably, he orients his arguments towards reception in an explicit critique of Peter Bürger (among others), who, Wellmer argues, establishes a novel constellation of reality, art, and living praxis, but does so by abolishing the notion of "aesthetic semblance" and emphasizing "the significance of this constellation of reality for artistic production over its significance for reception" (*PoM*, 17). In other words, for Bürger the decisive issue is how artists relate their production to the institutions of art – reflexively embodying autonomy in modernist form or breaking with autonomy in the activist modes of avant-garde art – whereas Wellmer suggests that a focus on reception may mitigate some of the either-or dilemmas Bürger poses. Accordingly (and though he does not cite the essay, Wellmer here echoes Adorno's important late essay "Culture and Administration"[9]), while Bürger formulates the avant-garde break as an abolition of a culture of artistic experts, Wellmer argues that transforming the institution of art would entail a *democratization* of the communicative interchange between experts and a broader constituency with a plurality of interest and engagements with art: "I argue on the assumption that a transformation of the 'institution of art' cannot mean the abolition of the 'culture of experts,' but that it would amount rather to the establishment of a tighter network of connections between the culture of experts and the life-world on the one hand, and the culture of experts and popular art on the other" (*PoM*, 31). In turn, Wellmer argues, art can play a role in a broader process of democratic emancipation: "we can defend the idea of an altered relationship between art and the life-world in which a democratic praxis would be able to draw productively on the innovative and communicative potential of art" (*PoM*, 31).

In developing this view, Wellmer sets out from the everyday communicative competencies of both makers and receivers of artworks. Both artists and audience members are, in this view, socialized individuals who have histories of participating in everyday practices of communication, both oral and written (and increasingly, televisual and digital). Their everyday competencies include a range of functions, from pragmatic, instrumental uses to aesthetically, emotionally, and existentially expressive uses of language, images, performative acts, and other signs. Their multifaceted participation in everyday communication will have shaped, to a greater or lesser degree, their abilities to use discourse consciously and make deliberative judgments about the discourse of others. In the course of performing everyday communication, in particular, they will have become competent in making and evaluating discursive claims to "truth" in a number of different dimensions. These truth-dimensions include: the *factual dimension* of how a statement representing a state of affairs measures up against our experience of the state of affairs itself; the *expressive dimension* of a statement's "truthfulness" or authenticity in relation to a speaker's personal beliefs, feelings, and way of life; and *the dimension of moral, practical, and emotional "rightness"* of a statement with respect to a concrete situation of life, measured against a background of culturally shared or even universally human values and norms. Moreover, not only do they gain communicative competencies in performing and evaluating claims to truth in these different dimensions; even in the relatively loose contexts of everyday life, they may also have become aware of the potential for dissonance between these different dimensions of truth employed in discourse. What we know to be true factually, for example, may nevertheless be morally repugnant to us or contrary to our personal, existential sense of who we are. Lastly, as part of their own personal and professional biographies, individuals may have succeeded in composing and integrating these different truth-dimensions into larger, more coherent wholes that are characteristic of their characters and lives. Everyday discourse, however, tends to shift sequentially between these dimensions and connect them at most in only loosely coordinated ways. It tolerates wide latitude for dissonance, bad faith, lack of awareness, and outright contradiction in the relations between these discursively embodied domains of truth.

In taking up the question of how art relates to these different dimensions of truth, Wellmer makes two specifications. First, he suggests, art does not so much literally represent truth as mobilize a *potential* for truth: "The truth content of works of art would then be the epitome of the potential effects of works of art that are *relevant* to the truth, or of their potential for *disclosing* truth" (PoM, 24). This potential for truth in artworks is, however, related to a second specification: the claims to truth that artworks carry are related to their claims of aesthetic validity. To put it otherwise, only insofar as a work is aesthetically "right" does it realize its potential relevance to other sorts of truth; the aesthetically valid work allows us to focus on and evaluate some potential truth that previously was imperceptible, before being represented to us in a concentrated, specially framed experience of art. Wellmer goes on to suggest that insofar as art mediates its relation to truth through aesthetic validity, through its complex "rightness" as composition, it is particularly suited to reveal the interactions and interferences of the different sorts of truth comprised in everyday communication: factual, moral, and expressive dimensions. As Wellmer writes:

> It transpires . . . that art is *involved* in questions of truth in a peculiar and complex way: not only does art open up the experience of reality, and correct and expand it; it is also the case that aesthetic "validity" (i.e. the "rightness" of a work of art) *touches on* questions of truth, truthfulness, and moral and practical correctness in an intricate fashion without being attributable to any one of the three dimensions of truth, or even to all three together. We might therefore suppose that the "truth of art" can only be defended, if at all, as a phenomenon of interference between the various dimensions of truth. (PoM, 22–3)

Aesthetic reception attends to the intimate connection between the formal dimension of artworks (or works, events, and performances that, by virtue of compositional qualities have been assimilated to art) and this reflexive work on a pluri-dimensional truth. To put this another way, aesthetic reception seeks to reveal how aesthetic validity (the "rightness" of artistic choices and structures) shapes a particular complex vision of truth – the possible interferences of factual, subjective, and moral truths in concrete human situations, and the ways in which, over time, these interferences may be negotiated. Focused in this way, this conception of the aesthetic helps us to interpret in a more rigorous light certain loosely shared aspects and background motivations of the critical, reflexive tendencies of modernist art and literature. Modernism represents an intentional practice of composing artworks that aim to reorient the communicative life of the works' receivers, offering them new ways of making sense not only within the microcosm of the artistic encounter, but also within the broader parameters of their everyday communication.

Wellmer's aesthetic writings are most directly related to the *Aesthetic Theory* of Adorno, as an immanent critique and reconstruction of Adorno's thought on reception-related and "communicative action"-oriented grounds. Adorno, as I noted in my earlier chapter, developed his aesthetic theory teleologically around its contemporary endpoint, to establish and justify the fragile possibility of a critical modernism in an age tending towards the abolition of art. Critical modernism, as Adorno discerned it in a few singular, communicatively resistant works by Schönberg, Picasso, Kafka, and Beckett, gave testimony to the trace of "something else" in the hour of its disappearance into the night of indifference. In his focus on the experience of art as potentially disrupting the ease with which we ascribe cognitive, moral, and personal-existential "truth" not only to the aesthetic event, but also to everyday and perhaps even specialized statements and acts, Wellmer retains Adorno's sense of art's special relation to truth. Moreover, it is easy to see that Adorno's justification of difficult, complex modernist art can be encompassed by Wellmer's revisionary perspective. When, for example, we puzzle over whether Beckett's "Molloy" and "Moran" in the novel *Molloy* are versions of the same character rather than two different ones, our inability to resolve the question may unsettle the self-understood existential truth that whatever else we might know or not know, we know *who we are*. Beckett's disruptions of character-identification might lead us to believe that holding onto a sense of self might not be so easy in the world we live in. Similarly, listening to a piece of atonal or electronic music, which has been emancipated from traditional principles of organizing the musical materials, we may perceive with new vividness various forms of local order that alternate throughout the longer piece. These organizational patterns may relate to intensified or novel application of compositional techniques as repetition and variation of rhythmic figures, sharp alternations between high and low pitches, uses of resonance and overtones, dynamic contrasts of very loud and very soft sounds, manipulation of sound shape and spatial volume, surprising dissemination of motifs among instruments of contrasting timbres, unconventional ways of producing instrumental and vocal sounds, and so on. Obviously, within the aesthetic experience of music, these various interacting forms of post-harmonic patterning call for different modes of attention and evaluation on the part of listeners. But new perceptual, affective, and cognitive intuitions originating in the experience of music need not remain encapsulated within the purely musical, but can extend by analogy to other dimensions of moral, existential, affective, and cognitive life. Indeed, Adorno himself is an extreme example of the contrary, insofar as he carried his musical training into a whole new way of writing philosophy and conceiving the nature of philosophical reflection. Martin Jay captured this translation of modernist music into philosophy well in his characterization of Adorno's negative dialectics as "atonal philosophy."[10]

Despite this proximity to Adorno – rendered even closer by Wellmer's intimate knowledge of modern and contemporary music, unique among the major followers of Habermas – Wellmer also diverges from Adorno on a number of key points in his interpretation of modernist art. First, since his focus is on how artworks impact listeners, viewers, and readers as agents within a plurality of communicative practices (a Habermasian perspective), rather than on the production of artworks as complex constellations of subjective and objective elements mediated by artistic form (Adorno's perspective), Wellmer abandons a key element of Adorno's theory: the strongly prescriptive focus on "progress" in the disposition of "artistic material," which in turn leads Adorno to dichotomous formulations such as the Schönberg / Stravinsky opposition elaborated in *Philosophy of the New Music*. Wellmer, in contrast, puts the receivers of artworks at the center of his account, listeners who, even as they experience works of music ranging from the rock song on the radio to the new music composition in a Frankfurt concert hall, also remain complex social agents living, acting, thinking, working, and speaking within a differentiated, plural set of social institutions, rules, and discourses. It is the relationship between this context and the act of listening that, for Wellmer, is determinative of the musical work's social significance, not the characteristics of the work alone. The question of what sort of artwork might play a critical or even emancipatory role cannot be unilaterally derived from formal-material features, rooted in the artist's production of advanced artworks. The "progressive" effects of artworks depend on situational aspects of reception as well, which can positively motivate a far wider range of artistic forms, registers ("high" culture to "popular" and "counter" culture), and modes ("classical," jazz, pop, etc.) than Adorno was himself willing to contemplate.

This artistic pluralism – comparable to that advocated by Bürger – is most striking precisely where Wellmer moves upon Adorno's signature artistic territory, in the field of modern classical and post-serialist "new" music. Wellmer's recent collection of musicological writings, *Essay on Music and Language*, offers a wide-ranging treatment of different musical examples, including a sympathetic examination of two major composers who represent opposing, influential directions in post-war "new music": John Cage, as the anarchist advocate of non-intentionality, indeterminacy, and chance in musical composition, as well as the expansion of musical materials to the whole range of natural and human sounds; and Helmut Lachenmann, as a rigorous, militantly politicized inventor of musical methodologies that extend serial techniques to new dimensions of instrumental and vocal sound, timbre, rhythm, and text. Rather than setting up an Adorno-like dichotomy of Cage's anarchic informality and Lachenmann's political and formal rigor, Wellmer offers a measured assessment of their artistic projects as complementary, if antipodal paradigms of new music.

The final chapter of *Essay on Music and Language*, entitled "Transgressive Figures in the Field of New Music," affirms a concept of "postmodernism" that is "equivalent neither to turning away from *the* modern nor with the return of an emphatic claim for art, but rather much more with a *pluralistic* modernism" (*VMS*, 302). Wellmer not only argues for this modernist pluralism philosophically, but goes on to survey an open field of musical possibilities represented by particular composers and their works. Having rejected Adorno's notorious either-or opposition of Schönberg and Stravinsky, Wellmer follows the lead of Pierre Boulez in presenting these two exemplary modernist composers as complementary figures by whom the structural apparatus of tonality was disrupted and dismantled, with one having focused on the destruction of tonal hierarchy through serial formalization and the other on "informal" rhythmic and instrumental violence to tonal organization.[11] Wellmer goes on, however, to suggest other ways in which the emancipation of the musical field has proceeded – exemplifying not a dialectical logic of opposites (Schönberg / Stravinsky, progress / regression, formalization / dissolution of form), as in Adorno, but rather a progressive differentiation of musical experience through the enrichment of compositional technique. Thus, for example, Wellmer enumerates: the expansion of the field of sound through electronic and aleatory musics; the exploration of microtonal elements through tremolo, glissandi, new vocal articulations, and use of non-Western and historical musical materials that reveal the contingency of classical and twelve-tone music's chromatic scale; the recourse to parts of the overtone series and other features of physical sound suppressed by tempered harmonics; the focus on gestural and tactile aspects of instrumental sound, as well as the dramatic aspects of their performance; the highlighting of spatial features of musical sound; the structuring of musical pieces as a direct intervention into the listener's perceptual faculties and bodily sensations; and the hybridization of new music with cross-overs into jazz, hiphop, gypsy music, rock and roll, and other forms of popular music. Accordingly, he incorporates into his open, non-exclusive canon of pluralistic modernism in music such highly divergent composers as John Cage, Giacinto Scelsi, Pierre Boulez, Pierre Schaeffer, Karlheinz Stockhausen, Helmut Lachenmann, György Ligeti, Hans-Werner Henze, Luigi Nono, György Kurtág, Luciano Berio, Heinz Hollinger, Mauricio Kagel, Iannis Xenakis, Cornelius Cardew, Alvin Lucier, Claus-Steffen Mahnkopf, Erhard Grosskopf, Georg Friedrich Haas, Hans Zenders, Hilda Paredes, Clemens

Gadenstätter, Gene Coleman, Bernard Lang, Klaus Huber, and Isabel Mundry: a very diverse, multi-generational catalogue of post-war composers that could undoubtedly be extended greatly beyond Wellmer's largely German and Central European "new music" focus. The modernist pluralism represented by this list, moreover, allows Wellmer to reach back into Adorno's modernism and open up the historical past that Adorno's philosophy of music mediated to future generations of critical theorists and musicologists. He refers not only to Adorno's canon of authentic modernists – Gustav Mahler, Arnold Schönberg, Alban Berg, and Anton Webern – but also to Claude Debussy, Igor Stravinsky, Oliver Messiaen, Edgard Varèse, Henry Cowell, Charles Ives, Béla Bartók, Ivan Wyschnegradsky, and Alois Haba, all of whom Adorno either spurned or ignored. "Postmodern," Wellmer writes, "would be . . . the consciousness of an infinite plurality of musical materials, including that of extra-European traditions, as well as the various procedures at the disposition [of composers] since the second half of the twentieth century" (VMS, 302). Wellmer's "postmodern," however, does not come *after* modernism, but is rather the pluralization of modernism itself, which branches forward in a field of ever-greater differentiation as it extends into and past the later twentieth century.

Moreover, in a passage in which he discusses the use of highly complex rhythmic structures and speeds and their effects on the senses and bodies of listeners, we catch a glimpse of the utopian, futuristic possibilities that works of the historical avant-garde, from Marinetti and Khlebnikov to Schwitters and Breton, adumbrated – the total reinvention of the human sensorium. Describing the unaccustomed relations to the human body that the soundscapes of recent music establish, Wellmer evokes the utopian suggestion of a transfigured body that would be adopted to the textures and speeds of a virtual world:

> Many of these rhythms race more swiftly ahead and oscillate more rapidly than would ever be possible for the body; many have a strongly gestural character, yet correspond to no known bodily or linguistic movement. While the early postwar composers presented the structures and skeletons for new, strange worlds, contemporary composers now create the flesh, muscle, and nervous systems not of traditional bodies, rather of completely new creatures that accordingly advance along an unfamiliar border of a "virtual movement." (VMS, 310)

Wellmer's evocation of creatures with radically different bodily and sensory characteristics harkens back to our discussion of Paul Scheerbart's *Lesabéndio* and Walter Benjamin's fascination with the utopian atmospheres of his fictional planet. Scheerbart describes the sonorous space of the double funnel-shaped asteroid-planet, Pallas, which is designed by the author as a kind of total musical environment in which the inhabitants, with their extraterrestrial alien bodies, are continuously immersed. The planet itself is a kind of natural wind instrument, which has been adapted by the Pallasians into an enveloping musical and sound-space:

> Refined music resounded out of the depths of the funnel, including strange tones that were held and sustained for long periods of time.
>
> This music emanated from the Central Hole connecting the north and south funnels.
>
> Here in the Center, where the funnel walls were steep and sometimes separated from each other by no more than half a mile, here in the very heart of the star, winds caused by the speedy descent of the cobweb-cloud at nightfall made the hole emit wonderful sounds.
>
> Because of the interior music of Pallas, which, naturally, could be heard best from the star's southern funnel, the Pallasians had set up many large, thin pieces of skin to strengthen the sounds and to link them into a melodious sonic flow. These hides were stretched and mounted in such a way as to cause the tones brought forth by the steep cliff walls to vary in a marvelous fashion. The pieces of skin were set up so that they would be easy to move to different spots in the larger system. The moveable skins created fantastical harmonies naturally amplified by the acoustics of the funnels. Certain capacious metal instruments could even make the noises seem orchestral.[12]

One could imagine that this is just the sort of music that creatures whose bodies are nothing but a "rubbery tube leg with a suction-cup foot at one end," an umbrella-shaped flexible head, and telescoping eyes would enjoy hearing. Yet turning around the perspective in light of Wellmer's discussion of contemporary music, we might also say that such a sound environment as Scheerbart describes, not unlike that of a contemporary composition exploring the resonant properties of materials and spaces and immersing the listener in slowly pulsating rhythms, also *evokes* bodies more like those of the Pallasians than the bodies with which the listeners walked into the concert hall. Their harmony with such an environment implies that human bodies, such as we possess, would find it very, well, alien. Yet in *Lesabéndio*, as in the musical worlds created by contemporary composers, we are also asked to imagine and empathize with creaturely forms radically other than our own: to become them for a time. For the duration of the musical experience, as for the duration of our reading of Scheerbart, our bodies are aesthetically stretched and compressed, broken and reassembled, in ways that give us a sensuous intuition of new Pallasian bodies, a shimmering succession of virtual bodies evoked by the dissonances and tensions between our natural bodies and the techno-compositional environments to which we have submitted ourselves. Wellmer concludes that this temporary plunge into strangeness, into apparent senselessness or nonsense that is characteristic of avant-garde art, is the occasion for the production of new thought and feeling. "Upon such new thought and feeling produced by new music," he quotes Karlheinz Stockhausen, "we can successively construct experiences, *learning processes*" (Stockhausen, quoted in *VMS*, 311). The extension of the key Habermasian concept of "learning processes" to aesthetic experience – for Stockhausen and Wellmer, to the non-discursive sonorous intensities of new music – will also, in a different context, prove crucial to the author and filmmaker Alexander Kluge, whose work I take up in my concluding section.

ALEXANDER KLUGE: ADORNO POSTHUMOUS, OR DANCING WITH THE DEVIL IN THE ICE AGE

In his voluminous body of work in media ranging from fiction and theoretical essays to film and television, Alexander Kluge has explored the concept of "learning processes" in an ever-expanding framework over the course of his fifty-year intellectual career. He has broadened outward from the German social, historical, and institutional dimensions that constituted the focus of early works such as his 1962 collection of stories, *Case Histories*, and his 1966 feature film *Yesterday's Girl*, to a vast array of literary, mediatic, technological, anthropological, scientific, natural-historical, and cosmic perspectives. He represents different dimensions of human learning processes, both good and bad ones ("learning processes with a deadly outcome," as he entitled his 1973 collection of science-fiction stories), through his signature use of documentary, fictional pseudo-documentary, and collaboratively produced montage. His books resemble arrangements of historical, news, and scientific items, including both textual and visual elements. These materials are sometimes the occasion for short narrative elaboration, sometimes the object of brief essayistic or theoretical reflection, while other entries simply appear as factual or documentary registrations without further comment, contextualized only by an open-ended set of implicit relations of similarity, contrast, and contradiction with other elements of the montage.

By tirelessly shifting between a welter of factual and fictional material in several different contextual frames, Kluge's literary and theoretical opus redirects the "long march through the institutions" that the German student movement leader Rudi Dutschke projected as the necessary means of radical change in the post-war period. In the influential theoretical work he co-authored with Oskar Negt, *Public Sphere and Experience*, Kluge had embraced Dutschke's Maoist metaphor, which dialectically advanced apparent retreat (from the hot years of student activism) as a means of regrouping and recuperating force for a later resurgence into action.[13] In his later work, however, he abandoned the implicit military resonances of the image and highlighted, instead, the image of contemporary social learning processes as a slow, painstaking, dangerous wandering through treacherous, icy terrain. Accordingly, I would summarize Kluge's trajectory as moving through three major phases, which are not so much chronological as theoretical and ideological; these phases overlap chronologically across his corpus of works and their various media. First, Kluge was strongly influenced by his friendship with Adorno and other representatives of the classic Frankfurt School, and he sought to draw implications from their attempts to work through the Nazi past and offer directions for a post-fascist democratization of society, while guarding against the closure of social imagination threatened by an ever-more pervasive capitalist culture industry. He advocated a form of critical modernism that was influenced by Frankfurt School Critical Theory, though his writing was also politically "engaged" in ways that contradicted Adorno's emphasis on incommunicability as the crucial index of art's critical relation to present-day society. Second, he would increasingly incorporate into his work the political, theoretical, aesthetic challenges to Adorno's modernist, classic Frankfurt School heritage. Throughout the 1960s and '70s, these challenges came, on the one hand, from more activist Marxist tendencies (and their artistic correlates, which favored Benjamin's and Brecht's legacy over Adorno's), and on the other hand, from Jürgen Habermas and his followers, within Critical Theory, who were advocating a reconstructive turn to "communicative action." Particularly compelling in these various challenges to Adorno was the jettisoning of the underlying philosophical anthropology, philosophy of history, and implicit theology in Adorno's work. In his theoretical writings, Adorno viewed modernity as the last turn of the screw in a deep historical process of human self-creation through repression and alienation, which could only be interrupted by a theologically tinged redemption. Authentic works of artistic modernism testified to and lamented this historical predicament but could not exercise, without betraying themselves, any further agency to break free of it. For Adorno's critics, accordingly, "action," whether political or communicative, was notably missing from his framework, and they sought to displace his dialectic of subjectivity with a renewed emphasis on intersubjectivity and intersubjective action. Kluge himself would increasingly take up the question of action, its conditions, and its implications, both in his artistic works and in his theoretical / political writings. He thus carried out a thickly textured, ongoing research into the avant-garde heritage, in search of means to break free of the shrinking field of communicative efficacy that Adorno's "dialectic of enlightenment" and his aesthetic theory left to artistic and political practice. Thirdly, however, Kluge would ultimately return to Adorno's provocative philosophical anthropology, philosophy of history, and dialectical natural history, reframing the question of human action in an ever-expanding perspective.

In this regard, Kluge has moved in a direction contrary to Habermas and his followers. If for them the communicative turn in Critical Theory meant rejecting Adorno's anthropology and philosophy of history once and for all and constructing a "post-metaphysical" theory of action that is not grounded in principles other than the pragmatics of social life, Kluge suggests that the shortcomings of Adorno's work lie elsewhere: that his anthropology and philosophy of history were too narrow in their speculative reach to accommodate the full possibilities of human action, learning, creativity, and change (including change precipitated by contingent or catastrophic causes, which by definition cannot be accounted for in a closed, systematic framework). Kluge has thus has expanded Critical Theory's anthropological frame to take in a vast array of new scales, from the subatomic scale of quantum events to the natural historical scale of the earth and its various macro-processes to the cosmic reaches of the universe. Key motives of his earlier work – action, learning processes, and the critical functions of art – are recontextualized in an exceedingly capacious philosophical ambit. Kluge considers the human capacities formed through our individual and collective metabolism with material nature, the ongoing evolution of human skills and knowledge, and the human ability to invent and innovate in the face of changing climate, environmental conditions, natural disasters, and cosmic events. This latter frame especially characterizes his work from the 1990s to the present.

Kluge had a long, extensive history with Critical Theory, which was a formative influence on him throughout his intellectual career. He first encountered the Frankfurt School in the late 1950s when as a young jurist he served as the Institute's legal advisor. As an artist and intellectual his relation to the Frankfurt School has gone through many twists and turns, but steadily deepened. In the preface to the English-language abridged edition of his 2002 volume of stories *The Devil's Blind Spot*,[14] Kluge explicitly positions himself within their legacy:

> Among my teachers are the philosophers of the Frankfurt School of CRITICAL THEORY (Theodor W. Adorno, Walter Benjamin, Max Horkheimer), who interested me in the *Dialectic of Enlightenment*. At the time of my birth this theory was already facing up to the advance of Fascism. The worth of a philosophy may be gauged by the effect it has on its opponent. And so, even if they come from the Devil's poisons a philosophy must also contain antidotes. This is the tradition in which I tell stories. (*DBS*, viii)

Notably, if it begins with this direct homage, *The Devil's Blind Spot* also includes a partly satirical, partly allegorical elegy for his friend and intellectual mentor Theodor Adorno, in a chapter entitled "Moment of Danger for the Last Survivors of Critical Theory at Adorno's Funeral" (this chapter, in fact, concludes the English edition, though not the much more extensive German edition).[15] He presents the tersely designated "disagreeable situation" of Max

Horkheimer's "bungled" arrangements for the funeral, including his unwill-
ingness "to give an opinion as to what music Adorno would have approved
of or considered appropriate" (*DBS*, 307). Members of the student movement
appear uninvited, perhaps to kidnap the coffin and reclaim the mantle of
genuine critical theory from those Kluge designates "the Old Men of Critical
Theory," the "Scholarly Men," or the "Scholarly Elders." Their intent is
unclear to the authorized members of the funeral, and in fact, as Kluge ironically underscores, the interloping students themselves "hadn't even fully discussed" whether they wanted to strike a threatening attitude or express their
sympathy and respect for the deceased philosopher.

This sad and confused ceremony culminates in a rainstorm, which drenches
the elders of Critical Theory, who have been so impractical as not to have
armed themselves against the cruel revenge of nature on enlightenment:

> A thundery downpour surprised the funeral procession when it was
> halfway. The heads of the SCHOLARLY MEN wet, their clothing, too,
> soaked. No one from "Critical Theory" had an umbrella. Further lengthy
> speeches at the graveside. Slow work by the cemetery workers as the
> coffin was lowered into the grave. There were still handfuls of earth, indi-
> vidual bunches of flowers, to be thrown down. The line to pay respects to
> the widow. All of this with a wet head. (*DBS*, 308)

In order to save the last founding Frankfurt School thinkers from catching
cold and dying themselves, pots of warm beer are ordered, which, the narrator
tells us on the authority of the Brothers Grimm, help rewarm the blood and
banish the danger. Yet this victory against the cold of death, a metonymy of
the political ice age soon to set in across Germany in the 1970s and the spreading winter of failed utopian hopes across the earth, is short-lived. As Kluge
knows, the student leader Hans-Jürgen Krahl, who makes a cameo appearance
at Adorno's funeral, would himself be killed in an auto accident at the age of
twenty-seven, less than six months later. Nor would the "Old Men of Critical
Theory," including such venerable figures as Max Horkheimer, Herbert
Marcuse, Leo Loewenthal, and Friedrich Pollock, be more than temporarily
spared the icy fate adumbrated at Adorno's funeral: "For the moment they
were saved: not emotionally, but physically. Twenty years later the planet dis-
charged the last of these wise thinkers. The world was never the same again"
(*DBS*, 308).

With this compact, self-consciously fairy-tale like story of the funeral of one
of Critical Theory's founding fathers, Kluge signals that his own approach
to both the Frankfurt School and aesthetic modernism will be shaped by an
emphatic *posthumity* with respect to Adorno, coming *after* him and living
through the mournful moment of his departure, an extended historical interval in which the grievers themselves may be threatened by the spreading cold.

Kluge's image of spreading coldness, which he extends across millennia to a natural historical meditation on the ice age, has its deeper genealogy in the work of the Frankfurt School, however – in the writings of Walter Benjamin and Adorno. We can thus trace in Kluge's increasing engagement with the problematic of coldness as his attempt to renew the Frankfurt School's critical conception of modernism, which the founding thinkers saw as the attempt to employ negativity to create moments of exception in what appeared to be a deterministic historical fatality. If Benjamin viewed this modernistic critical activity as rooted in a logic of montage, supporting new political and pedagogical functions for art, and Adorno saw modernist art's critical potential in its tense, dissonant coupling of rational technique and intense subjective expression, then Kluge recasts art's critical function as a cunning dialectic of warmth and coldness, which, like Adorno and Horkheimer's dialectic of enlightenment, has natural-historical and archaic as well as more recent parameters.

Already in the mid-1920s, Walter Benjamin had introduced the motif of coldness in a passage in his "Imperial Panorama" in *One-Way Street*. He writes:

> Warmth is ebbing from things. The objects of daily use gently but insistently repel us. Day by day, in overcoming the sum of secret resistances . . . they put in our way, we have an enormous labor to perform. We must compensate for their coldness with our warmth, if they are not to freeze us to death . . . From our fellow men we should expect no succor. Bus conductors, officials, workmen, salesmen – they all feel themselves to be the representatives of a refractory matter whose menace they take pains to demonstrate through their own surliness. And in the degeneration of things, with which, emulating human decay, they punish humanity, the country itself conspires. It gnaws at us like the things, and the German spring that never comes is only one of countless phenomena of decaying German nature. (*SW* I, 453–4)

Benjamin articulates the affective and dispositional side of late-capitalist experience, touching both the object-world and social relations, which converge in coldness. Indeed, coldness appears here as a kind of indifference zone in which instruments and their human operators, commodified products and their consumers, have become increasingly indiscernible. Although Benjamin often espoused a positive view of the "mimetic faculty" – the human capacity to appropriate qualities of the object-world imitatively rather than conceptually – this passage presents an unambiguously negative "cold" version of it.

Benjamin here adumbrates the concept of regressive mimesis that would later be more fully developed by Roger Caillois and Theodor Adorno in the 1930s and '40s. The genesis of this concept is a complex one, in which various sociological and anthropological theories, literary concerns, and social contextual factors such as the emergence of mass political ritual under fascism and Stalinism played a role. However, Benjamin's text, written in the mid-1920s, suggests its deeper roots in the rapid cultural and social transformation that found their most intense concentration in Weimar Germany's "imperial panorama." Already in the first decade of the century, Georg Simmel – a strong influence on Benjamin's theories of urban experience – had diagnosed a cool, blasé outer demeanor that served to protect metropolitan subjects from the excessive stimulus of the big European city. The large city dweller faces the external world of the metropolis with heightened inner consciousness and lowered external expressiveness; at the same time, according to Simmel, the outer face that the metropolitan dweller presents to the world is a more consciously prepared, tactical, calculated pose.[16] Recent scholars broadly influenced by the general Frankfurt School critical paradigm, such as Peter Sloterdijk in *Critique of Cynical Reason* and Helmut Lethen in *Cold Conduct*, have emphasized how interwar aesthetic modernism such as the work of Dadaist Walter Serner's *Manual for Swindlers* and Bertolt Brecht's *Hand Oracle for City Dwellers* reflected the mass propagation of "cold," matter-of-fact (*sachlich*) social dispositions in German urban society in the 1920s.[17]

So too, Adorno, in his important address "Education After Auschwitz," saw the conditions of possibility for fascism and the Nazi genocide in the increasingly universal disposition of coldness in individual and social life. He set out this connection with unusual starkness:

> If coldness were not a fundamental trait of anthropology, that is, the constitution of people as they in fact exist in our society, if people were not profoundly indifferent toward whatever happens to everyone else except for a few to whom they are closely bound, and, if possible, by tangible interests, then Auschwitz would not have been possible ... Society in its present form – and no doubt as it has been for centuries already – is based not, as was ideologically assumed since Aristotle, on appeal, on attraction, but rather on the pursuit of one's own interest against the interests of everyone else. This has settle into the character of people to their innermost center.[18]

Adorno saw no direct antidote to this spreading coldness, which was the dispositional correlate of a modernity that had developed over a very long span of history and had come to culmination in the twentieth century. The first duty of thought "after Auschwitz," Adorno believed, was to not disavow coldness by rushing to a temporary, ultimately illusory source of warmth, but rather to reflect on coldness, bringing it to conscious and critical scrutiny:

> If anything can help against coldness as the condition for disaster, then it is the insight into the conditions that determine it and the attempt to

combat those conditions, initially in the domain of the individual . . . The first thing therefore is to bring coldness to the consciousness of itself, of the reasons why it arose.[19]

The full-length German edition of *The Devil's Blind Spot* includes a section entitled "Adorno on the Cold Stream [*Kältestrom*]." Notably, this particular terminology was used not only by Adorno to designate cognitive and affective dispositions of contemporary humanity, but also by Ernst Bloch, who used the conceptual pair *Kältestrom/Wärmestrom* (cold/warm stream) to designate the characteristics of analytical critique and enthusiasm that together, dialectically, constitute the affective dimensions of a genuinely revolutionary Marxism.[20] But Adorno was concerned especially with the cold side, related to the post-Auschwitz, Cold War social environment of the West, and intended to explore it in philosophical depth. Kluge's "story" stands in for Adorno's unwritten book. I quote Kluge's passage in full:

> In the year of his death, Theodor W. Adorno made notes for a book that he intended to write after completing his AESTHETIC THEORY. He waited for the end of a terrible negotiation about the division of the Institute's budget between students, assistants, and directors. For four hours he had sat in the smoke-filled seminar room. His eyes were teary. It seemed as if he was writing down the words of the speakers. In fact, he was conceptualizing his book.
>
> Coldness, which it was to discuss, is one of the dominant currents of modernity. It is, Adorno noted, "derived from the libidinous energies of human species-being, similar to achievement of knowledge. In contrast, however, it produces indifference, the cold stream."
>
> The "primal history of the subject" is sketched out in the *Dialectic of Enlightenment*; there, however, the MODERN METAMORPHOSIS of the subject is lacking (which crumbles ever more into particles). How so? It is contained in Marx's observation that the human being, as producer of his life, as producer of commodities, comes to stand *close to* the production process. This is alienation. It underpins the observation that where human beings and their reality are severed from one another, coldness arises.
>
> The book should have begun with a description from the early ice-age. How above the oldest rocks of the planets, on the Canadian plate, an endlessly extended glacial lake formed. How then the power of such cool masses of water, which were however on the way to warming up, broke through the constraints of the glacier, which cut off the east coast of ancient America. The powerful flood-wave raised the watertable of the ocean six meters higher, flooding the polar caps and lands (also Egyptian) and so unleashed the ice-ages in which we continue to find ourselves.

This "natural history" produced by the "intelligence that came in from the cold," thus actually the art of keeping warm, which brings fire into the world, Adorno wanted to set apart against the ice-heap that overflowed from fantasies and feelings. In this regard, the comfortableness of the individual family group that settled in the Reich were a part of Auschwitz. Warm-hearted production of feeling plus exclusion = the cold stream.[21]

Kluge returned to Adorno's unfinished book on coldness in a recent film montage entitled *Who Dares Pull Coldness from Its Horse* (2010), which is accompanied by a short book *Straw in Ice*. Here he reveals his own direct connection to Adorno's reflections on coldness in the late 1960s. In a letter to Kluge dated March 13, 1967, Adorno acknowledges that he has thought about the question of coldness for a long time, and goes on to speak about a possible film by Kluge on the topic:

> I would very gladly have spoken to you about it, how and whether this intention could enter into your plans – it may be that precisely this, as I almost suspect, is already your intent. Such a film would touch very closely upon the matter that has occupied me ever more: the question of coldness. In the lecture about Auschwitz I spoke about it, but I plan, when my bigger plans have advanced somewhat, to write an essay about coldness.[22]

Adorno refers in his letter to a passage in Kluge's film *Yesterday's Girl* in which Anita G., played by Kluge's sister Alexandra (referred to familiarly as "Lexi" by Adorno), gives an explanation to a judge why she stole a colleague's sweater in July. She answers: "I'm freezing even in summer," which resonates metaphorically throughout the film, as she drifts through the icy post-war German social landscape of rentiers, bureaucrats, therapists, technicians, and policemen. Kluge's extraordinary film montage, which ranges from meditations on the earth's atmosphere and history to various historical and artistic representations of ice, snow, and cold, is a sort of posthumous monument in the place of this joint essay-never-written and film-never-made. It can be seen, perhaps, as a pendant to the representation of Adorno's funeral in *The Devil's Blind Spot* – another product of Kluge's long work of mourning for a Critical Theory that has vanished from the earth.

Among the avant-garde, however, there was a more utopian connotation to coldness, in the metaphor of crystallization and the imaginary creation of a crystal world that intersected with modernist fantasies about glass architecture. The poet and Communard Arthur Rimbaud, for example, in his poem "After the Flood," evoked the construction of the Hôtel-Splendide "in the chaos of ice and polar night" as a prelude to the revolutionary imagination of another flood that would sweep away the bourgeois trappings that had accumulated in the time since the last great cleansing. The expressionist architect Bruno Taut, who collaborated with Paul Scheerbart to imagine an earth transformed by glass architecture, in 1917–18 developed a series of drawings that spelled out a vision of an "extra-political," "cosmic" city of glass constructed in the mountains, his *Alpine Architecture* (1919). In a late homage to this tradition, in his novel *The Crystal World* (1966), which imagines a spreading crystallization of the organic world including human beings, J.G. Ballard made otherwise seemingly unmotivated allusions to the avant-garde legacy, using character-names such as the third-person protagonist "Edward Sanders" (who shares the name of the underground New York poet and co-founder of the '60s rock group The Fugs) and names from surrealist and Soviet avant-garde culture: the smuggler *Aragon*, the journalist Louise *Peret*, the physicist Professor *Tatlin* (part of a Russian scientific team led by *Lysenko*), Captain *Radek*, and Father *Balthus*. The novel hinges upon a decision that may be understood as a judgment upon the epochal project of modernism itself: should Ballard's protagonist Sanders resist or surrender to the crystallization that the avant-garde once imagined, figuratively, as a utopian overcoming of human life, and that in the world of Ballard's story has become a terrifyingly literal, environmental condition?

Kluge too refers directly to this avant-garde reversal of coldness into aesthetic utopia in his short chapter in *The Devil's Blind Spot* entitled "Origin of a Sense of Beauty in the Ice," which he captions as "Episode from the First Epoch of Globalization." Kluge's reference here is dual. On the one hand, as he explains in an interview, "the first epoch of globalization" is the comparatively rapid "spread of life across the whole planet" deep in natural historical time, the "first globalization of the living."[23] But it is also reiterated, he hints, in human history in the globalization of technological and capitalistic "second nature" in the early twentieth century, the period in which Taut envisioned his architectural utopias. The first three decades of the twentieth century, Kluge suggests with this ambiguous caption, were the dawn of a globalized planetary consciousness in the form of avant-garde utopian fantasies, shaped by a burgeoning planetary technology, a shattering world war, the collapse of empires and the sudden appearance of new republics, and the imagination of total world revolution unleashed by the unexpected Bolshevik victory in Russia.

Kluge refers to Taut as the source of the idea that the sense of beauty is rooted in a deep historical, anthropological experience of the ice age. In fact, the sense of beauty is only a derivation of an even more primal capacity to imagine, which meant that humans could stretch their temporal horizons beyond the boundaries of the present, remembering better times that once were and projecting those to come, threading through imaginative representations and stories the dimensions of the past, present, and future:

> In planning his *Alpine Architecture* ... Bruno Taut claimed that he
> was able to go back to PRIMAL EXPERIENCES OF THE HUMAN
> IMAGINATION. Not the sense of beauty but the power of the imagination
> was primary. It was engraved in the collective memory of the human race
> when the herds of animals and the humans following them, moving par-
> allel to the mighty barriers of the glaciers, migrated for decades across the
> plains, which were already turning into deserts under the influence of the
> advancing ice. Those were terrible years, without hope, and only in
> the hearts of man and beast did a kind of glow of former times, promis-
> ing warmth, remain. In the end, only stories. (*DBS*, 37)

Human beings lived for centuries under the conditions of hard necessity, with
many dying out, and others reaching the oceans and discovering caves. But at
last, the atmospheric and cosmic forces that had led to the ice age shifted and
the thaw began:

> After long ages of deprivation the earth's alignment to the sun changed:
> a portion of the mass of clouds, which had been reflecting the light of the
> sun back into the cosmos, fell to earth, and open stretches of water stored
> heat. The memory of sharpened powers of discernment, developed in the
> cold years, was sealed in the hearts of men. There, according to Bruno
> Taut, it is often mistaken for the sense of beauty. (*DBS*, 37)

In the interview to which I have previously referred, Kluge states that the
"source of the sense of beauty is the memory of warmth – the genesis of beauty
from an experience of need and expansion."[24] Here, Kluge argues that beauty
is the human response to a vital upsurge in biological life that came from both
the planet and human beings being embraced by a new atmosphere of warmth.
Yet its original, prefigurative nucleus had been preserved during the hard years
of the ice age, when human beings' survival depended on a memory of warmth,
even as the herds that nourished them, in this poetic paleontology, gradually
disappeared into narratives, images, and myths. This capacity to recall better
times made ice-age humans discerning readers of signs, trackers, interpreters of
faint hints and traces amidst the seemingly uniform landscape of ice and snow:
tools for persisting in the face of a dire adversity without any end in sight.

Ultimately, though, it is not just this deep natural historical and anthropological past, nor just the avant-garde past of the early twentieth century that Kluge
has in mind, but also his own present and future. Kluge wrote this passage
in the wake of the disappearance of the greatest twentieth-century planetary
utopia, the dream of world socialism embodied, with increasing decrepitude,
by the countries of "actually existing socialism" (including, importantly, the
eastern half of pre-unification Germany). Moreover, as Kluge was aware,
the visionary anarchism of an avant-gardist like Taut is unthinkable without

the social forces, technological horizons, and collective imaginaries of revolution that also fed more politically actual planetary utopias like early Soviet communism. If the opening decades of the twentieth century, with their avant-garde and politically vanguardist dreams, were a period of collective warmth, Kluge suggests, the period after 1989, twenty years after the death of Adorno and the disappearance of the remaining "elders of Critical Theory," shows emphatic signs of another ice age setting in. A post-avant-garde, post-socialist art – such as Kluge's own later fiction and films seek to adumbrate – has the task of thinking through and revising, in a deeper and more emphatic sense than was possible in the relative heat of the 1960s, Adorno's strategy of "hibernation," as Jürgen Habermas once critically characterized Adorno's valorization of difficult, scarcely communicable modernist art and literature. "Adorno follows a strategy of hibernation," Habermas wrote, "the obvious weakness of which lies in its defensive character. Interestingly, Adorno's thesis can be documented with examples from literature and music only insofar as these remain dependent on techniques of reproduction that prescribe isolated reading and contemplative listening (the royal road of bourgeois individuation)."[25] Rather than defend Adorno against the charge of having a "strategy of hibernation," or shedding it as an element of Adorno's critique that has outlived its moment, Kluge vigorously embraces the metaphor, seeking to enrich the concept of hibernation and lend it new resources of warmth and dreams to weather the polar night. Art in the future will need, he implies, to preserve the remembered warmth of the modernist and avant-garde imagination of the past, as not only as an ember to carry into the future, but also as a critical tool to use in the present: a retraining of the senses, to discern the remaining sustenance on our spreading planetary desert of ice.

Notes

1. See, for example, Rosalind Krauss, *The Originality of the Avant-Garde and Other Modernist Myths* (Cambridge, MA: The MIT Press, 1986); Craig Owens, *Beyond Recognition: Representation, Power, and Culture* (Berkeley and Los Angeles: University of California Press, 1994); Hal Foster, *The Return of the Real: The Avant-Garde at the End of the Century* (Cambridge, MA: The MIT Press, 1996); and above all, Benjamin H.D. Buchloh, *Neo-Avantgarde and Culture Industry* (Cambridge, MA: The MIT Press, 2003).
2. David Roberts, *Art and Enlightenment: Aesthetic Theory After Adorno* (Lincoln: University of Nebraska Press, 1991).
3. Peter Bürger, "The Problem of Aesthetic Value," in *Literary Theory Today*, ed. Peter Collier and Helga Geyer-Ryan (Ithaca, NY: Cornell University Press, 1990), pp. 27–8.
4. Peter Bürger, "The Decline of the Modern Age," trans. David J. Parent, *Telos* 62 (1984–85), pp. 117–30.
5. Bürger, "The Decline of the Modern Age," p. 125.
6. Bürger, "The Decline of the Modern Age," p. 130.
7. For a discussion of recent work in the Frankfurt School, contextualized in relation

to earlier work, see Joel Anderson, "The Third Generation of the Frankfurt School," available online at http://www.marcuse.org/herbert/scholaractivists/00Jo elAnderson3rdGeneration.htm, and "Selected Writings of German Members of the 'Third Generation' of the Frankfurt School," at http://www.marcuse.org/herbert/scholaractivists/00JoelAnderson3rdGenBibliography.htm (last accessed October 30, 2013).

8. Albrecht Wellmer, "Truth, Semblance, Reconciliation: Adorno's Aesthetic Redemption of Modernity," in *PoM*, pp. 1–35. Other relevant sources not directly cited here include Wellmer's discussions of philosophy of language and interpretation in *Endgames: The Irreconcilable Nature of Modernity*, trans. David Midgley (Cambridge, MA: The MIT Press, 1998), and *Wie Worte Sinn machen: Aufsätze zur Sprachphilosophie* (Frankfurt a/M: Suhrkamp Verlag, 2007).

9. Adorno, "Culture and Administration," in *The Culture Industry*, pp. 107–31.

10. Martin Jay, *Adorno* (Cambridge, MA: Harvard University Press, 1984).

11. Pierre Boulez, "Style or Idea? – In Praise of Amnesia" and "The Stravinsky-Webern Conjunction," in *Orientations: Collected Writings*, ed. Jean-Jacques Nattiez, trans. Martin Cooper (Cambridge, MA: Harvard University Press, 1986), pp. 349–59 and 364–9. David Roberts calls attention to Boulez's essay in *Art and Enlightenment*, pp. 117–21.

12. Scheerbart, *Lesabéndio*, pp. 26–7.

13. Oskar Negt and Alexander Kluge, *Public Sphere and Experience* (Minneapolis: University of Minnesota Press, 1993), p. 129.

14. Selected from Alexander Kluge, *Die Lücke, die der Teufel läßt* (Frankfurt a/M: Suhrkamp Verlag, 2003).

15. *DBS*, pp. 307–8; *Die Lücke, die der Teufel läßt*, pp. 640–1.

16. Georg Simmel, "The Metropolis and Mental Life," in *On Individuality and Social Forms*, ed. Donald N. Levine (Chicago: University of Chicago Press, 1971), pp. 324–39.

17. Peter Sloterdijk, *Critique of Cynical Reason*, trans. Michael Eldred (Minneapolis: University of Minnesota Press, 1987); Helmut Lethen, *Cool Conduct: The Culture of Distance in Weimar Germany*, trans. Don Reneau (Berkeley and Los Angeles: University of California Press, 2002). See also Lethen, *Unheimliche Nachbarschaft: Essays zum Kälte-Kult und der Schlaflosigkeit der philosophischen Anthropologie im 20. Jahrhundert* (Freiberg: Rombach Verlag, 2009); and Jessica Burstein, *Cold Modernism: Literature, Fashion, Art* (University Park: Penn State University Press, 2012).

18. Theodor W. Adorno, "Education After Auschwitz," in *Critical Models: Interventions and Catchwords*, trans. Henry W. Pickford (New York: Columbia University Press, 1998), p. 201.

19. Adorno, "Education After Auschwitz," p. 202.

20. *Bloch-Wörterbuch: Leitbegriffe der Philosophie Ernst Blochs*, ed. Beat Dietschy, Doris Zeilinger, Rainer Zimmermann (Berlin: Walter de Gruyter, 2012), pp. 224–31.

21. Kluge, *Die Lücke, die der Teufel läßt*, pp. 750–1, translation mine.

22. Alexander Kluge, *Wer sich traut, reißt die Kälte vom Pferd* (Berlin: Suhrkamp Verlag, 2010), DVD and book. Letter reprinted in "Vorwort," pp. 4–5.

23. Alexander Kluge and Rainer Stollmann, *Die Entstehung des Schönheitsinns aus dem Eis: Gespräche über Geschichten mit Alexander Kluge* (Berlin: Kulturverlag Kadmos, 2005), p. 13.

24. Kluge and Stollmann, *Die Entstehung des Schönheitsinns*, p. 13.

25. Jürgen Habermas, "Walter Benjamin: Consciousness Raising or Rescuing Critique?," in *Philosophical-Political Profiles*, trans. Fredrick G. Lawrence (Cambridge, MA: The MIT Press, 1983), p. 144.

INDEX